WOMEN IN CONTEMPORARY INDIA

Women in Contemporary India

Traditional Images and Changing Roles

Edited by

ALFRED DE SOUZA

MANOHAR
2021

To the men and women
who contributed to the continuous
publication for 25 years, 1951-1975,
of SOCIAL ACTION

First published 1975
Reprinted 2021

ISBN 978-81-943521-8-1

Published by
Ajay Kumar Jain *for*
Manohar Publishers & Distributors
4753/23 Ansari Road, Daryaganj
New Delhi 110 002

Printed at
Replika Press Pvt. Ltd.

CONTENTS

CONTRIBUTORS

ZARINA BHATTY lectures in Sociology at the College of Jesus and Mary, New Delhi

SUMA CHITNIS is Head of the Unit for Research in Sociology and Education, Tata Institute of Social Sciences, Bombay

VICTOR S. D'SOUZA is Head of the Department of Sociology, Punjab University, Chandigarh

VERITY SAIFULLAH KHAN is currently on the staff of the Runnymede Trust, London

URSULA KING is lecturer in Comparative Religion at the University of Leeds

JOSEPH MINATTUR is a Barrister-at-Law of Lincoln's Inn and Associate Research Professor at the Indian Law Institute, New Delhi

J. MURICKAN is Professor of Sociology at Loyola College of Social Sciences, Trivandrum

ANDREA MENEFEE SINGH is Associate Director of a research project at the Indian Social Institute, New Delhi

HELEN E. ULLRICH is visiting Professor at the University of Texas at Austin

SYLVIA VATUK is Associate Professor of Anthropology at the University of Illinois at Chicago Circle

MARJORIE R. WOOD is a former Research Associate of the Institute of Asian and Slavonic Research, University of British Columbia

INTRODUCTION

In India, as in other countries of the world, there is a great discrepancy between the idealised concept of woman and the real life situation in which women find themselves. In both the industrially advanced and less developed countries, women are burdened with cumulative inequalities as a result of socio-cultural and economic discriminatory practices which, until recently, have been taken for granted as though they were part of the immutable scheme of things established by nature. All over the world women are denied equal access with men to opportunities for personal growth and social development in education, employment, marriage and the family, professional and political life. In India as in the developed countries, women are less likely than men to continue their education to higher levels and are more likely to be found concentrated in female occupations like teaching, nursing, social work, typing and stenography—all of which have low status and low remuneration. Even those women who have surmounted the hurdles to professional education are disadvantaged as women because of the difficulty of reconciling the competing and often incompatible demands of a professional carrier with culturally defined homemaking responsibilities.

While women in India share many of their disabilities with women in the developed countries, their experience of discrimination is more extensive because of the sex segregated character of society, the conditions of poverty and the traditional value system. In sex segregated societies in South

Asia, Papanek[1] notes, there is a preoccupation with the sexual and reproductive behaviour of females. Allowing for variations of behaviour across regions and between higher and lower castes, it is generally true that in India a woman's sense of personal worth is related to her fertility performance and the social standing she achieves as a mother of sons. The typical Indian woman, Mandelbaum[2] points out, "knows of no acceptable alternative role for herself than that of wife-mother" and the "mark of her success as a person is in her living, thriving children." By the time she has completed her reproductive span an Indian woman has an average of five to six live births. In the rural areas where the economic advantages of having many children, particularly sons, is widely recognised, high fertility becomes less a personal choice of the woman than an outcome of a combination of socio-economic factors such as poverty, high infant mortality, the requirements of the family work force and old age security.

Though none of the papers in this book deals directly with the question of fertility, it is being increasingly realised that an important step in inproving the position of women in India is to break the vicious circle of poverty and high fertility. "People are not poor because they have large families", Mamdani concludes after his study of Manupur, a village in the Punjab. "Quite the contrary: they have large families because they are poor."[3] Again, he reports that while the richer Jat farmers were in favour of family planning, the poorer farmers "responded to adversity not by decreasing their numbers, but by increasing them. In numbers they found security and the opportunity for prosperity."[4] It has been

1. Hanna Papanek, "Men, Women, and Work: Reflections on the Two-Person Career," in Joan Huber (ed), *Changing Women in a Changing Society* (Chicago: University of Chicago Press, 1973), pp. 90-110.

2. David G. Mandelbaum, *Human Fertility in India* (Berkeley and Los Angeles: University of California Press, 1974), p. 16.

3. Mahmood Mamdani, *The Myth of Population Control* (New York: Monthly Review Press, 1972), p. 14.

4. *Ibid.*, p. 127. The Statement of the Indian delegation to the International Women's Conference at Mexico points out that "Without social security, the poor in the rural communities will continue to see in their children an investment for the future." (June 23, 1975), mimeo.

suggested by Chandrasekhar[5] that in conditions of high fertility and mortality, the reduction of fertility is not as crucial as the reduction of the infant mortality rate which may even be a precondition for the reduction of fertility. His argument is that parents are unlikely to have large families if they have reasonable certainty of the survival of their first two or three children. In India where sons constitute old age security, the reduction in infant mortality—fifty per cent of all infant deaths occur in the first four weeks of life—would bring about a reduction in fertility. This may at first sight appear strange but it could make practical sense in the cultural situation of India.

High fertility in a sex segregated society affects the status of women in several ways. First, the birth of the first child at a very early age and repeated pregnancies combined with malnutrition leads to high maternal mortality and fetal wastage. The maternal mortality rate (1971) was estimated at 376 for 100,000 live births; in Bangladesh one-third of all adult female deaths were maternally related. Second, women are so completely tied down by child care, housework and agricultural labour that few options are open to them for their personal growth apart from their main role of wife-mother. Third, since such a high value is attached to the reproductive function, formal education tends to be seen as irrelevant for girls who are destined for marriage and motherhood at an early age. Though the mean age at marriage for females is reported to have increased from 16 years in 1951-61 to 18.3 in 1961-71, girls continue to be married before puberty and, especially in the rural areas, the age at affective marriage is at least two or three years lower than the mean.[6] This pattern of early marriage and the attitude to female education is largely responsible for the high female illiteracy rate. According to the 1971 Census,

5. S. Chandrasekhar, *Infant Mortality, Population Growth and Family Planning in India* (London: George Allen & Unwin Ltd, 1972).

6. *Country Statement: India* (Bucharest : World Population Conference, 1974); A.P. Barnabas, "Population Growth and Social Change", in Anthony A. D'Souza and Alfred de Souza (eds), *Population Growth and Human Development* (New Delhi : Indian Social Institute, 1974), pp. 57-66.

the literacy rate for females was only 18.7 per cent in contrast to 39.5 per cent for males.

That the decline in fertility is a crucial factor in improving the social position of women has been recently documented by Titmuss in a study of fertility and mortality trends in Britain.[7] He reports that "the typical working-class mother of the 1890s married in her teens or early twenties, and experiencing ten pregnancies, spent about fifteen years in a state of pregnancy and in nursing a child for the first year of its life. Today, for the typical mother, the time so spent would be about four years. A reduction of such magnitude in only two generations in time devoted to childbearing represents nothing less than a revolutionary enlargement of freedom for women brought about by the power to control their fertility." Titmuss interprets this fall in the birth rate, which could not have occured without the consent of the husband, "as a desired change within the working-class family rather than as a revolt by women against the authority of men on the analogy of the campaign for political emancipation." He also attributes the dramatic improvement in female health and mortality rates to the progressive decline in the size of the family after 1900.

In Indian cities, excluding the urban slums, it has been found that high school education for girls is significantly associated with smaller family size.[8] Though education of women has tended to raise the age at marriage and lower the birth rate, it has not brought about any radical change in the traditional pattern of arranged marriage with dowry. In a study of three villages in the Punjab that was made to assess the impact of education on marriage, caste and occupation, Bhatnagar[9] found that most of the educated villagers were in favour of intercaste marriage and marriage without dowry, but in actual practice there was not a single intercaste marriage in these villages and in all cases dowry was

7. R.M. Titmuss, "The Position of Women: Some Vital Statistics," in M.W. Flinn and T.C. Smout (eds), *Essays in Social History* (London: Oxford University Press, 1974), p. 279.

8. Mandelbaum, *op. cit.*, pp. 52-53.

9. G.S. Bhatnagar, *Education and Social Change* (Calcutta: The Minerva Associates, 1972).

accepted. In another study of Indian students, Cormack found that girls were ready to go to college and mix with boys but they wanted their parents to arrange their marriage. "Many want new opportunities, old securities; new freedom, old protection."[10] Apart from the fact that viable alternatives to arranged marriage are not easily found in a sex segregated society, it would appear that arranged marriage is an important mechanism for ensuring compatibility of life styles of husband and wife within the framework of caste and religious norms regarding the traditional roles of men and women within the family.[11] Though educational and occupational opportunities are providing women with new roles outside the home, their social position in the family remains largely unchanged because the system of arranged marriage reasserts the authority of caste norms and the obligation of conformity to the traditional image of woman as wife-mother with low ritual status. It seems most unlikely that the requirement of dowry will be discontinued with the education and employment of women. The problem of dowry is rooted in the system of arranged marriage and, while it may provide the bride with security and facilitate upward social mobility, it also encourages a view of woman as a commodity with a market price that varies according to her education and complexion and the boy's occupation. Since all girls are destined for marriage and motherhood, the obligation of dowry tends to make parents consider a female child a liability right from birth. The prejudice against a daughter and the preference for a son is expressed in folklore, and a Punjabi tradition asserts that "boys are conceived on moonlight nights, girls on dark ones."[12]

In spite of over two decades of planned economic development the structure of employment opportunities for women in the rural areas remains relatively unchanged. Nearly 80 per cent of the total female work force is employed in agricultural activities either as cultivators or farm labourers. Women

10. Margaret Cormack, *She Who Rides a Peacock* (Bombay: Asia Publishing House, 1961), p. 109.

11. See Papanek, *op. cit.*; Cormack, *op. cit.*, p. 128.

12. Mamdani, *op. cit.*, p. 141.

usually perform unskilled or semi-skilled tasks that are poorly paid, but they are also involved in different ways in dairying, poultry and gardening. Rural women have not only to do their share of subsistence farming for the survival of the family but they are also entirely responsible for the female tasks of child care and housework. Very little attention has been paid in practice by social planners to improving the social situation of the rural woman. For example, it has been pointed out that agricultural extension services are directed to men though women are heavily involved in agricultural production and marketing. Instead of formal education that is largely irrelevant to their needs, the situation of rural women could be improved if they are given opportunities in the village for informal education in production and marketing, nutrition, hygiene, cooking and basic child care skills.[13] In the sex typed division of labour in the village, women are primarily responsible for the supply of water for drinking and other needs of the family. The Fifth Five Year Plan envisages a massive programme to provide villages with an adequate supply of drinking water. This is very much in line with the thinking of the Draft Plan of Action which recommends that "easily accessible water supplies should also be provided. . . to improve health conditions and reduce the burden of carrying water which falls mainly on women and children."[14]

In the cities, if we exclude women in the industrial labour force and the urban slums, the employment patterns of educated women are strikingly similar to those of women in the developed countries. In the industrial labour force as well as in the informal urban sector, the occupations considered appropriate for women belonging to the lower income groups are determined by caste and regional norms. In the modern sector,

13. See *Women in India: A Compendium of Programmes* (New Delhi: Women's Welfare Division, Department of Social Welfare, 1975).

14. *Draft Plan of Action*, n. 93 (see Appendix); George Macpherson and Dudley Jackson report that a village in northern Tanzania had been supplied with about 32,000 gallons of water annually by village women and children who carried it in four gallon containers from a pipe nearly a mile away from the village, "Village Technology for Rural Development: Agricultural Innovation in Tanzania", *International Labour Review*, 111 (February, 1975), p. 112.

both in India as also in the developed countries, because of occupational segregation based on a sex-typed division of labour, high proportions of educated women are found in such female occupations as nursing, teaching and clerical work; only an insignificant number of women seek careers in engineering, technology and science, in politics and administration. In every stratum of the labour force and the professions, men monopolise the more responsible positions which are better paid and also enjoy a wider range of opportunities for career advancement and occupational mobility. The increase in the number of women in the professions and the service sector has not led to sexual equality in the distribution of occupational positions having power, status and privilege. In a recent cross-national study[15] of professional work opportunities for women in European countries, North America, Australia and New Zealand, it was found that "the rate of female professional participation was not significantly associated with greater sexual equality within the professional sector." Granting that the professions constitute a special occupational group, this study suggested that though increased female participation in the labour force may promote egalitarian relations within the family, it did not seem to be associated with greater sexual equality *within* the labour force.

There are several reasons why this pattern of occupational segregation and the exclusion of women from positions of executive authority and leadership are maintained. First, socialisation in the family and education in the school reinforce "gender roles", that is, cultural definitions of the traits and behaviour that are considered appropriate for men and women.[16] In school, girls are encouraged to aspire to a limited range of occupations which are believed to be "feminine" and compatible with the demands of their primary gender roles of housewife and mother. Second, women lack role models in the scientific and technical occupations, in management, politics

15. Rosemary Santana Cooney, "Female Professional Work Opportunities: A Cross-National Study", *Demography*, 12 (February, 1975), pp. 107-120.

16. Wilma R. Krauss, "Political Implications of Gender Roles: A Review of the Literature", *The American Political Science Review*, LXVIII (December, 1974), pp, 1706-1923.

and public administration. In India there have been several outstanding women associated with the freedom movement, but they were largely in the political arena. The occasional woman vice-chancellor of a university or airline pilot or IAS officer tends in fact to reinforce the general belief in the appropriateness of the existing occupational segregation to which, of course, laudable exceptions may be tolerated. Third, it has been suggested that women, as a subordinate group in society, have internalised "self-sacrificing" and "expressive" values and developed a "false consciousness" which includes "beliefs in the appropriateness of lower pay, of doing menial work, and of eschewing leadership positions and politics."[17] Thus women are expected to seek occupational roles which stress the aspect of service and cooperation with men, not competition. It is interesting to note that Gandhi[18] whose salt compaign, he believed, had brought thousands of women "from their seclusion and showed that they could serve the country on equal terms with men," expressed a strong belief in woman as the "embodiment of sacrifice" and that "equality of the sexes does not mean equality of occupations."

The requirement to be self-sacrificing for the fulfilment of their subordinate gender role is seen most clearly in the conflict which women experience because of the demands of marriage and career. Apart from the general expectation that all wives must be housewives, Bernard notes that "when occupational sacrifices have to be made, the wife is usually happy to be the one to make them, subordinating her own career to that of her husband's."[19] It has been widely assumed that household chores are the responsibility of the wife, irrespective of whether she is employed outside the home for the benefit of the family. In effect, with the belief that child-rearing and housework are "women's work", women are compelled to manage two full-time jobs with little or no support

17. Krauss, *op. cit.*

18. M. K. Gandhi, *Womcn and Social Injustice* (Ahmedabad: Navajivan Publishing House, 1958), p. 167.

19. Jessie Bernard, *Social Problems at Midcentury* (New York: Holt, Rinehart and Winston, 1957), p. 350.

of the husband. In a study[20] of the role conflict experienced by nurses, social workers and researchers in Delhi with regard to their family responsibilities, it was found that all these women experienced the greatest difficulty in combining their professional work with their role as *mother*.

Two approaches have been suggested for the resolution of the conflict experienced by working wives. One is to reorganise the traditional division of work in the home so that husband and wife share in the rearing of children and the various household tasks which so far have been considered to be female work. A pioneering effort in this direction was made by Szalai through "time-budget" studies to document the prevailing sexual division of labour within the home in several developed countries.[21] His general conclusion is that when the wife is employed outside the home there is a tendency for the husband to help her in the housework. As a result, there is a trend in urban-industrial societies towards a "symmetrical family" in which a more equitable sexual division of labour prevails. He reports that a time-budget study of ten countries with regard to child care activities showed that fathers were only minimally involved in the basic child care tasks of feeding, washing, clothing and other tasks such as playing, talking or walking with the child or supervising schoolwork. "Mothers, be they full-time employed women or housewives, have no choice except to do all the rest." Szalai notes that working women adjust to this inequitable distribution of parental tasks by having recourse to "preferences and prejudices about feminity." In India traditional concepts about women's work persist and, according to Kapur, the tendency of husbands to act on the belief that household jobs and child care are the wife's duty, is one of the "most significant factors" in marital discord.[22] Though the tasks associated with housework and child care are looked

20. Rama Kapur, "Role Conflict Among Employed Housewives", *Indian Journal of Industrial Relations*, 5 (July, 1969), pp. 39-67.

21. Alexander Szalai, "The Situation of Women in the Light of Contemporary Time-budget Research" (United Nations: E/CONF./66/BP/6, 15 April, 1975).

22. Promilla Kapur, *The Changing Status of the Working Woman in India* (Delhi: Vikas Publishing House, 1970), p. 27; *Draft Plan of Action*, n. 102.

upon as women's work, it seems likely that Indian husbands will be under increasing pressure to assist their employed wives. It seem doubtful, however, if the "symmetrical family" will develop in the near future in India because, apart from the cultural attitude to the wife-mother role, womcn themselves in the prevailing system of arranged marriage tend to find their emotional fulfilment in the mother-son relationship.[23]

The second approach to the resolution of the conflict between family responsibilities and employment outside the home is to consider working wives as a "special employment group" and to reorganise the conditions of work. Rama Kapur suggests that employers should provide working housewives with "suitable adjustments" such as flexible working hours, housing facilities, transport and facilities for child care. These improvements in the conditions of work within the existing pattern of occupational segregation are important to ease the housewives' burden of two full-time jobs. But it is not often realised that career patterns of high status that are tailored to male life styles are a pervasive source of inequality because they discriminate against women who have family responsibilities and force them into female occupations.[24] In view of this institutionalised inequality in the structure of occupational opportunities, it seems strange to find the Statement of the Indian delegation to the International Women's Conference, asserting that "Once opportunities are provided to (women) to fulfil their political, biological and social role, women should compete on equal terms with men and should not expect favoured treatment. Only then, will the concept of equality be truly meaningful."[25] The issue of inequality in occupational opportunities has unfortunately been obscured by the concern with legislation to guarantee equal pay for equal work. The Indian government intends to commemorate International Women's Year by legislation on equal pay for equal work and one can only hope that this legal provision will be better observed than

23. Aileen D. Ross, *The Hindu Family in its Urban Setting* (Toronto: University of Toronto Press, 1967), p. 177.

24. *Education and the Working Life in Modern Society* (Paris : Organisation for Economic Cooperation and Development, 1975), p. 16.

25. See the Statement of the Indian delegation to the International Women's Conference at Mexico, mimeo, p. 4.

the labour laws designed to ensure special protection to women in industry. Cook's[26] comment on the question of equal pay laws in the American context is also relevant to the situation of women in India. She writes that equal pay laws or policies alone "can even provide reinforcement to employers' biases against women in jobs in the mixed or male labour market. The crux of the problem lies not in providing for equal pay alone, but in the adoption of policies on equal opportunities which are unambiguous and enforceable."

From what has been said above it will be seen that the position of women in India is influenced by a number of social factors that are specific to sex segregated, less developed countries; in the modern urban economy, however, the problems of Indian women, particularly with regard to education and employment in the professions and the service sector, are comparable to those experienced by women in the developed countries. While the problem of social change in the largely traditional societies of South Asia has been the focus of wide ranging studies by sociologists, the implications of change for the place of women in the social, cultural, economic and political life of these societies in transition is a neglected field of sociological inquiry. The Report of the Committee on the Status of Women in India notes the "paucity of data" on important social and economic variables affecting the personal development and patterns of social behaviour of Indian women. On the occasion of International Women's Year, this book on contemporary Indian women offers a fresh perspective on women and social change through empirical studies of the interaction between the traditional images of women and their new social roles in the family and the wider society.* This book is divided into four parts. The first paper presents an overview of the situation of women in India and discusses the problems of urban and rural women in the context of the objectives of International Women's Year. This is followed by a set of four research studies which cover a wide geographic

26. Alice H. Cook, "Equal Pay: Where is it ?" *Industrial Relations*, 14 (May, 1975), p. 176.

*Most of the papers in this book appeared in the special number of *Social Action*, 25 (July-Sept. 1975).

spread from Uttar Pradesh in the north to Gujarat and down south to Karnataka and Kerala. The third part comprises a set of five papers which examine the "special case" of women and the law, women and religion, women and employment, aging women and Indian and Pakistani women migrants in Britain. The book concludes with an extended analysis of the methodological problems which are peculiar to the study of women in India.

In her insightful discussion of the significance of International Women's Year for women in India, Suma Chitnis provides a documented overview of the participation of women in the economy and their integration in the process of national development, participation in political life, and the promotion of sexual equality in the family and the wider society. Though women comprise a small proportion of the agricultural labour force, it seems likely that changing conditions in agriculture will require women to assume new tasks and, in the future, increased agricultural productivity will depend to a greater extent on women workers. The survey of trends in urban female employment shows that there is a higher participation rate of women in female occupations and that the problem of urban unemployed women is largely a problem of unemployed educated women. In the political sphere the performance of women, measured by the level of political awareness and voting behaviour, has been disappointing. The promotion of equality between men and women, Chitnis argues, requires not only that priority should be given to the economic and political participation of women but also to the complex problem of the redefinition of sex roles within the family and the wider society.

Zarina Bhatty examines the pattern of social stratification of a Muslim village in Uttar Pradesh to study the institutionalised differentiation in status and life styles of Ashraf and non-Ashraf women. The life style of Ashraf women, who belonged to the upper social strata, were determined by the characteristics of a *purdah* society : confinement to the home, subordination to male authority and no alternatives to the role of wife-mother. On the other hand, non-Ashraf women did not observe *purdah*, enjoyed relatively more freedom from male authority and worked outside the home with their husbands.

Education and urbanisation are altering the traditional life style of Ashraf women and there is a tendency to come out of *purdah* and seek employment outside the home. But among non-Ashraf families that are upwardly mobile, the direction of change is towards the traditional *purdah* life style. Through a process of "emulation" non-Ashraf women are retiring into *purdah*, withdrawing from the family work force and regressing towards less egalitarian relations in the family.

In an intensive study of a sample of urban middle-class women in Gujarat, Majorie Wood explores the changes in their life style and ritual behaviour that seemed to be associated with employment outside the home. A striking change was seen in the reduction of the size of the family, none of the women having more than two children. A pragmatic approach was seen in attempts to accomodate household tasks and child care to the requirements of the job: fewer meals were prepared, part-time servants were engaged and children were made to help with housework. Customs regarding dietary habits had changed significantly and rituals pertaining to life cycle events were either abbreviated or omitted altogether. Unlike life cycle events, calendrical occasions were celebrated more fully than in their homes of orientation. The extent of any modification in ritual behaviour depended on a number of variables such as composition of the household, type of marriage and caste affiliation; but the direction of modification, the basic pattern of change, appeared to be directly related to the women's employment outside the home. This study suggests that, when men and women are employed outside the home, new ways of thinking and behaviour are introduced in the home.

By studying the forms of address used by women belonging to different castes in a village in Karnataka, Helen Ullrich reveals the place of women in the social structure of the village and the family. In this village there were six major caste groups—Havik Brahmins, Divaru (a Sudra-group), Lingayats, Vokkaligas, Girijans and Harijans. The analysis shows how the three basic forms of address used by the women express dimensions of ritual and economic power and reinforce the basic social divisions in the village as well as their hierarchical character. Within the family the relative position of the women is discussed with reference to the ways Havik Brahmin and

Divaru wives address their husbands. In the Havik family the husband has complete authority in the running of the household and in decisions regarding marriage and even food. The wife regards her husband as a personal god and is completely submissive to him. Though Havik women tend to view their identity in terms of their husbands, there is a tendency among educated younger Havik women to be more independent. Divaru women, on the other hand, are in charge of their household, work with their husbands in the fields and have no inhibitions about criticising their husbands in public. The more egalitarian relationship between Divaru husband and wife is reflected in the use of a common term for both boys and girls whereas among Brahmins the terms for male and female children are distinct. This analysis suggests that the changes taking place in the forms of address are reflected in the changing relationships between the various caste groups that are moving from the more strictly hierarchical to what is more egalitarian.

Women in Kerala differ from their counterparts in other states of India in several ways: life expectancy for females is higher than for males, the age of marriage is higher at about 20 years, and there is hardly any disparity between male and female participation rates in education at all levels. Jose Murickan reports the findings of several empirical studies in three urban centres of Kerala—Trivandrum, Cochin and Kottayam—in order to study the participation of women in the political sphere and their attitudes to religion, marriage and dowry, and to delineate the characteristics of the self-image which women in Kerala have of themselves. This paper reports that younger women see themselves differently from their mothers and this change in perception is also reflected in changing attitudes to politics, religion, marriage and dowry. This study suggests that education and urbanisation have had an impact on the values and attitudes of the younger generation of women but it is uncertain to what extent these attitudinal changes are predictive of corresponding change in actual behaviour.

India has remarkable body of social legislation that is aimed at safeguarding the rights of women in marriage, education, industrial employment and education. While one of the Directive Principles of the Constitution requires the state to secure equal pay for equal work for men and women, a provision of the Constitution, after having laid down that the state shall not discriminate against any citizen on the grounds of sex, among other things, permits the state to discriminate in favour of women if this is found necessary. Joseph Minattur examines the provisions of the more important legislation on marriage, dowry, divorce, succession, adoption and abortion, with respect to their effect on the status of women and sexual equality. Legislation on marriage and divorce, though socially motivated, has been relatively ineffective because of loopholes in the law. Thus the Child Marriage Restraint Act which made it an offence for a man to marry a girl under fifteen years of age has been ineffective because the law recognises the validity of a marriage which violates the age requirement. Similarly, though dowry is prohibited, "presents" are permitted at the time of marriage. Though the Hindu Marriage Act of 1955 respects equality of the sexes in the matter of grounds for divorce, there is some discrimination against the right of the wife to divorce in customary law and the Indian Divorce Act. But the Hindu Succession Act of 1956 and the Hindu Minority and Guardianship Act of 1956 invest the Hindu woman with equal rights to inheritance and adoption. The problem with progressive social legislation is that the new rights given women are opposed to prevailing social and cultural norms. Thus a woman may assert her right to divorce, but a divorcee and her remarriage will meet with strong social disapproval.

All religions, Ursula King maintains, are facing a new challenge. Women who have attained sexual equality with men in the secular sphere are questioning the secondary status accorded them in the major religious traditions of the world. Women have not always and everywhere been excluded from active participation in religious life as can be seen from the presence of women magicians, healers, seers and priestesses in both primitive and ancient religion. With the institutionalisation of religious roles in the higher religions, sacred authority, like secular authority, was invested in men and the exercise of religious functions became a male prerogative. This regressive trend can be found in all the major religious traditions—Hinduism, Jainism, Buddhism, Islam and Christianity. This examination of the image of woman leads to a threefold conclusion: whenever the ascetical ideal gained ascendancy in a religion, the position of women deteriorated; no religion appears to have a model that corresponds to contemporary woman's self-understanding; and an adequate theology or religious interpretation is only possible if both men and women participate in its elaboration.

In an attempt to explain the marked decline in the rate of female work participation from rural to urban and from smaller to larger communities, Victor D'Souza focuses on the interaction of certain social structural factors. On finding a curvilinear relationship between female work participation and the education of women, he uses empirical data from an earlier study to examine the relationship between the participation rate of women and the occupational prestige of their husbands and between the occupational prestige of husbands and wives. The remarkable association between the occupational prestige of wives and husbands leads him to consider the asymmetry hypothesis or family status consistency, according to which a wife should enter an occupation which is almost equal in prestige to that of her husband's or slightly inferior to it. If the wife is not able to fulfil this condition she withdraws from the work force. This study suggests that legislation on the right of women to work and to equal employment opportunities may not be effective if the social structural factors are not taken into account.

To delineate the social and cultural framework of aging in India, Sylvia Vatuk studies the life cycle and social roles of aging women belonging to the Rayā Rajput caste in an "urbanised village" in metropolitan Delhi. In this study "old age" was deffined primarily with reference to life cycle criteria—e.g., son's marriage. The joint family household of three generations was the common pattern of residence of these elderly women. Great effort goes into the preparation for old age and the first step is to have a son to care for one's needs in old age; various alternative arrangements are made if there are only female children such as remarriage, adoption or the taking of a *ghar jamāī*. The perceptions of these women of their own old age and of what a woman's old age ought to be are discussed in the context of their work activities, the pattern of their participation in religious life and their sexual life.

In the wider perspective of the "Imperial connection" and the exploitation of migrant labour, Verity Saifullah Khan analyses the major determinants of the nature and the quality of the Asian woman's life in Britain. The majority of Indian and Pakistani women migrants are from rural areas and they know little or no English: most of them remain at home with the young children and their contact with British society is minimal. These women entered Britain as dependents and it is the Asian woman's status as a dependent which makes her husband or group. Though the problems of adjustment of these women are those of all migrants in a new environment, there are some factors which are specific to women migrants from India and Pakistan: the first experience of urban life and another culture; the separation of work from the family, physically mobility, the absence of the "women's world" of the village. The way in which adjustments are made in family life and the socialisation of the children and patterns of work outside the home reveals that behavioural changes are a response to new circumstances without necessarily involving the loss of their traditional cultural values.

The concluding paper by Andrea Menefee Singh, a comprehensive review of some of the methodological problems which have been inherent in sociological studies of women in the past, attempts to clarify ways in which these problems can be resolved in future studies of women. In the past the study of women tended to be reserved for women while male sociologists often acted as though male roles, activities and aspirations were representative of society as a whole. Singh argues for a more integrated approach with regard to both community studies and the study of women as a special category. Other methodological problems analysed relate to attitudinal and survey research. It is stressed that because of the special social and cultural factors which influence the position of women in India, special importance must be given to the ways in which region, religion, caste, family structure and systems of kinship and marriage affect the occupational patterns, social mobility, relative freedom of movement and life styles of women.

This book represents a collaborative effort of several men and women scholars. First of all I would like to express my deep gratitude to all the contributors for their willingness to share the results of their research. I would also like to acknowledge the help I received from Anthony A. D'Souza of the Centre for the Exploration of Values and Meaning, A.M. Shah of Delhi University and Sheila Allen of Bradford University. I am especially indebted to my colleague Andrea Menefee Singh whose comments and suggestion were most helpful.

ALFRED de SOUZA

Indian Social Institute
August 15, 1975

1

SUMA CHITNIS

*International Women's Year: Its Significance for Women in India**

The central theme of International Women's Year—equality, development and peace—emerges from the major objectives set for IWY by the United Nations: To promote equality between men and women; to ensure the full integration of women in the total development effort, especially by emphasising women's responsibility and important role in economic, social and international levels, particularly during the Second United Nations Development Decade; to recognise the importance of women's increasing contribution to the development of friendly relations and cooperation among States and to the strengthening of world peace.[1]

Although the basic objectives of the integration of women in development, the promotion of their equal rights and the strengthening of peace have universal relevance, International Women's Year will have a different meaning for different countries. The operationalisation of these objectives will differ according to the situation in which women within each country actually find themselves. More specifically, it would

*An earlier version of this paper was prepared for the Indian Council of Social Welfare.

1. United Nations' General Assembly's resolution No. 3010 (XXVII), December 18, 1972.

differ according to developmental needs of each country, the constraints that have traditionally been placed on equality for women, and according to how favourable the climate for change happens to be. Whatever the specific nature of the changes required in a country may be, these changes are almost invariably likely to be in the direction of the removal of differences, disparities and inequalities between men and women. Inasmuch as change will involve disturbance of age-old structures it is a threat to established norms and values. Thus, the challenge to societies all over the world is to bring about peacefully changes that secure equality for women and promote their participation in development.

SCOPE

The purpose of this paper is to discuss the significance of the objectives of IWY—equality, development and peace—in the Indian situation. The first two sections of the paper focus on the problems and opportunities of integrating women more effectively in the process of national development. The third section discusses the complex issue of the redefinition of sex-typed roles in the family and society, and the concluding section outlines some concrete action programmes to help women to work in partnership with men for integral human development in India.

In India, as probably in most developing countries of the world, the issue that occurs foremost to the mind while considering possibilities for integrating women in development, is their participation in economic activities. The 1971 Census data on the percentage of workers in the female population of the country indicate that women workers constitute 19.6 per cent of the age group 15-59.[2] Although women comprise about 48 per cent of the total population of the country they constitute only 13.8 per cent of the total work force. If this overall picture of the participation of women in the economy of the country is discouraging, details regarding interstate variations are even more so. In some states like Andhra, Maharashtra and Himachal Pradesh women constitute between 21 and 25 per cent of the work force, but in Haryana, Punjab,

2. Census of India, 1971, Series 1: India, Paper 3 of 1972, Economic Characteristics of the Population, p. 2.

TABLE 1

Workers and Non-workers According to Main Activity

	Total Population			Total Workers	
	Persons	Males	Females	Males	Females
Total	5479.5 (100.0)	2839.4 (51.3)*	2640.1 (48.2)	1490.7 (86.6)	313.0 (17.4)
Rural	4388.6 (100.0)	2252.2 (51.3)	2136.4 (49.7)	1204.1 (81.2)	279.7 (18.8)
Urban	1090.9 (100.0)	557.2 (53.8)	503.7 (46.2)	286.6 (89.6)	33.3 (10.4)

	Cultivators		Agricultural Labourers		Livestock, Forestry, Fishing, Hunting and Plantations, Orchards and Allied Activities	
	Males	Females	Males	Females	Males	Females
Total	689.1 (88.1)	92.7 (11.9)	316.9 (66.7)	157.9 (33.3)	35.1 (81.8)	7.8 (18.2)
Rural	674.2 (88.1)	91.3 (11.9)	303.6 (66.7)	152.1 (33.3)	30.4 (81.0)	7.1 (19.0)
Urban	14.9 (91.5)	1.4 (8.5)	13.3 (69.6)	5.8 (30.4)	4.7 (87.3)	0.7 (12.7)

	Mining and Quarrying		Manufacturing, Processing, Servicing and Repairs: Household Industry		Manufacturing, Processing, Servicing and Repairs: Other than Household Industry		Construction	
	Males	Females	Males	Females	Males	Females	Males	Females
Total	8.1 (86.6)	1.2 (13.4)	50.2 (79.0)	13.3 (21.0)	98.5 (91.9)	8.7 (8.1)	20.1 (90.8)	2.0 (9.2)
Rural	5.1 (84.8)	0.9 (15.2)	37.6 (79.0)	10.0 (21.0)	29.7 (87.2)	4.4 (12.8)	9.9 (90.2)	1.1 (9.8)
Urban	3.0 (89.8)	0.3 (10.2)	12.6 (79.1)	3.3 (20.9)	68.8 (94.1)	4.3 (5.9)	10.2 (91.4)	0.9 (8.6)

TABLE 1 (continued)

	Trade and Commerce		*Transport, Storage and Communications*		*Other Services*		*Non-workers*	
	Males	Females	Males	Females	Males	Females	Males	Females
Total	94.8 (94.5)	5.6 (5.5)	42.5 (96.7)	1.5 (3.3)	135.4 (85.9)	22.3(14.1)	1348.6 (36.7)	2327.1 (63.3)
Rural	33.4 (92.2)	2.8 (7.8)	11.7 (96.7)	0.4 (3.3)	68.5 (87.7)	9.6(12.3)	1048.1 (36.1)	1856.7 (63.9)
Urban	61.4 (95.7)	2.8 (4.3)	30.8 (96.7)	1.1 (3.3)	66.9 (84.0)	12.7(16.0)	300.5 (39.0)	470.4 (61.4)

Source: Census of India, 1971, Series 1. India, Paper 3 of 1972, Economic Characteristics of the Population

Note: Figures are in lakhs

*Figures in parentheses indicate percentage

West Bengal, Assam and Jammu and Kashmir the figures drop to between 2 and 6 per cent.[3]

The types of occupation in which women are found indicate the low level of their participation in the economy. Table 1 presents a comparative statement of rural and urban employment of men and women. It will be seen that agricultural labour and household industry are the only two categories of occupations in which the representation of women is relatively high (33.3 and 21 per cent respectively). In the other seven categories women constitute less than 20 per cent of the work force, and their representation is particularly poor in trade and commerce, transport, storage and communications, in industry other than household industry, and in the urban sector. It is obvious that the participation of women in rural occupations like agriculture, livestock, animal husbandry, fisheries, quarrying and household industry needs to be improved as also in urban occupations like trade, commerce, transport and other non-skilled and professional services. In what follows we will consider the possibility of developing opportunities for the employment of women in a wide range of rural and urban occupations.

PARTICIPATION OF WOMEN IN AGRICULTURE

According to the Census of 1971, agriculture accounts for as much as 73.91 per cent of the total working population of women in India. Of these 46 per cent are agricultural labourers and 28 per cent are what are described as cultivators. The issue at stake, however, is not what the size or the share of their involvement actually is, but what it can or should be. And from this point of view it is important to understand the factors that influence the participation of women in agriculture.

Economists have observed that in societies that practise shifting cultivation the participation of women in agriculture is fairly high.[4] Apparently in this type of agriculture, men and

3. *Women in India* (Bombay: S.N.D.T. University, 1975), p. 44.

4. The discussion on the participation of women in agriculture is based on Ester Boserup, *Women's Role in Economic Development* (London; George Allen and Unwin, 1970).

young boys perform the heavy tasks of felling trees and clearing the ground for cultivation, but it is the women who perform all subsequent operations like the removal and burning of felled trees, sowing, weeding, harvesting and storing the crops for consumption. In societies that have progressed to settled agriculture, on the other hand, the participation of women is much smaller. There is a little need for female labour except in the harvest season. Ploughing, sowing and most other activities need to be done by men. This situation, however, tends to last only as long as settled farming is simple and extensive, but when it becomes labour intensive the participation of women increases.

TABLE 2

Average Hours Worked per Week by Family Members

	With crops		With animals		Total in family farm	
	Women	Men	Women	Men	Women	Men
Western India						
Sample B	13	18	3	15	16	33
Sample C	16	23	3	12	19	35
Central India	14	14	2	14	16	20
Southern India	9	16	11	14	20	30
Delhi Territory	9		22	31		

Source : Ester Boserup, *op. cit.*, p. 31

Apart from the type of agriculture practised, the kind of crops produced and the availability or non-availability of hired labour, are other factors that have been observed to influence the participation of women. For instance, in settled agriculture the participation of women is relatively higher in rice cultivation than in farming for wheat, sugarcane or cotton. Further, as may be seen from Table 2, the involvement of women is likely to be much greater in tasks concerned with crops than it is with tasks concerned with animals. Female work participation is high where hired labour is little used but it is low when hired labour is liberally used. Mechanisation of farming does not seem to effect the participation of women adversely. In developed countries, where farming is highly mechanised women workers have generally increased to approximately the size of the male work force. These considerations suggest that the participation of women in agriculture tends to increase (a) as society makes the transition from shifting to settled cultivation; (b) as agriculture becomes labour intensive; (c) as land belongs to owner cultivators rather than to landlords who depend on hired help; and (d) as animal husbandry becomes a prominent feature of agriculture.

NEW TASKS

This has serious implications for the Indian situation since the transition from shifting cultivation to settled agriculture generally takes place as the pressure of population on land grows. Similarly change from extensive to intensive farming has been the mechanism through which societies have met the demands of increasing population. Given the current rate of the growth of population in the country both the transition from shifting cultivation (wherever it is practised) to settled agriculture and the movement from extensive to intensive farming are inevitable. The latter change would call for a rapid increase in the size of the labour force in agriculture. The change from shifting to settled agriculture may have the opposite effect but the growing pressure of the population is such that those who make the transition will have to move rapidly towards intensive farming. Land policy in India which is positively oriented in favour of ownership farming is another factor that is likely to call for greater involvement of women in agriculture. Finally, the fact that poultry, animal husbandry and other forms of agricultural production will have to be increased substantially to meet the needs of the growing population implies that men will have to be released for animal husbandry. This is possible only if women take on more of the tasks of cultivation traditionally performed by men. On the whole, it seems that in the years to come agricultural development in the country will depend heavily on the proportion of women workers and the quality of their contribution.

Not only will women have to take on some of the tasks in agriculture now being undertaken by men, it will be necessary for them to bring greater knowledge, skill and sophistication to the tasks they have traditionally performed. Women will have to be trained and organised for their new responsibilities in agriculture, for more effective methods of sowing, harvesting, winnowing and storing, and for new activities like cheese-making, curing of meat, production of honey, and canning of fruit, vegetables and animal products.

Neither the education of women for greater effectiveness in traditional agricultural tasks nor their involvement in new agricultural occupations is likely to be easy. Boserup notes that in developing countries "agricultural change is being held back because men—or women—refuse to do more work than is customary, or to do work which according to prevailing custom should be done by persons of the other sex."[5] Programmes for the education, training and organisation of women for their new responsibilities in agriculture and a massive effort to alter the attitudes and values that are likely to inhibit an increase in their participation in agriculture could be taken up as a major challenge in International Women's Year.

TRENDS IN URBAN OCCUPATIONS

Since agriculture constitutes the backbone of the Indian economy greater and more productive participation of women in agricultural and allied rural occupations should be the major feature of any programme for increasing their integration in economic development. However, the promotion of their participation in urban non-agricultural occupations is equally important.

While the data in Table 1 clearly indicate that the participation of women in urban occupations is generally poor, they do not bring out one of the most serious problems of their employment in the urban sector—the progressive decline in the number of employed women. More detailed statistics on the situation of women in urban employment show that the percentage of women employed in industry other than household industry has been dropping steadily.[6] The figures in Table 3 relate to the decade 1952-1962 and, though more recent data are not available, the decline in the employment

5. Ester Boserup, *op. cit*, p. 35.

6. V.B. Karnik, "Status of Women: Economic and Employment Aspects" in *Women in India* (Bombay : S.N.D.T. University, 1973), mimeo.

of women in the industries listed is not likely to have been arrested substantially. Further evidence of a declining trend in the employment of women in industry can be noted from their situation in mining, an occupation which is not strictly urban but which by character belongs to the urban industrial rather than the rural agricultural sector. In 1961, 106.3 thousand women were employed in mines. This number dropped to 100.3 thousand by 1966, 84.3 thousand by 1968 and 78 thousand by 1969.

TABLE 3

Employment of Women in Industry, 1952-1962

Industry	Women as per cent of total employed 1952	1962
Textiles	9.2	5.8
Processes Allied to Agriculture	43.7	40.8
Paper Products	5.0	3.8
Chemical Products	15.5	9.9
Mineral Products	16.7	17.6
Basic Metal Industries	7.0	3.1
Miscellaneous	8.5	6.8

Source : V.B. Karnik in "Status of Women : Economic and Employment Aspects" in *Women in India* (Bombay : S.N.D.T. University 1973), mimeo

Unemployment in the country seems to have affected women in the sectors listed in Table 3 the most. Given the choice, employers seem to prefer male labour for the simple reason that it is "uneconomic" for them to provide the basic service conditions with which labour legislation protects women. The injustice of this tendency of employers is deplorable but the fact remains that the drop in female employment means that employers find it more profitable to employ men than women. As a consequence, a great deal of the nation's potential for productivity remains unutilised. If it is impossible to absorb available women in the sectors which register a decline in their employment, alternate ways and means of utilising this female labour for productive purposes need to be worked out.

While the employment of women in the sectors listed in Table 3 has dropped their employment in nursing, teaching, secretarial and clerical jobs, the pharmaceutical and telephone industry, has risen noticeably. The remarkable growth in the employment of women in these fields suggests that, by entering these fields in larger numbers, they have something special to offer and could make an even greater contribution to national development. Meanwhile, taking into consideration the large proportion that women constitute in nursing and teaching it would be extremely useful to concentrate on the improvement of the quality of their service in these fields. By improving the quality of their work and commitment, women in these occupations could launch a major revolution in improving work values and performance standards in the country. Are women in these and other occupations in which they are to be found in large numbers able to contribute according to their potential? What are the factors that promote or inhibit the quality of their performance? What are the constraints on the effective participation of women in occupations which they have entered? Are the impediments largely in the nature of structural constraints within the organisations in which women work? Or, do they arise out of the expectations Indian society has of women in their roles as mothers, wives and daughters? These are questions which must be considered by those who are concerned with the contribution of women to economic development.

EDUCATED UNEMPLOYMENT

Improvement in the quality of the output of working women is only one way of enhancing their contribution to economic development. The other and probably the more important aspect, is that of drawing into productive work women who are equipped to produce but do not. We have referred above to the non-utilisation of the potential of the female labour force in industry. Equally, and perhaps even more important, is the problem of the non-utilisation of the potential of women in the service sector and professions of different kinds. A reference must specifically be made to the non-utilisation of the potential of educated women. During the two and a half decades since independence the education of women has expanded enormously but the gainful employment of educated women has not increased proportionately. While unemployment of the educated is a general feature of the slow development of the Indian economy, the unemployment and underemployment of educated women is particularly distressing. It is not possible to estimate the character of the underemployment of educated women, but the 1961 Census data provide a clue to the magnitude of their unemployment. Only 36 per cent of unemployed women aged 15 and above are illiterate.[7] The majority are school educated. As many as 49.3 per cent are educated up to matric and above. Thus, it seems that the majority of the illiterate or marginally educated women find some employment, but it is those who are educated above middle school level who are unemployed in larger numbers.

Inasmuch as the state invests heavily in all education, both unemployment and underemployment are a national waste. It is sometimes argued that educated women "choose" to remain unemployed, but this argument fails to take note of the possibility that, at least for some women, the "choice" to opt out of employment is forced on them. The reasons for this are complex and related to family responsibility and the structure and organisation of work. However, even those women who are unable at present to take up employment outside the home should be offered opportunities for social and civic service to society.

Apart from gainful employment or unpaid voluntary service, women can contribute significantly to economic development through savings and organised consumer movements. Women are in a position to exercise considerable control over savings since they are largely responsible for domestic expenditure; they can also determine whether savings will be put into productive investments or locked up in jewellery and gold. Again, by exercising discrimination regarding the price and the quality of the goods they purchase, and by resisting smuggled or black market goods, they can exercise healthy consumer control over the economy. Unfortunately, the extent to which conscientious saving, wise investment of savings and discriminating and well-organised consumption can contribute to the growth of the economy has yet to be appreciated. Interna-

7. Census of India 1961, Vol. I, Part II B (11) General Economic Tables. Table B. VIII Parts A & B, p. 26.

tional Women's Year could make a beginning by exploiting these new ways of involving women in economic development.

POLITICAL PARTICIPATION

The success of a democracy depends on how informed, alert and aware the electorate is and how well the interests of the different sectors are represented and fought for in legislative bodies. Thus the quality of the participation of women in politics may be gauged by the character of their behaviour as voters and by the extent to which their interests are represented in Parliament, in the State Legislative Assemblies, and in other policy and decision-making bodies.

In countries like the U.S.S.R., Czechoslovakia and Yugoslavia, where the number of women in legislative bodies is the largest in the world, women constitute about 27 to 28 per cent of the membership. At present women comprise less than 5 per cent of the total membership of Parliament in India. This proportion is far smaller than that in some East European socialist countries but higher than in some developed countries of the West. For instance, only 4.1 per cent of the members of the British Parliament are women, while in Egypt, Iraq and Ethiopia women are not represented in legislative bodies at all.

The election of women to public office is another indicator of their participation in political life. Not only do we have a woman Prime Minister but we have several women Ministers as well. In 1952, 3.8 per cent of the Union Cabinet consisted of women, 5.2 per cent in 1957, 9.8 per cent in 1967 and about 7.5 per cent today. Further, women are included in twelve out of the nineteen state cabinets in the country. Yet, although the representation of women in Parliament, in the Assemblies and in Union and state cabinets in India is larger than it is in many other countries in the world, it is not proportionate to their number in the total population and does not even approximate the figure that political parties consider to be a fair allocation. At the time of the selection of candidates most political parties promise to reserve 10 to 15 per cent of their seats for women candidates, but the maximum number of seats allotted has never exceeded 7 per cent and, of course, the percentage of the seats actually contested and won is even smaller.[8]

Membership of political parties and the exercise of voting rights are other indicators of political involvement. As far as the former is concerned the record of Indian women is quite unsatisfactory. Exact figures are not available but it is estimated that in no party does membership of women exceed 20 per cent. As may be imagined, the number of women performing policy-making functions in political parties is almost negligible. Women lag behind men as voters too. In 1952 only 37.1 per cent of females eligible to vote as compared to 55 per cent of males exercised their franchise. The percentage of women voters rose from 46.6 in 1962 to 60 per cent in 1971 while the corresponding figures for men were 61.1 in 1962 and 69.7 in 1971. But the difference between the percentage of males and females who voted has narrowed down from 17.9 per cent in 1952 to 15.0 per cent in 1962 to 9.7 per cent in 1971.[9]

UNINFORMED AND CONSERVATIVE

While increasing the number of women voters is important, equally crucial is the improvement in the quality of their political participation. One of the basic questions in this connection is the extent to which the problems and the concerns of women are taken up in the State Assemblies or in Parliament. Do male representatives fight for issues concerning women? Do women at least? Do the issues concerning women receive adequate support? Identification of social injustice to women and the formation of pressure groups for redress and removal of these injustices is one of the more important aspects of the political development of a nation. India has a healthy tradition in this matter but Indian women are not yet politicised enough to fight for their own cause.

Another important matter concerning the quality of the political participation of women is the quality of the vote. While most of the electorate in the country is illiterate, politically uninformed and unaware, this is especially true of female

8. Usha Mehta, "Political Status of Women," in *Women in India* (Bombay: S.N.D.T. University, 1973), mimeo.

9. *Ibid.*

voters. In a public opinion survey conducted in Bombay at the time of the Fourth General Elections, 110 women having radios were interviewed regarding the programmes they listen to.[10] The findings indicated that 41 were interested in news and only 8 had heard talks on elections, as against 99 who regularly listened to music programmes. The poor exposure of women to the mass communications media is brought out even better by a recent comparative study of husbands and wives with respect to the press, radio and cinema.[11] Among the couples interviewed it was found that twice as many husbands (10.5 per cent) as wives (5.3 per cent) read newspapers; fewer wives (25.2 per cent) than husbands (37.2 per cent) went to the cinema, and nearly twice as many husbands (19.4 per cent) as wives (10.5 per cent) listened to the radio.

Election studies have revealed that female voters are more conservative than men and more likely to be influenced by religious considerations, that women's voting behaviour is heavily influenced by others, especially their husbands. For instance, in two Bombay studies on the extent to which husbands and wives influenced each other's vote it was found that 45 and 28 per cent of the women consulted their husbands, and as many as 10 per cent voted "solely" on the advice of their husbands.[12] In contrast to this it was found that 2 per cent of the men voted according to the advice of their wives. The issue of improving women's participation in political development then is not merely that of increasing the number of women who exercise their franchise, but also one of educating and motivating them to be more informed, more aware, more independent and more purposive as voters.

MODERNISATION AND CHANGE

The possibilities for women's contribution to economic and political development have been discussed above. The economic and political participation of women must be given high

10. *Ibid.*

11. *Family Planning Practice in India : First All India Report* (Baroda : Research Group), p. 5

12. Usha Mehta, *op. cit.*

priority, yet, from the point of view of national development, there are several other areas in which more active and purposive involvement on the part of women would be invaluable.

The complaint is often heard that women are heavily tradition bound and that they obstruct the progress of healthy modernisation and change. In movements for the secularisation of life the inability of women to depart from convention is a major obstacle. Similarly, measures such as more liberal divorce laws, the legalisation of abortion, or the anti-dowry legislation which were introduced specifically for the liberation of women and to give them equal rights with men, fail because women remain unconvinced of the propriety of using them. Again, opportunities for the education of women and occasionally even for their employment, and services for their health and medical care are ineffective because women do not utilise them adequately. Programmes that are deliberately aimed at releasing women from tradition and convention and motivating them to make optimum use of the facilities provided for their benefit could be of tremendous benefit to the development of Indian society.

While women can, by stepping out of restrictive tradition, make a valuable contribution to social development, it is probably as mothers that they can make the most significant impact on society. The country is committed to the ideals of equality, secularism and national integration. It is struggling for the successful implementation of several schemes such as universal primary education and population control. Neither are national ideals, objectives and goals really attainable unless each generation of Indians grow up fully committed to their achievement. Educational institutions and mass communications media can assist in the development of this commitment but it is largely in the home that the new ideals and goals must be communicated and developed. It is up to Indian mothers to inculcate in their children the new values, ideals and norms. In International Women's Year a major breakthrough could be achieved in awakening Indian mothers to this responsibility and to prepare them for this important task.

One of the major obstacles to the integration of women in economic development is the slow growth of the economy. In the developed countries the employment of women has been a corrollary to economic growth. Women have been drawn into the economy because a larger work force was needed. With us the situation is altogether different. How can women enter the labour force in a situation in which the economy can not even absorb all employable men? This is a crucial question, but its answer lies in a counter-question. Why should the poor rate of economic growth affect women's right to gainful employment more than it affects man's right to work? Hopefully, the economy will grow to absorb more men and women in the labour force but one of the most important conditions for liberating women and increasing their involvement in development is that their employment should not be conditional on the full employment of men. The equal right of women and men to work must be respected even in a situation of relatively high general unemployment.

LIMITATIONS

There are ample possibilities for involving women in the economy of the country. It is largely a matter of educating them for new responsibilities, and of designing and organising mechanisms to draw them in. However, it is important to recognise that neither the equipment of women with the new skills and knowledge that are required nor practices and procedures designed to involve women can be effective unless women themselves are motivated to contribute. It is true that the poor involvement of women in development is a consequence of slow economic growth and of the fact they are not equipped to participate; but the apathy of women and the lack of awareness of their own capacities and potentialities are as important as limitations on their more productive involvement in the economy. Their apathy and lack of awareness in turn originate in anachronistic notions about what women 'may' or 'may not' do. For instance, it is widely believed that the gainful employment of women, particularly their employment outside the home, is detrimental to the "status" of their families. Where the financial circumstances of a family make it absolutely necessary for women to work, only certain jobs are considered "respectable" or "suitable". Jobs that involve travelling or contact with men or jobs which have been so far the preserve of males are considered unsuitable.

Another major limitation on the participation of women is that Indian society is still so structured that it is not easy for women to have time for work outside the home in addition to homemaking. Labour saving devices, processed goods, water and fuel facilities, services for removal of garbage, creches and day-care centres for children are required to liberate women from being restricted to traditional household tasks.

The limitations on women's involvement in political and social development are largely similar. Few women have the time or inclination for politics. Although we have a woman Prime Minister most women leave politics to men. They consider politics to be too "dirty" and "rough" for women. On the whole, women are diffident about their abilities for political participation and unaware of the impact they can make on social development. They are not even aware of their crucial and far-reaching impact on national development through the influence that they exercise as mothers on the younger generation.

Efforts to involve women in development will have to take account of these limitations. Plans and programmes will have not merely to educate women for new responsibilities and provide them with opportunities for employment and in public life but also to promote an entirely new set of attitudes and values concerning the role and status of women.

REDEFINITION OF SEX ROLES

In a sense, the involvement of women in national development may be considered to be a process wherein they are encouraged to discover and develop their own potential and to live a life that is richer and socially more purposeful. Inasmuch as this is in effect the emancipation of women, we may say that the movement for the involvement of women in development is simultaneously a movement for their emancipation. This equation between development and the emancipation of women is what is unique about the movement for the liberation of women in India.

Basically, the liberation of women calls for an examination and redefinition of the roles of women both in and outside the home. The roles of women, however, cannot be redefined in isolation but in relation to the roles of men. So far, it has been believed the world over that the social apportioning of male and female roles is biologically conditioned. Today this belief is being seriously questioned. In many of the Western countries this questioning is the major thrust of the movement for women's liberation. In India, we have not yet started questioning the traditional allocation of sex roles. There is, however, a major danger in this questioning and we need to guard against it. In some parts of the world the movement for the revision and redefinition of sex roles has taken the form of ugly conflicts between "liberationists" and "traditionalists". The consequence of this is that a world already torn by dissensions has one more division—that between the "feminists" and the "male chauvinists". Divisions of this sort are damaging to human life and purpose. Developing countries like India need to integrate men and women in development and cannot afford such divisions.

Fortunately, Indian men have not resented the advance of women. The reasons for this are probably rooted in the Indian respect for womanhood, and Indian notions regarding the male obligation to "protect" women. It is possible that the tolerance of the Indian male also has something to do with the non-competitive and non-aggressive ethos of Indian life. But the question that we need to ask, before we set out to examine and redefine sex roles, is whether Indian men will continue to be as tolerant if they have to compete with large numbers of women. Will Indian men and women go the way of the West or will they discover for themselves and offer to the world some new adaptation that provides for a sharing of roles and allows both mobility and freedom to women and men?

CONSEQUENCES FOR THE FAMILY

While "male chauvinism" is the major obstacle to the redefinition of sex roles in society, there is also a genuine fear regarding the unhappy consequences it may have for the family. It is feared that the emancipation of women from traditional household functions may lead them to neglect their obligations to their homes and children. It is believed that in order to reach out to new avenues of self-fulfilment they will neglect old obligations. The position taken by extremist feminists, is particularly alarming. They say that they would willingly sacrifice the institutions of marriage and the family if these prevent the liberation of women. But, it is important to recognise that there are thinkers who believe that the emancipation of women will not damage the family; on the contrary, they believe that it will benefit family life. They envisage interesting possibilities for the redistribution of familial functions and believe that the new patterns of family living that will emerge will make for richer companionship in the family.

Obviously, neither the restructuring of sex roles nor the repatterning of family life will be easy. But these tasks are likely to be easier to handle in a country which is consciously "developing" and in which feminist demands have not yet aroused antagonism between the sexes. If attempts to conceptualise concrete alternatives to the existing division of tasks between the sexes are made, and if carefully guided experiments to operationalise these alternatives are undertaken, India could perhaps succeed in advancing peacefully in a sensitive area of human relations unlike some of the most developed nations in the world that are highly agitated over the demands of women.

While considering possibilities for the Indian woman's discovery of herself, and for her self-development and self-fulfilment, it is important to recognise that we are, on the whole, a society in which the individual personality is poorly developed. Shortcomings like a lack of confidence in oneself, an inability to estimate one's own capacities or to identify and cultivate one's interests—which are obstacles to the achievement of personal fulfilment and freedom—are not restricted to women. Even men in India suffer from the same deficiencies. These personality characteristics seem to be related to a society in which both men and women have always submitted to the authority of age, kinship, caste and custom, and have not asserted their individual freedom. It would be shortsighted to formulate programmes for the personal growth and emancipation of women without taking the social factor into account. The movement for the emancipation of women in India has to be viewed as part of the wider process of the liberation of the individual.

If the liberation of women and men is seen as part of a wider movement for individual freedom, and is planned as an integrated process, men and women will be better able to appreciate and respect each other's freedom. If both men and women together launch out on a quest for personal freedom, instead of antagonism between the sexes, there will be a tendency to look upon each other as partners in a common quest and to avoid the unhappy course that the women's liberation movement has taken in some of the developed countries.

ASSERTION OF EQUAL RIGHTS

In most of the developed countries of the world the achievement of equality for women still means a struggle for the basic rights and opportunities enjoyed by men. Unlike women elsewhere, Indian women have not had to struggle for their rights to vote, to education and to work which were granted to them even before they organised themselves to demand them. During the past century and a half Indian reformers—most of them men—have struggled ceaselessly and with determination for a better life for women. Suttee, female infanticide, infant marriage, the dowry system, polygamy, the ban on the remarriage of widows and several other practices detrimental to the status of women, have been systematically attacked and counteracted by legislation. Tremendous efforts have been made to promote education among women. If, in spite of this, the life of most Indian women continues to be confined and restricted it is largely because the regeneration of attitudes and values that is required to motivate women to assert their rights and to reach out to a richer life has not yet taken place. What Indian women need for their liberation is a revolution for the transformation of traditional notions concerning equality and the status of women.

What has been said above may perhaps convey the impression that Indian women do not suffer from inequalities and discrimination. Although the legal position of women in India is better than in many parts of the world, inequality in various forms continues. Article 13 of the Indian Constitution assures all citizens equal protection before the law, and Article 15 expressly prohibits discrimination on the ground of sex. But "personal" laws are excluded from the scope of this Article with the result that in matters of marriage, divorce, inheritance, maintenance, guardianship and custody of children, adoption and other matters affecting personal life, women still experience inequalities and injustices. There is an urgent need for a uniform civil code based on principles of social justice and full equality for men and women. Although the Directive Principles of the Constitution accept this in principle a uniform code applicable to all citizens, irrespective of their religion, has yet to be framed.

Although the country is committed to equal opportunity for all, women lag far behind men in education. According to the Census of 1971 only 18.74 per cent of Indian women are literate compared to 39.5 per cent of Indian men. The enrolment of women, at all stages of education is far below that of men. For instance, it was estimated that in 1970-71 girls enrolled in classes I-IV constituted only 68.6 per cent of the relevant age group whereas boys constituted 109.8 per cent.[13] The disparity increases as we compare the enrolment of girls and boys at successively higher stages. Girls in classes V-VII constitute 33 per cent of the relevant age group and those who are enrolled in classes VIII-IX only 12.2 per cent. The corresponding figures for boys are 67.7 per cent for classes V-VII and 34.2 per cent for classes VIII-IX. Enrolment figures for higher education are even more discouraging.

The fact that working women carry the burden of two full-time roles of worker and homemaker makes for enormous inequalities for working women. Over and above this, in spite of I.L.O. requirements, women do not receive equal wages. Table 4 illustrates the scale of the disparity in wages. Again, we find that the health of females in the country is far inferior to that of men. For every age group the female death rate is higher than that of males. Female infant mortality is higher than male infant mortality, especially after the first six months of life. Evidence on the point is not particularly reliable, nevertheless it seems consistently to indicate that the higher level of female mortality has a great deal to do with the fact that in society the health and well-being of women is much more neglected than that of men.

13. *Report of the Education Commission, 1964-66* (New Delhi: Ministry of Education, Government of India, 1966) pp. 161, 167.

TABLE 4

Comparison between Male and Female Wages

Process	Daily wage in paise	
	Male	Female
Ploughing (Sowing)	100	82
Weeding	82	52
Transplanting	111	69
Harvesting	98	58
All agricultural occupations	96	59
All non-agricultural occupations	107	62

Source : V.B. Karnik, "Status of Women: Employment and Economic Aspects" in *Women in India* (Bombay: S.N.D.T. University, 1973).

TASKS FOR IWY IN INDIA

The previous sections of this paper discussed the potential for the integration of women in development, the obstacles to their involvement and the importance of the removal of the inequalities from which they suffer. There is much that needs to be done to liberate women and to involve them in the process of national development, and we now suggest some tasks that could be undertaken to achieve the goals of IWY.

Involvement of women in the economy

Task 1. To identify the economic activities in which women can be involved, and to specify more precisely the nature of the functions they can perform. It is important to take note of the fact that possibilities for the employment of women would differ from state to state and also between urban and rural areas.

Task 2. To prepare state and district level plans for the involvement of women in the economy. Such plans would have to take note of the skills women have and their levels of education. Provision would have to be made for gainful as well as unpaid, voluntary participation for part-time, own-time or full-time work. Further, the plans would have to devise measures to overcome anticipated constraints and difficulties.[14]

14. Much of the work of Tasks 1 and 2 will be simplified by the fact that data on the situation of women are now available on a scale unheard

Task 3. To set up organisations to promote the employment of women, by maintaining liaison between the female work force and employers and by undertaking programmes to motivate women to work.

Task 4. To establish centres to educate and prepare women for new economic responsibilities and for the effective performance of their traditional tasks. In the rural areas these centres could train women in modern methods of harvesting, threshing and storing grain, and preserving, processing, packing, canning and marketing of orchard, garden, poultry, dairy and farm products; in setting up cottage industries and cultivating traditional crafts. In urban areas such centres could train women in skills not provided by formal education: development of entrepreneurial skills for ancillary industries, training in the organisation of day-care centres and creches, provision of catering services to schools, hospitals and offices.

Task 5. To establish cooperatives especially designed to assist women involved in all kinds of production, encourage them to market their own products, and to provide services to simplify housework and thus free women for employment.

Task 6. To develop a women's consumer movement.

Involvement of women in political development

Task 1. To organise programmes to educate women about their political rights and responsibilities and to make them aware of how our political system works.

Task 2. To encourage women to participate in party politics and seek election to positions of power and influence in decision-making bodies.

Social development

Task 1. To design programmes to inform women about national goals and objectives and the changing values and needs of a modernising society, and to stimulate them to think about and discuss their own role in social development.

of before in India. Apart from the information available through the Census, the National Sample Survey and Manpower Planning and Research, valuable data are to be found in the material collected by the National Committee on the Status of Women.

Equality

Task 1. To organise movements for a uniform civil code and the elimination of disparities in remuneration between men and women.

Task 2. To promote education among women by providing services and facilities to attract more girls to school, to prevent them from dropping out and to improve their academic performance.

Task 3. To revise school and college curricula with a view to making them relevant to the lives of women.

Task 4. To foster among both men and women a deeper understanding and appreciation of the need to redefine sex-typed roles according to which tasks and functions are traditionally regarded as being exclusively "male" and "female".

The dynamism of the women's movement in India will depend on how effectively these tasks are understood, accepted and performed. Much will also depend on how the movement is organised. Already there is talk of the appointment of a special body on the lines of the Backward Classes Commission with state and district level units, but experience has shown that the utility of such bodies is extremely limited. What is necessary is a determined and concerted effort by both governmental and voluntary organisations to facilitate the integration of women in the process of national development. Existing women's groups, clubs and organisations will have to be restructured for action, university and other governmental and voluntary research centres will have to share the responsibility for relevant fact finding studies, and the mass communications media will have to create, through the dissemination of information, a new awareness among women and a desire for change in attitudes and outlook—these are some of the important challenges that all, including women, have to face if they are seriously concerned about International Women's Year in India.

2

ZARINA BHATTY

Muslim Women in Uttar Pradesh : Social Mobility and Directions of Change

Muslims in India are a heterogeneous community. While there is conformity in ideals and beliefs, derived from the Quran and the *Hadis* (sayings of Prophet Mohammad), the general pattern of living, the system of social stratification, customs and attitudes regarding women have been greatly influenced by the dominant Hindu culture of India. Early conversions to Islam usually meant the acceptance of a different faith while the mode of living remained more or less unchanged. What Ibbetson says of the Muslim convert of Punjab is also true of Uttar Pradesh: "... His customs are unaltered, his rules of marriage and inheritance are unchanged, and almost the only difference is that he shaves his scalp lock and the upper part of his moustache, repeats the Mohammadan creed in the mosque and adds Mussalman to the Hindu wedding ceremonies."[1]

An important reason for the retention of Hindu customs was that very often instead of a few individuals in a village community, a caste group as a whole accepted Islam. Such a group escaped the brunt of social pressures to abandon its cultural heritage. In Kasauli[2] —a village in the former Oudh

1. D.C.J. Ibbetson, *Punjab Castes* (Lahore : Government Printing Press, 1916), p. 14.

2. Kasauli is a pseudonym for a village which is 25 miles east of Lucknow and 8 miles from the town of Bara Banki. The majority of the

region of Uttar Pradesh which I studied and shall frequently refer to for empirical support of my comments and conclusions —the Sakkas (the caste of water carriers) still have the symbolic fire as a part of their wedding ceremony, the bride and her groom do the ritual rounds along with the Muslim *nikah*. The position of women in Indian Muslim society is thus influenced both by Islamic injunctions and Hindu traditions. And, as has often happened in the compounding of two sets of influences, the conservative and restrictive elements of one have tended to dominate or neutralise the liberal elements of the other. This has become glaringly apparent since the enactment of Hindu Code Bill which has given equal rights, at least in law, to Hindu women while the tenacious adherence to the outmoded Muslim Personal Law continues to keep the lot of Muslim women unaltered.

Islam, at its inception, also represented a reformist movement.[3] In Arabia, at that time, women were no more than chattels and even female infanticide was practised. Islam brought about significant improvements in the attitude towards women and their rights so that Muslims were usually considered to have a higher social status than their Hindu sisters before the passage of the Hindu Code Bill. However, the reforms of centuries ago are completely outmoded and absolete in the realities of the twentieth century. It is this fact that Muslim society in India has persisted in not recognising.

SOCIAL STRATIFICATION

Muslim society in India is sharply divided into two distinct sections—the Ashrafs and the non-Ashrafs. The Ashrafs represent the upper social strata and comprise the equivalent of a hierarchy of four castes: the Sayyads, the Sheikhs, the Mughals and the Pathans, in that order. It is believed that these upper castes are of foreign origin and thereby superior, while the non-Ashrafs are mostly converts and inferior. In the Oudh

population is Muslim. This paper is based on data collected during field work in 1962, 1964 and again in 1973.

3. Zarina Bhatty, "Social Status of Muslim Women in India," *Roundtable* (March, 1975).

region of Uttar Pradesh, Ashrafs form the bulk of the Muslim landlord class. One reason for this may be that the Nawabs continued to rule in Oudh till as late as 1856. This might also explain why a distinctly feudal culture is associated with the Muslims of Uttar Pradesh and, particularly, with those who hail from the region of Oudh.

The division between the Ashraf and the non-Ashraf strata of Muslims is clearly reflected in their attitudes towards women. The Ashraf concept of a woman is derived entirely from her role as a wife and a mother and is garnished with the traditional feminine virtues of pre-marital virginity, beauty, tenderness, modesty, self-denial, graciousness, sensitivity and devotion to the family. These virtues, however, are not superfluous trimmings but prerequisites for the role assigned to her in which she upholds the honour of the family, ensures the continuity of the lineage and passes on to the new generation the 'noble' tradition. A girl, right from birth, is moulded for marriage and motherhood. Romance, an inevitable adjunct of her assigned role, is sung about but in practice tabooed. The daughter, in fact, is regarded as a potential alien in her father's house, for she belongs to the patrilineal lineage of her future husband. She is referred to as *amaanat* or *paraya dhan* (another's property). Mrs. Hassan Ali, an English lady married to an Indian Muslim, who lived with her husband in Lucknow in the early years of this century, writing about Ashraf Muslim families in Uttar Pradesh says:[4] "It is generally to be observed in Mussalman families even in this day that the birth of a baby girl produces a temporary gloom, while the birth of a boy gives rise to a festival in the Zenanah. Some are wicked enough to say that it is more honourable to have sons." Today, three quarters of a century later, the gloom at the birth of a girl baby persists.

The reason for this gloom among Muslims is the same as that advanced in Hindu society, namely, that the girl is a liability, her birth commits the family to exorbitant outlays for her dowry or marriage gifts and expenses, and though she does not really belong to her parents, she must be cared for,

4. M. Hassan Ali, *Observations on the* Mussulmans of India. (ed.) William Crooke (London : Oxford University Press, 1917), p. 186.

guarded and preserved until she is claimed by those who expect her to be thus guarded and preserved for them. It is not surprising, therefore, that Muslims, while expressing their displeasure as begetting a daughter, use the phrase "a guest of four days" to describe her.

PATTERNS OF MARRIAGE AND WORK

Islam does not envisage a woman having the liberty to choose her own man to marry, but it does give her the privilege to approve the man she is married to. The Quran is quite explicit on this issue: "A woman ripe in years should have her consent taken (in marriage). While she remains silent her silence is her consent, but if she refuses she will not be married by force."[5] But in Uttar Pradesh, particularly among Ashraf Muslims, not only is a girl's consent not taken but it is regarded as scandalous if she expresses her preference for a man. The custom of *purdah* which is enjoined upon a Muslim woman, whereby she has to cover herself with a superfluous garment specially designed to conceal her feminine appearance, drastically curtails her freedom and ability to move about. This custom springs from the attitude that women must not be seen by men lest they be attracted towards them. The implicit presumption is that once being attracted the men are not expected to exhibit any self-restraint. The onus of protecting themselves lies with the women. Thus if a man misbehaves with a woman, the fault most likely is hers and hence no sanctions in this respect need be invoked against the man. And there are none.

Clearly a life so hemmed in by constraints, so laden with impositions, could not possibly come naturally to women. Indeed, the desired attitude of complete submission to male authority, whether it is the father, brother, husband or father-in-law is assiduously taught to girls. A song that is sung when a bride departs from her natal to her conjugal home depicts this attitude very aptly :

5. T.P. Hughes, *Dictionary of Islam* (London : W.H. Allen, 1835), p. 314.

Babul ham tore khoonte ki gayyan,
jhidhar baandho bandh jayen
(We are your cows, O Father;
whichever stake you tie us to,
There we shall remain bound.)

Non-Ashraf women by comparison are freer. To begin with, they do not as a rule observe *purdah*. And since *purdah* is one of the insignia of respectability, these women are not considered as respectable as Ashraf women. While they play the role of wives and mothers, they are also partners in the daily struggle for earning a livelihood and, the harder this struggle, the greater is the importance of woman as a partner in work. The dominance of this struggle, often pursued grimly in the midst of poverty, leaves little room for the leisurely feminine virtues though they may be admired and even aspired to. Non-Ashraf women too are subordinate to male authority, though they need not be as submissive as their Ashraf sisters. Their movements are less restricted and, being equal partners in earning the daily bread, they have more opportunities for asserting themselves. Virtue is valued and expected of a woman more than it is of man, but it is not so rigidly conceived nor are deviations so severely frowned upon. Non-Ashraf women, therefore, find room for their emotional fulfilment; romances are not uncommon and even elopements occur. Divorce permitted by Islam still carries a strong stigma among the Ashrafs, but to a much less degree among the non-Ashrafs. In Kasauli I found that divorce, remarriage after divorce and marriage of widows were more frequent among the non-Ashrafs than among the Ashrafs.

Legally, a Muslim man can take upto four wives. He can also divorce his wife at will, without assigning any reason, and simply by saying "I divorce you". He is not required by law or custom to pay any maintenance to the wife thus divorced, though he is obliged to pay a compensation of *mehr*[6] fixed in the marriage contract provided the divorced

6. *Mehr* can be literally translated as dower. This is the amount fixed at the time of *nikah* which a husband is required to pay to the bride before consumating the marriage but in actual practice it is not paid unless or until husband wants to divorce the wife. But if wife initiates the divorce proceedings then he is not obliged to pay the dower. But since a Muslim man

wife or her family insists on it. On the other hand, it is very difficult for a woman to secure a divorce. Not only does she have to go to court but the conditions under which she can seek divorce are also very stringent. Even if she succeeds in getting a divorce, she forfeits the *mehr*. Incidentally polygamy is not recognised as a reason for seeking a divorce. Fortunately, however, polygamy is almost negligible. Nevertheless, the absence of any safeguard for the woman clearly demonstrates the inequality in the status of man and woman in Muslim society.

In matters of inheritance too a woman is discriminated against in law as well as by custom. Islam stipulates that a daughter is entitled to one-third of her father's property, that is, to half of what her brother gets. This rule seldom applies to landed property which is almost never inherited by daughters. I found in Kasauli that, to camouflage this denial, the custom of cousin marriage with a preference for parallel cousins has become well established. In fact, this custom is common throughout Uttar Pradesh and particularly among those who have landed property. Non-Ashraf families generally do not own land or any other property worth considering and therefore the occasion for any discrimination in inheritance does not arise. There is a sense of common ownership of whatever little is possessed because it is acquired through the joint effort of both husband and wife.

The fact of joint effort at making a living is perhaps the most important differentiating feature of the non-Ashraf families. I found non-Ashraf women in Kasauli moving about freely with their men and working alongside with their husbands in the fields or at crafts in which the family specialises. A division of labour based on sex is commonly practised. For example, among Manihars (the caste of bangle sellers) men manufacture the bangles or journey to the nearby city to buy their stock of bangles, while both men and women sell them in the village streets or at their shop. Women have an edge over men in selling because they can reach Ashraf women in their home which the men, on account of *purdah*, cannot. The

can have up to four wives without divorcing the previous wives, it is seldom that a man starts the divorce, he can always discard his wife unofficially and marry another.

division of labour between men and women is more clearly defined in the caste of Nais (barbers). Men cut hair and shave, carry messages regarding births, deaths or marriages and cook at ceremonial occasions for Ashraf as well as non-Ashraf families. Nai women carry and deliver sweets that are customarily distributed among relatives and neighbours at festivals or ceremonial occasions, help Ashraf women in their toilette and at childbirth (it is usually a woman of the Nai caste who delivers the baby) and also massage new mothers and the new born babies. These women are paid a wage for their services or, as in Ashraf homes, they receive a traditionally fixed payment at harvest time and other customary gifts.

EDUCATION AND EMPLOYMENT

A change in the attitude towards women is clearly observable both in Ashraf and non-Ashraf sections of Muslim society, but the change is in different directions. It was discouraging to find that, while upper class Ashraf Muslims in Kasauli were moving towards a more liberal attitude, the non-Ashrafs were becoming more conservative and were trying to emulate those very traditional customs of Ashraf society which the Ashrafs themselves were giving up.

The greatest change in Ashraf attitudes towards women has come about in the matter of their education. The worth of education has come to be established so well in their own minds that they not only find it impossible to deny it to women but also actively encourage it. The partition of India, in this respect, had an advantageous effect on those Muslim families which decided to remain in India. Immediately after partition many families allowed their sons to go to Pakistan either out of fear of discrimination or to exploit the job opportunities in the new country, while the girls remained with their parents. Older people from families which owned land tended not to migrate for reasons which included the prospect of losing their property.

This happened in Kasauli too. While hardly any from the older generation migrated, quite a few young men opted to do so. Many joint families broke up on this account and, in some families, the burden of earning a living even fell on the women. Necessity forced many families to yield to the pressures of time and to allow their daughters to take up jobs. Further, a side effect of the Hindu-Muslim riots immediately after partition was that many Muslim women gave up *purdah* because in *Burqa* they were immediately indentified as Muslim. Once a woman gave up *purdah*, though for a short-term practical reason, she seldom returned to it. Meanwhile, the doors of education were opening to girls and both these changes made more and more women to come out of their seclusion to seek jobs and take their place in spheres which had hitherto been closed to them.

In Kasauli today several girls, married and unmarried, are not only holding paid jobs, one of them is a Minister in the State cabinet. However, I found that while higher education for women is now desired and even facilitated by male members of the family, when it comes to taking up a job, some resistance is still encountered. Here, traditional attitudes towards women and values regarding status and prestige both play a role. At the time I was doing my study in Kasauli, an unmarried daughter of the leading Muslim family was working as a teacher in the village school. Another woman of the same family, now a Minister, was a member of the U.P. Legislative Assembly. While the family showed no resistance to the candidature of the latter for the Assembly seat—in fact, was proud of it—it debated for long whether the other girl should be allowed to take up school teaching in the village. This, notwithstanding the fact that the Assembly candidate was forced to mingle with all sorts of people on terms not consistent with the traditional values of her class. Such exposure was tolerated because to be a member of the State Assembly carries high prestige, but similar exposure in the midst of the village folk at the relatively low prestige level of a school teacher was clearly undesirable. This lingering resistance in fully accepting the break is evident in many other ways as well.

It should be noted that though the worth of education is being accepted, at least among families that can afford it for their daughters, in matters of marriage and the granting of other personal choices, women are still treated differently from men. The alternatives available to them are still very limited and traditional attitudes continue to regulate their lives. In Kasauli girls are not encouraged to make their own choice of husbands or even to express their preference. They marry whoever is chosen for them by their parents and the majority of marriages take place within close relatives. Some deviations have taken place in the last decade or so, but these were resisted and strongly disapproved. In the matter of accepting jobs too the resistance has not worn off. Two years ago when a girl from the leading landlord family took up a university lecturership, the echoes of disapproval from the older members of the family were clearly audible.

Judged in the context of the present day urge for equality, the status of Muslim women in Uttar Pradesh surely falls short of the desired. Let me add immediately that I do not hold with equality in the sense of similarity of roles for men and women in society. But an individual's status in society does depend on the totality of rights—political, legal, economic and social—enjoyed by him or her. In other words, the status of an individual within any social system varies inversely with the impediments imposed by society deliberately or otherwise to restrict self-realisation. On this criterion Muslim society has been and still is discriminating against women. A Muslim woman has the assigned role of mother and wife, but this role is looked upon as inferior and serious constraints are placed on her if she wishes to supplement it with out-of-home interests. The encouraging sign, on the other hand, is that some rethinking is taking place and a few deviant women are emerging even in the Muslim society of Uttar Pradesh.

SOCIAL MOBILITY AND EMULATION

The situation among the non-Ashrafs is almost the reverse. Women in this segment of Muslim society are losing the freedom they had in an effort to emulate the Ashrafs. In Kasauli I found that the Ashrafs were acting as a reference group for the non-Ashrafs.[7] On the one hand, urban influences were percolating both directly and through the upper classes and on the other, rising incomes and a greater social and political awareness were giving them a more palpable stake in the

7. For a fine discussion of reference group behaviour and "emulation" in a caste structured society, see Owen M. Lynch, *The Politics of Untouchability* (New York : Columbia University Press, 1969).

village community and its traditions. The net result of these two strands of influences was rather curious. The lower class women were trying to imitate the upper class women, who are now more urbanised, in matters of dress styles, manners and language. This imitation extended further to attitudes towards education, religion and family structure.

But the desire was to become more like the upper class families in the traditional village structure rather than in their present day context. For example, the urge for education has expressed itself in the opening of Madarsas in the village, where the Quran along with some Urdu is taught. The practice of religion has become more ostentatious. There is a marked tendency among those non-Ashraf families who have done relatively well to put their women in *purdah* and to withdraw them from the family work force. It is now said in praise of a husband that he is able to give his wife the leisure to "stay on bed", instead of forcing her to work in the field.[8] In Kasauli, a family of Telis (caste of oil pressers) made good and built a partly *pucca* (brick) house. Previously the women in the household used to help in working the *ghani* (oil press) and also in vending mustard oil in the village streets. Now the young daughter-in-law does not work and has taken to *purdah* while the mother-in-law continues to work and does not observe *purdah.* Consequently, the authority of the husband has also increased and the woman has been pushed back into the limited roles of wife and mother.

The same regressive process with respect to the status of women in lower classes has been observed by Srinivas who describes it as the process of "Sanskritisation" among the lower caste Hindus.[9] Thus in Hindu society too it has been found that while the upper classes are becoming more modern and are according a better status to women, the lower classes, in an attempt to emulate them, are accepting the attitudes and values which these upper classes are discarding.

8. Zarina Bhatty, "Status and Power in a Muslim Dominated Village in U.P.," in Imtiaz Ahmed (ed.), *Caste and Social Stratification Among the Muslims* (Delhi: Manohar, 1973); Zarina Bhatty, "The Problem" in Seminar 165 (May, 1973), pp. 10-12.

9. M.N. Srinivas, *Caste in Modern India* (Bombay: Asia Publishing House, 1970).

Two new segments of society have emerged exhibiting new patterns of behaviour. In its attitude to women, one represents a backward and the other a forward step. These directions of

Diagram: Social Mobility and Directions of Change

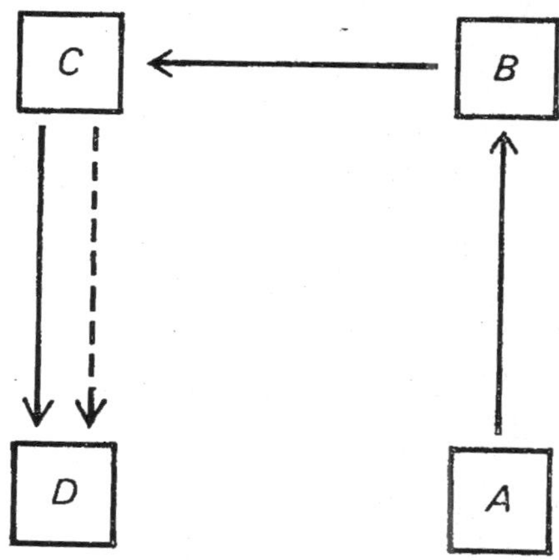

A poor class families; *B* lower class families who become relatively well off; *C* traditional upper classes; *D* liberal upper class families.

change are shown in the diagram which describes the dominant character of change in Muslim society of Kasauli. In the future, since the traditional upper class is itself in flux and the lower classes are motivated to emulate them, change from B to C can be expected to be followed by a change from C to D shown in the diagram by the dotted arrow. Similarly, while no change is visible between A and D its emergence in the future cannot be ruled out.

DIRECTIONS OF CHANGE

The major influence for change operating on the upper classes are education and urbanisation. On the lower classes, the major influence is economic progress, or more specifically, a rise in per capita income. It is the latter influence that needs to be examined further because it concerns the bulk of the Muslim society. The starting point here is poverty or near poverty—a condition in which work is hard (made harder by poverty, and physical incapacity for hard work) and the rewards meagre. Women work because they have to, and not because they find in it the means for greater freedom, economic independence or self-expression. In a measure they already have these. When income rises and it becomes possible to substitute the labour of the woman in the family by a hired hand, or the addition to the income contributed by the woman does not seem worthwhile, the attraction of withdrawing from work appears too strong. While the modulation of women's working hours or character of work or both with the possibility of giving the increase in family income a greater impetus might appear a more rational solution, it is rejected due to the psychological satisfaction of appearing closer to the behaviour pattern of the upper classes.

This analysis shows that while there are similarities in the status of women in the liberalised sections of the upper classes and the poorer lower classes (no *purdah*, freedom of movement, participation in economic activity) and the distance between them may appear relatively small, at least in one respect the similarity is entirely superficial, namely, the approach to work. Since this is fundamental, a direct movement from A to D in the diagram must be viewed as highly improbable at least in the foreseeable future. The process of change as far as the lower classes is concerned, therefore, would continue to be circuitous, though its time span will be less the faster the rate of growth of family income.

Despite the dynamics of change, whose alternate directions appear to be towards a more liberal and a more egalitarian status for women, there is an island of stagnant rigidity—the Muslim Personal Law. Unless this can be submerged and replaced by legislation similar to the Hindu Code Bill, it will stand solidly in the way of Muslim women attaining what their sisters in this country or abroad are now likely to achieve.

3

M. R. WOOD

*Employment and Family Change : A Study of Middle-Class Women in Urban Gujarat**

In Urban Gujarat, as elsewhere in India, the roles of most middle-class women are familial roles.[1] While women of poorer communities often work outside the home for economic reasons, and women of the urban elite frequently participate in non-earning activities for social reasons, the majority of Gujarat's middle-class women confine themselves primarily to the home-centred roles of daughter, sister, daughter-in-law, wife, and mother. Until recently, a middle class woman's employment for economic gain could compromise her family's secular status. On the other hand, non-earning activities outside the home were considered "Western", and could threaten a family's ritual status. Even today, the initiation of such activities often requires economic resources and social connections not always available to middle-class families. In other words, the urban middle-class Gujarati woman may

*An earlier version of this paper was presented at the Annual Meeting of the Canadian Society for Asian Studies in Ottawa, 1972.

1. By "middle-class" is meant individuals or families having a moderate standard of living, a moderate amount of liquid wealth, and a moderate degree of economic security, relative to others in the same urban area.

remain conservative in her activities because she is neither poor enough nor wealthy enough to ignore traditional mores. As such, she represents "the stronghold of Gujarati tradition."

To assess patterns of familial behaviour and attitude among urban middle-class women, a survey of thirty-two respondents was conducted in Ahmedabad in 1968-69. From this larger sample, twelve women who held B.A. degrees, who worked outside their homes and who had children under ten years of age were selected for in-depth interviewing.[2] The selection was made in a non-random fashion: five female clerks in a particular division of a large company who met the above criteria were interviewed, as were five primary school teachers and two social workers. After each respondent had been met informally, an open-ended questionnaire was administered, usually on two successive days. Finally, frequent visits were made at the invitation of the women to their homes of procreation and orientation, and to their places of work and their children's schools. In getting to know each respondent, the primary aim was to evaluate how her behaviour and attitudes with regard to her present family life varied from the behaviour and attitudes manifested in her family life of orientation.

Six of the twelve respondents thus interviewed were employed as a result of what they considered to be economic necessity. The other six, although not less well-off financially, worked for reasons of personal inclination. Cross-cutting this variable was that of caste: half the respondents belonged to Hindu or Jain Bania castes, and half to Brahmin castes. The original study hypothesised that the women working for economic reasons would make fewer changes in their family lives than would those who were employed because they wished to be. This hypothesis was not strongly supported by the evidence; indeed, the variable of caste affiliation proved more relevant to the number and nature of changes made than

2. Marjorie R. Wood, *Changing Patterns of Family Life in Urban Gujarat : A Study of Twelve High Caste Working Women* (unpublished M.A. thesis, University of British Columbia, 1972). A revisit to Ahmedabad in 1974 indicated that while employment among middle-class women is becoming more widespread, the basic findings of the thesis remain the same.

did the variable of reason for employment.[3] Most striking of all, however, was the degree of similarity in the family lives of the respondents as compared to the family lives of their childhoods, and it is to this change phenomenon that the present paper is addressed. Because all respondents work, the relationship between their employment and the changes found in their family patterns can only be suggested. But it is hoped that the hypotheses arising from this analysis will lead to further studies comparing the lives of working and non-working middle-class women in India.

SIMILARITIES IN BACKGROUND

Analysis of the respondents' life-histories suggests that certain factors, or a combination of factors, may predispose Gujarati middle-class women to seek activities outside the home. Information summarised in Table I indicates first of all that birth order may be related to the respondents' inclination towards non-familial roles. Half of the twelve women are either the only daughters or the youngest daughters of their parents.[4] Their childhood recollections indicate that particularly a youngest daughter is often indulged. She is kept at home beyond the age at which her sisters are marrried. Her wish to continue studying is granted. Even her choice of husband is usually given at least formal parental consent. As a youngest daughter, her behaviour cannot jeopardise her sisters' chances of making good marriages. She tends to be treated as an individual, and continues to expect such regard.

A second possible factor in the women's decisions to work is an economic one. As Table 1 shows, all but three respondents have experienced financial loss, five during childhood and four after marriage. High caste families may be "poor but pure" for generations, in which case economic circumstances may not motivate female members to seek employment. But for nine women in this sample, economic hardship

3. Wood, *ibid.*, pp. 172–174.

4. See Promilla Kapur, *Marriage and the Working Woman in India* (Delhi : Vikas Publications, 1970). Kapur does not present birth order information in tabular form, but the number of subjects who are mentioned as youngest daughters is striking.

occurred suddenly and without precedent. They sensed a double disparity, that between the status of their caste and their own economic status, and that between their past and present levels of prosperity.

The seriousness of economic loss suffered by the respondents may to some degree be due to the gradual but perceptible decine in the caste and family emphasis of urban Indian culture. All five women who first experienced loss during their childhood did so when the hereditary positions of their families were dissolved after Independence, or when their fathers died. In the past, according to the respondents, a family left without earning males could usually depend on relatives for support. But as these particular life-histories indicate, relatives today are not always willing or able to assume the extra financial burden, nor is the pressure of caste-community opinion strong enough to oblige them to do so. Similarly, of the four women whose economic circumstances first declined after marriage, three suffered because they had transgressed familistic principles by making love matches, and their families denied them any financial support.

The third fact possibly related to the women's positions as employees also concerns the decline in familistic ties and obligations. As indicated in the last column of Table 1, seven respondents grew up in "fatherless" families, either because of the death of the father, his absence on business, or his religious withdrawal. In traditional Hindu families, an uncle or elder male cousin could be expected to serve as a "father figure": to look after the family's budget, supervise its children's education, and help arrange marriages for the daughters and jobs for the sons. But the mothers of six of the seven "fatherless" respondents received a minimum of such support. They coped with financial and educational matters as well as with household affairs. It may be that daughters raised in such "fatherless" families are predisposed by their mother's examples to act with a degree of assertiveness, and ultimately to assume a traditionally male role, that of wage-earner.

INTRAFAMILIAL RELATIONSHIPS

Certainly an unusual amount of self-assertion is reflected in the structure and nature of the respondents' family ties (Table 2).

Only three women married men selected for them in the customary manner, whereas nine made "love matches": two with the whole-hearted blessings of their elders, four with formal

TABLE 1
Selected Aspects of Respondents' Life-Histories

Respondent	Birth Order	Economic Loss	Absence of Father
Urmila	2nd of 3 Dau 2nd of 8 Chn	Fa' position dissolved	Sanyasi when R. 10 yrs.
Aruna	2nd of 4 Dau 3rd of 7 Chn	Hu had to resign job	-present-
Nandini	5th of 5 Dau 8th of 8 Chn	Fa' position dissolved	bed-ridden when R 10; died when R 15 yrs.
Kamla	only Dau 3rd of 3 Chn	Hu' business small, unstable	-present-
Hansa	4th of 5 Dau 5th of 7 Chn	Hu supports joint family	-present-
Kusum	4th of 4 Dau 7th of 7 Chn	Fa died, Bros' jobs dissolved	died when R.3 yrs.
Sharda	1st of 2 Dau 1st of 2 Chn	Fa ill ; Fa died	bed-ridden when R 6 yrs.; died when R 10 yrs.
Champa	4th of 4 Dau 5th of 6 Chn	-none-	away on business 8-9 months a year
Malti	only Dau 1st of 3 Chn	-none-	away on business 8-9 months a year
Asha	1st of 2 Dau 1st of 2 Chn	Hu without money or family	-present-
Jaya	5th of 5 Dau 8th of 10 Chn	-none-	-present-
Janu	1st of 2 Dau 3rd of 4 Chn	Fa died, Bro ill	died when R 7 yrs.

R respondent; Fa father; Hu husband; Bro brother

parental consent, and three without consent. Seven of nine love matches were particularly deviant in that they involved partners from different castes.[5]

5. Three of the inter-caste marriages occurred between Banias and Brahmins, two between Jain Banias and Hindu Banias, one between a Brahmin and a Moslem, and one between a Brahmin and a Sindhi. Ironically, two of these out-of-caste marriages were given whole-hearted parental consent, while two of the in-caste marriages were vehemently opposed by the elders concerned.

When asked what they considered the traditional marital relationship to be, the women replied something to the effect that a Hindu wife ideally gives unquestioning obedience and unending assistance to her husband. In return, she receives "provision and supervision" for herself and her children. But eight women in the present sample, including one whose marriage was arranged, have established give-and-take or egalitarian relationships with their husbands. They desire and receive a demonstration of interest in their own activities, and they participate in decisions concerning such issues as their husbands' jobs, shifts in residence, and their children's schooling.

TABLE 2

The Structure and Nature of Respondents' Intrafamilial Relationships

Respondent	Marriage		In-laws		Children	
Urmila	love	E	joint	E	1	E
Aruna	love	E	joint	E	2	
Nandini	love		nuclear		2	E
Kamla	love	E	nuclear		1	E
Hansa	arranged	E	joint	E	2	E
Kusum	love	E	nuclear		1	E
Sharda	love		nuclear	E	2	
Champa	love	E	nuclear	E	2	E
Malti	arranged		joint		1	E
Asha	love	E	nuclear		2	E
Jaya	love	E	nuclear	E	2	E
Janu	arranged		nuclear		2	E

E egalitarian relationship

Table 2 also suggests a changing relationship between the respondents and their in-laws. Although eight women lived jointly with their husbands' families after marriage, the same number now live in nuclear households. One couple shifted because the husband was transferred to another city, but the other three reported that they left the husbands' families in part because the latter disapproved of a daughter-in-law's being employed.

Regardless of the place of residence, a woman's devotion to her husband is normally reflected in her respectful behaviour with his family, particularly his mother. Among my respondents, however, only those women who visit their in-laws infrequently comply with the dutiful daughter-in-law ideal: touching the elders' feet in greeting, covering their heads at all times, and remaining silent unless addressed. In contrast, respondents who interact with their in-laws on a daily basis do so in a relatively egalitarian manner. They sit and chat with them, they take meals with their husbands or mothers-in-law, and, with one exception, they discuss differences of opinion directly with their mother-in-law.

It is with regard to the planning and rearing of their own families that the women most noticeably demonstrate changing attitudes (Table 2). No doubt several social and economic factors contribute to the decrease in the number of children between the women's families of orientation (average 5.58) and their families of procreation (average 1.66). But the adamantine manner in which the respondents advocate having no more than two children indicates a strong personal motivation as well. This motivation weakens in one circumstance only: each woman whose first two children are female plans of a third child in the hope that it will be a male.

The respondents felt that a woman is expected to raise her children according to the dictates of her husband's family, for the children "belong" to that family and constitute its future. In fact, my respondents do follow the advice of relatives on how to deal with new-born infants. But once a child can walk and follow simple sentences, most of the women begin to implement book-learned child-rearing methods, methods which emphasise a democratic orientation within the nuclear family and a direct, positive relationship between father and child as well as between mother and child.[6] Ironically, half the respondents find that they tend to be stricter with their children than their husbands are, and less "democratic" than they wish to be, facts which they attribute to the pressures of time and fatigue resulting from their employment.

6. Eight respondents studied some child psychology in college, and another has read extensively on the subject.

It could be argued that an Indian woman who is married to a man of her own choosing, who lives independently of her in-laws, and who has only one or two children is enabled by these circumstances to participate in activities outside the home. However, eight of the present respondents sought employment before marriage, and seven worked while residing jointly with their husbands' families. Thus it appears that for this sample at least, family ties of a non-traditional structure and nature are concomitants of women's employment rather than prerequisites for it.[7] The aspects of character which motivate an Indian woman to assume extra familial roles may also move her to select her own husband, limit the size of her family, and establish egalitarian relationships within her own household, regardless of traditional expectations and obligations.

LIFE-STYLE

With one exception, all the respondents were born into families long associated with Gujarat's urban areas. For generations they had been accustomed to a monetary economy, to literary and cultural institutions, and to an awareness of social and political developments taking place outside their communities. But industrialisation came relatively late to Gujarat, and its social consequences were delayed until the First World War.[8]

The city where the women live, like many indigenous Indian cities once occupied by the British, contains three distinct residential areas: a crowded urban core with clusters of buildings known as *pōls*, an old suburban ring composed of large bungalows, and a new suburban periphery composed of smaller bungalows. In the first instance, industrialisation began to pull the place of business away from the place of residence: the fathers of half of the respondents conducted business in the home, but none of the respondents' husbands does so.[9]

7. Kapur, *op. cit.*, pp. 57, 65 and 67, found that 64 per cent of her working women had made love marriages, 44 per cent lived in strictly nuclear families, and 64 per cent had no more than two children.

8. K. L. Gillion, *Ahmedabad: A Study in Indian Urban History* (Berkeley: University of California Press, 1968 p. 7.

9. Seven fathers but only three husbands were/are in business on their own—yet another consequence of industrialisation.

Secondly, by luring workers into the city to the factories and mills, and by opening up new and more spacious residential areas outside the city, industrialisation both pushed and pulled wealthier *pōl* residents to the suburbs. Thus, from an economic point of view, a division now exists between urban and suburban neighbourhoods, the latter having more prestige. The *pōls* in which half the respondents grew up and into which half married are now considered lower middle-class, and only three respondents have not yet moved to the suburbs (Table 3).

Thirdly, to avoid impoverishment after the loss of their well-to-do residents, *pōls* and old suburbs, which had originally housed members of a single caste, began to admit members of different castes.[10] From a social perspective, then, the main division in residential areas occurs between homogeneous, "traditional" neighbourhoods and heterogeneous, "modern" ones. As Table 3 shows, eight respondents were raised in single-caste *pōls* or suburbs, but only three live in such "traditional" areas today.

Finally, industrialisation affected residential patterns in that it facilitated an increase in mobility. Nine women never shifted residence until they were married, but the same number have moved at least once since then, several on account of new job opportunities or the practice of inter-office transfer.

Changes in the household arrangements of the respondents also reflect the consequences of industrialisation. Most noticeable is the reduction in the size of residence and in the amount of living space. Whereas the families of respondents raised in inner-city areas occupied three-to-five-storey houses for both residential and business purpose, the three respondents living in *pōls* today occupy at the most one floor of a building solely for residential purposes. In the suburbs, because of the rising cost of living, portions of old bungalows are now let to tenants, and new bungalows are much smaller. Of the five women living in older bungalows. only one who lives jointly with her husband's fourteen-member family does not share her accommodation with unrelated persons. Of the four women living in new bungalows, only one enjoys more than three rooms.

10. See Harish C. Doshi, "Industrialisation and Neighbourhood Communities in a Western Indian City," *Sociological Bulletin*, XVIII (March, 1968).

TABLE 3

Sample Changes in Life-Style : Location of Residences and Social Composition of Neighbourhoods

Respondent		During Childhood	After Marriage	At Present (1968-1969)
Urmila		tP	mP	mP
Aruna		tP	tS	tS
Nandini		R	mS	mS
Kamla		tS	mP	mP
Hansa		tS	tS (later mP)	tS
Kusum		mS	mS (later mP)	mS
Sharda		tP (later R)	tP (later mP)	mS
Champa		tP	tS	tP
Malti		tP	mS	mS
Asha		tP (later mS)	mS	mS
Jaya		mS	tP	mS
Janu		mS	tP	mS
TOTAL	tP	6	3	1
	tS	2	3	2
	mP	—	2	2
	mS	3	4	7

t traditional homogeneous caste composition
m modern heterogeneous caste composition
P *pol* residential area of inner city
S suburban residential area beyond walls
R rural area

Industrialisation has also made available to the respondents a variety of consumer goods at reasonable prices. Moreover, it appears to have stimulated an interest in material possessions which contradicts the well-known Bania and, to a lesser extent, all-Gujarati, emphasis on saving. Most of the women grew up in homes furnished only with low wooden stools, thin mattresses or pallets, cooking and eating utensils, and religious articles. Today, all own at least a bed and a wardrobe, and three enjoy a complete range of Western style furniture.

With regard to the daily routine of my respondents, perhaps the most far-reaching effect of industrialisation has been the introduction of the concepts of "fixed time" and "regular programme". Hard work and long hours have always characterised Gujarati men's activities; but, unlike the fathers of the respondents, the husbands of all but two women now keep regular hours and work-weeks as dictated by their employers. Similarly, not only in response to their husbands' fixed schedules but more especially because they themselves are employed, my respondents also adhere to a fairly rigid programme, one which short-cuts many of the household chores previously performed by their mothers. Instead of preparing two meals a day, as their mothers did, the respondents living in nuclear families generally serve left-overs at either the mid-morning or the evening meal. Instead of supervising full-time servants and letting their children "make play of their assistance," the women work with part-time servants during the few morning hours that they have at home and pressure their children to help them according to their abilities.[11]

While industrialisation accounts for the *direction* of change noted in patterns of residence, material possessions and daily routine, the *extent* of change may well be determined in large measure by the fact of the women's employment. Most obviously, an extra income facilitates shifts in residence and the acquisition of more consumer goods. But more significantly, the women's exposure to new attitudes and modes of living may increase the rate at which consequences of industrialisation affect their families. Working women have the opportunity to develop a taste for material goods used by colleagues whose life-styles differ from their own. Their employment familiarises them to settings and may predispose them towards socially heterogeneous neighbourhoods. And women who work outside the home appear less reluctant to enjoy leisure activities outside the home.

11. Whereas the respondents were not expected to do anything "by the clock" until they entered school at about age six, their children started or will start school before their third birthday. An interesting question is whether the acceptance of pre-kindergarten nurseries has encouraged mothers to work, or whether the desire to work has prompted the acceptance of earlier schooling.

RITUAL BEHAVIOUR

Of all changes made in family life between the respondents' childhood homes and their homes of procreation, changes in ritual behaviour appear most directly related to the women's employment. With regard to rituals performed on a daily basis, the modifications pertain to children more than to adults, and to men more than to women. Yet, it is the women's attitudes towards the rituals which permit the changes. For example, the early morning bath which is prescribed by religious tradition continues to be part of each adult's morning routine. For their children, however, my respondents may postpone the bath until later in the day, although they themselves were never permitted to forego the activity in their own childhood.

TABLE 4

Sample Changes in Ritual Behaviour Between Families of Orientation and Families of Procreation

Respondents	Daily		Life-Cycle		Calendrical	
	Puja	Diet	Wedding	Naming	Feasts	Fasts
Urmila	—	—	—	—	+	0
Aruna	0	0	—	—	0	0
Nandini	—	—	—	—	+	0
Kamla	—	—	—	—	+	0
Hansa	0	0	0	0	+	0
Kusum	—	—	0	—	0	0
Sharda	—	—	—	—	+	0
Champa	—	—	—	—	+	0
Malti	—	0	0	0	0	0
Asha	—	—	0	0	+	0
Jaya	—	—	—	—	+	—
Janu	0	—	0	0	+	0

— decrease in ritual
\+ increase in ritual
0 little change

After bathing, adults and most children habitually acknowledge a god's image with a *namaste* and perhaps a *sloka*. But the morning hours, which the respondents' fathers spent in worship, the husbands use for household business (Table 4). Only three women, each married to a man of her own caste, report that their husbands spend "half an hour, sometimes an hour," in morning *puja*. With regard to the customary woman's *puja* in the evenings, change is again evident in that it has become a family affair. Several times a week, rather than on a daily basis, family members including husbands stroll in groups of two's or three's to the temple, stopping to chat with friends or visit relatives along the way.

Customs concerning dietary habits which are most dependent on decisions of the women, have also changed significantly. Only three respondents include in their diets items which were prescribed in their homes of orientation. But the prepared meal, which in their childhoods was offered first to the gods and could be eaten by Brahmin men only if they were wearing silk is now taken without ritual except on holidays. Only Brahmin women living with their husbands' elders stay away from the kitchen during menstruation; and only Bania respondents of the Jain religion forbid their children food from vendors (i.e., food prepared under unknown circumstances). All respondents dine with members of other castes and religions when at work, and all except one have eaten in restaurants—an activity strictly forbidden by most respondents' families of orientation.

Rituals pertaining to life-cycle events have also been minimised in the homes of the respondents (Table 4). Only five women had three-day wedding ceremonies, whereas the parents of all twelve had been wed in ceremonies lasting between three and five days. Similarly, only one woman participated in pregnancy rites for the birth of her second child, and even for first borns, two women celebrated in the traditional manner at their elders' insistence. Life-cycle events given by the respondents for their children, rather than by their parents for them, are even more abbreviated. For instance, the traditional name-giving ceremony normally involves many relatives, particularly the husband's sister who chooses the name. But seven of my respondents and their husbands named their children "with the approval" of the husband's sister and omitted the ceremony altogether.

Unlike life-cycle events, calendrical occasions appear to be celebrated more fully today than when the respondents were young (Table 4). The Gujarati calendar provides numerous occasions for celebration or lamentation, but the five most frequently mentioned by my respondents are festivals in which all castes participate: Diwali, Navratri, Rakshabandhan, Uthrarn, and Holi. In their families of orientation, the women celebrated these events by going to temples of their sects and by gathering at the homes of relatives. Today, almost every respondent exchanges visits and gifts with at least one family of a caste other than her own. Sweets are served which members of any caste or sect are permitted to eat, and festivities peculiar to a caste are either omitted or they take place early in the morning before guests arrive. Two women who made caste marriages and who live with their husbands' families do not receive visitors of other communities, but they and their husbands call on friends outside their castes and exchange gifts with them.

While the major occasions common to all castes are marked by feasting, minor occasions such as the moon's eclipse or a guru's day more often involve fasting. Certain fast days serve to absolve the abstainer from past sins. Others cleanse women after menstruation. Whatever the nature of the fast, a sense of blended humility and power is gained from the ordeal, and only one respondent will forego it unless ordered to do so by a doctor. Change is evident primarily in so far as not all the women require fasting of their children, as their mothers did require it of them.

As indicated above, the *extent* to which any given modification in ritual has taken place depends upon a number of variables such as the type of marriage (whether caste or cross-caste), composition of household (whether joint or nuclear), and caste affiliation (whether Brahmin or Bania). But the *direction* of modification, the basic pattern of change, appears directly related to the respondents' employment. In the first instance, women who work have fewer hours to devote to daily rituals, and they are less able to assume the household chores which facilitate their husbands' observance of daily rituals. Less obvious but just as important is the interest and personal satisfaction provided by a woman's employment. A woman who works may relegate her role as organiser of social and religious functions to fourth position, following those of wife, mother, and employee. By serving her family as wage-earner, she need not feel negligent for diminishing her role as transmitter of tradition. And by involving herself in her job, she satisfies a need for purposeful activity which may be satisfied for other women by ritual behaviour.

Why, then, the maintenance of and even increase in calendrical ritual occasions? In the case of fasting, no expenditure of time is needed. Indeed, a fast requires nothing but a bit of will-power, and it affords an opportunity to demonstrate selflessness. In the case of the major feast days, the necessary time is specifically provided. Because all castes participate in them, schools and businesses set aside days for the celebrations, and all members of the family enjoy their holidays together. If a working woman feels at all guilty about her abbreviation of daily and life-cycle rituals, she can compensate with full observance of calendrical occasions and fasts.

HYPOTHESES AND CONCLUSION

Since all the respondents in the present sample work, the relationship between their employment and their patterns of family life cannot be stated categorically. Nevertheless, the data do permit certain hypotheses warranting further investigation:

1. Middle-class Hindu women most likely to assume roles outside the home and manifest non-traditional attitudes within the home are youngest or only daughters, women raised in "fatherless" families, and women who have experienced significant economic loss.

2. Women who seek employment are more likely to make love marriages, have small families, and relate to members of their households in an egalitarian manner than are their unemployed counterparts.

3. Compared with the families of unemployed women, the families of working women tend to reside nuclearly in suburban areas of heterogeneous composition. They shift residence more frequently and acquire material possessions more readily.

4. In the homes of employed women, rituals pertaining to daily and life-cycle events become abbreviated or are omitted altogether. However, rituals pertaining to all-caste calendrical events are fully observed, as are fasts.

Possibly the most fundamental effect of a woman's employment is on her attitudes, attitudes which the behavioural changes reflect. Evidence of these attitudes may be found in the reasons which the respondents of the present sample give for the changes they have made in their patterns of family life. One group of changes in ritual behaviour and life-style is attributed by the women to the costliness of the previous mode of behaviour, its time-consuming nature, or its impracticality. But these customs were just as expensive, time-consuming, and perhaps impractical for the respondents' elders. Furthermore, the respondents do find money, time, and use for other items of behaviour which were not part of their parents' lives: life-cycle ceremonies are modified or omitted because they are too costly, yet expensive and inessential furniture is acquired for the home. Daily rituals are abbreviated and deleted because they demand too much time, but time is found for the women's jobs. In other words, my respondents have made certain changes in their patterns of family life because their priorities differ from those governing the patterns of family life in their homes of orientation. I suggest that these priorities reflect a dynamic and pragmatic approach to life.

Reasons given for a second group of changes indicate that the respondents also grant high priority to the interests and inclinations of the individual. Shifts in residence are made because the respondents or their husbands feel thwarted when living with the husbands' elders. Life-cycle events and daily rituals are abbreviated or omitted by some respondents either for lack of personal conviction or for lack of interest. Particularly in relation to their children, my respondents demonstrate an orientation towards principles of individualism.

A third group of behavioural changes made by the respondents indicates that their orientation is more cosmopolitan than was that of their elders. They have universalised all-caste calendrical occasions so as to include their friends, neighbours, and colleagues regardless of caste affiliation. They participate in activities outside the home and shift to heterogeneous neighbourhoods. In general, the respondents demonstrate a willingness to expand their realm of experience.

The novelty of pragmatic, individualistic, and cosmopolitan attitudes could easily be over-emphasised. As mentioned earlier, the families of the respondents have lived in urban, relatively cosmopolitan areas for generations. Sources of Indian tradition, such as Kautilya's *Artha Sastra*, the *Dharma Sastra*, and the *Manu Smrti* embody highly pragmatic and, in some respects, individualistic values. Particularly for Gujarati Banias considerations of time, money, and practicality are not new. And for Brahmins especially, the religious and philosophical focus on the "Self"—whether the Self is affirmed or denied—fosters at least a consciousness of individuality. But there is something different about the attitudes manifested in these respondents' patterns of family life, a difference which may in part be attributed to their employment.

Studies of change in Indian culture frequently indicate that although new patterns of behaviour and belief may characterise men's activities outside the home, traditional patterns continue to characterise the activities of both men and women inside the home.[12] The present study suggests that when women as well as men participate in outside activities, new ways of thinking and behaving are introduced in the home. A woman who works is aware of job opportunities and job requirements, and has a personal stake in the allocation of income. She develops a sense of identity and sense of purpose apart from those gained through her familial roles of wife, daughter-in-law and mother. And through her activities in the "outside world" she comes to know and accept differing behaviours and beliefs. In sum, employment may foster in women a dynamic and pragmatic approach to life, an individualistic view of self, and a cosmopotitan orientation — attitudes which are manifested in the working woman's patterns of family life and in her changing familial roles.

12. See, for example, Milton Singer, "The Indian Joint Family in Modern Industry", in Milton Singer and Bernard S. Cohn (eds.), *Structure and Change in Indian Society* (Chicago : Aldine Publishing Company, 1968).

4

HELEN E. ULLRICH

Etiquette among Women in Karnataka: Forms of Address in the Village and the Family

Recent studies on linguistic etiquette have focussed on a macro level of several languages[1] and of a language as a whole.[2] The emphasis has been on pronominal usage and on the use of "plural" forms to show "politeness".[3] There is a dearth of material regarding etiquette for women and linguistic etiquette for the structure of a caste stratified village. The purpose of this article is to show how forms of address are related to the social structure of a village in Karnataka State[4] and how these forms reveal women's place in the social structure on the village level and the family level.

1. R. Brown and A. Gilman, "The Pronouns of Power and Solidarity," in T. A. Sebeok. (ed.), *Style in Language* (New York: John Wiley and Sons, 1960).

2. S. S. Bean, "Meanings of Grammatical Number in Kannada", *Anthropological Linguistics*, XVIII : 1 (Jan., 1975); H. S. Biligiri, "How to be Polite in Kannada and Other Important Matters", unpublished paper, Symposium on Politeness Exchange in Indian Languages, (Mysore : Central Institute of Indian Languages, April 23-25, 1975); Clifford Geertz, "Linguistic Etiquette", *The Religion of Java* (Glencoe, Ill. : The Free Press, 1960).

3. S. S. Bean, *op. cit.*; S. S. Bean, "Two's Company, Three's a Crowd," *American Anthropologist* 72 (1970), p. 72.

4. Data for this study was collected during a year's residence in a Karnataka village. Field work was made possible by a Senior Research Fellowship, American Institute of Indian Studies.

Politeness as a term has frequently been used to refer to the use of plural forms of address for those in a position requiring deference. In a number of languages the plural form of address is used to people in a position of relative power, higher status, and unfamiliarity; whereas the singular form of address may be a manifestation of lack of power, low status, intimacy. To recognise the use of plural pronouns as indicating "politeness" seems to be confusing the issue. The implication is that one is more "polite" with those of greater power. I argue rather that etiquette is a preferable term and that the etiquette appropriate to those in various social positions differs. Hence the occasions for the use of singular address and the occasions for the use of plural address as well as the people to whom these various forms should be used all belong under the rubric etiquette. In examining etiquette appropriate to women in a Karnataka village, the family and village will be examined. The perspective, as revealed by means of address, will include ideal usage and actual usuage including attempts at change in the social system. Unless otherwise indicated the data were collected from women.

The methodology used in gathering the material was both participant-observer and direct questioning of the manner of address used. Women of the different castes were asked how they would address members of other castes whose names they knew and whose names they did not know. They were also asked how they would address members of their family. Another very important aspect of village intra-communication was observation of women who went to various hamlets and for what reasons.

SETTING

Material for this paper is drawn primarily from the women of six castes in Totagadde,[5] a village in the Western Ghats of Karnataka State. The village, numbering approximately seven hundred, has three major caste areas—the lower castes reside in the south of the village; the Havik Brahmins,

5. Totagadde is a pseudonym referring to the two major crops *tota* (areca nut plantation) and *gadde* (rice paddy)—grown in the village.

in the centre; and the Sudras, in the northern part of the village. The two lower caste hamlets, Harijans and Girijans[6] have little to do with each other. The Havik Brahmins, who occupy two hamlets, are the dominant caste economically, ritually and politically. They are the second most populous caste in the village—the most populous caste is the Divaru (Halepaika), a Sudra group which also occupies two Hamlets. The difference in numbers between the two castes, however is less than fifty. As a result of Brahmin dominance, the village apparently has more Brahmins than members of any other caste—an impression not borne out by census data. The four castes located in the northern part of the village are the Lingayat, Potter, Divaru (Halepaika), and Vokkaliga castes. The Potters, Lingayat family, and Vokkaligas reside on one side of the rice paddy fields; the Divaru, on the other (see Diagram). There is much visiting back and forth among the members of the Sudra groups. The six castes from whom data have been drawn are the Brahmins, Girijans, Lingayats, Vokkaligas, Divarus, and Harijans.

Schematic Diagram of Totagadde Hamlets

	North	
Divaru		Vokkaliga
	Rice Paddy	Potter
		Lingayat
Divaru		Vokkaliga
	Sudra	
Havik Brahmin	Areca Nut Grove Brahmin	Havik Brahmin
Girijans Harijans		
	Low Castes	
	South	

Totagadde is a structural entity in itself. An outsider asking a villager his *ūru* (village) would receive the answer, Totagadde.

6. Girijans, literally 'mountain people' are reputed to be former tribals. The terms Girijan and Harijan are used only by the Brahmins. Members of other caste groups are not familiar with the terms and refer to Harijans and Girijans by caste names.

It has its own post office, two stores, but more importantly the people are linked to each other ritually. At the Dipawali festival, for instance, Brahmins give all who ask items needed for worship and non-Brahmins reciprocate by providing ropes to tie a cow during the Dipawali cow worship. *Uru* has other usages showing the various levels of social identity for the village. When the temple god is taken on his annual tour of the village, he does not visit the Harijan hamlet. When a panchayat is held for the *ūru*, this usually means a particular caste panchayat. When the *ūru* is summoned to weddings, *ūru* refers to caste for the Brahmins, Girijans, and Harijans. Sudra groups, however, invite all other Sudras and the Lingayats. *Uru* 'village' then has four different points of reference in Totagadde—residential hamlet, caste, the northern area of town, and the village itself. In the next section just how closely this usage approximates linguistic divisions will be discussed.

FORMS OF ADDRESS: VILLAGE LEVEL

There are three basic types of address found in the village. For those considered inherently high in rank, the term *amma* is used. *Amma* for Brahmins and Lingayats designates the kinswoman mother; for all the other castes, it designates the kinswomen in the category, grandmother. This includes female kinfolk of the second ascending generation. Among those relatively close in rank kinship terms are reciprocally used. Among castes where kinship terms are used, there is a difference in ranking which is realised by not accepting food from the lower ranking castes and by the lower ranking castes' having to wash their own drinking vessels. While relative ritual purity and pollution are observed, those castes which use reciprocal terms have visiting and gossip patterns suggesting considerable interaction. In the one multi-caste hamlet this extends to intercaste borrowing of valuables such as gold ornaments. The third form of address is to those considered much lower in rank. The term used is *huḍugi* (girl).[7] Either this term or personal name without kinship term is used. Some use only personal name; others use *huḍugi* exclusively.

7. The retroflex form is indicated by a dot beneath the letter.

One might view the three forms of address as metaphorically referring to a family. The Brahmins as the parents have charge of remedying any problems and of the religious well-being of the village. To a large extent they also control the economic and political life of the village. The Sudras comprise a liminal category in which they are neither dependent nor completely independent of the Brahmins. The Sudras own and manage their own lands and are not completely dependent upon the Brahmins for religious services, but they do depend upon the Brahmins for economic assistance in times of need and advice for dealing with officials in town such as doctors and police. The low castes are to a large extent dependents on the Brahmins. Forms of address serve to reinforce the relationship with the use of *amma* (mother) and *huḍugi* (girl).

Chart 1 : Dimension of Power within Totagadde

	Brahmin	Sudra	Low Caste
Employer			
Permanent	+	—	—
Temporary	+	+	—
Employee	—	+	+
Adviser	+	—	—
Religious matters	+	—	—
Moneylender (outside of caste group)	+	—	—
Arbitrators in disputes	+	—	—
Land owners	+	+	—

From the perspective of power, one might regard different groups in the village as being marked by a distinctive feature. This feature has dyadic properties—a plus sign indicates the presence of the feature; a minus, its absence; plus and minus signs indicate that the feature is neutralised.

From a dyadic perspective one either has power or one lacks power. In Totagadde the various caste groups may be divided into those which have power and those which do not. This characterises intercaste relationships. Power may be regarded as possessed by those whose advice is sought, those who are requested to perform worship when illness occurs, those who lend money, those who serve as links between the village and the town, those who own land, and those who are the employers. The use of distinctive features along this classification may be seen in Chart 1.

DIMENSION OF POWER

With the exception that Sudras employ people on a temporary basis and that they own land, the Sudras and the low castes belong to the same category, the category without power. But taking into consideration terms of address, the Sudras fall into a middle category (see Chart 2) in which the highest group calls them by the term *huḍugi* (girl) whereas the lowest group, the Harijans, calls all higher ranking groups *amma* (mother). Note that the Girijans, one of the low castes, receive the *amma* form of address from Harijans. However, Girijans are subsumed under the low caste category because they are regarded as untouchable by some, are landless, and because they used to borrow marriage money from the Brahmins which resulted in a permanent indentureship. Those who are called *amma* are marked by power while those called *huḍugi* are marked by an absence of power (see Chart 2).

Chart 2 : Linguistic Dimension of Power within Totagadde.

	Power	
Brahmins	+	Called *amma* (mother) by all groups
Sudras	±	Called *huḍugi* (girl) by Brahmins; *amma* by Harijans
Low Castes		
Girijans	±	Called *huḍugi* by Brahmins, *amma* by Harijans
Harijans	—	Called *huḍugi* by all Castes

Amma (mother) is used exclusively as a form of address to Brahmin and Lingayat women (see Chart 3). In addition, it is used by Harijans to every group except the Lingayats. The

Chart 3 : Receivers of Respectful *Amma* (mother) Form of Address

All non-Brahmins	——→	*amma* (mother) to Brahmin women and occasionally to girls
Brahmins, all non-Brahmins with exception of Lingayat	——→	*akkamma* (elder sister-mother) *amma* (mother) to Lingayat women ; Harijans also use *akkanoru* (elder sister-respectful suffix)
Girijans	——→	*amma* (mother) Brahmins, Lingayat, much older women
Harijans	——→	*ammnoru* to Brahmin women and girls ; *amma* (mother) to all women in village with exception of Lingayat

use of the term *amma* to express ritual rank has dimensions of power which extend into the economic and political realms as well. Accompanying the use of *amma* is the use of the grammatical plural in commands, third person finite verbs, and personal pronouns of reference and address. The metaphorical distance which the use of *amma* and plural forms create also correlates with a lack of knowledge of the groups about each other's practices. Brahmin women are surprised that Divaru women have any ritual practices at all. Brahmin women even expressed surprise that Divaru marriages needed to be performed at a propitious time (*muhurta*). Divaru women in emulating Brahmin women develop a variant form as, for example, in the preparation of foods. The system of address forms is operating to such an extent that only Brahmins reported changes in forms of address; no other group openly objected to reported forms of address. This system of address in Totagadde seems to be stable with the beginning of change induced from the most powerful group.

LIMITED COMMUNICATION

For the Brahmin women the use of *amma* serves to reinforce ritual and economic rank as well as to indicate a lack of familiarity with non-Brahmins. People from all non-Brahmin groups request Brahmin men to perform *pūja* (worship) when disaster or illness occurs. Brahmin men are called upon to settle disputes and to provide one of three types of financial help—marriage money to low castes, money for oxen to the Divaru, and money in times of need to members of any caste. Only the first type is not expected to be repaid but rather indicates the beginning of a lifelong indentureship for the low castes.[8] Brahmin women and children share in the etiquette which requires the address by plural forms, of which *amma* may be regarded as an example. *Amma* may also symbolise the limited communication with Sudras. Although Brahmin women are no longer as restricted as they once were, they are rarely seen outside of their own hamlets. Rather Sudra women come to the Brahmin women to have clothing stitched or, in the case of the Harijans, to clean the barns or to do outside work. Both patterns reflect the differences in the skills of the women concerned. The Harijans provide unskilled labour whereas the Brahmin seamstresses provide skilled labour. For Brahmin women to work outside of the home or to work for other castes, is a new pattern. Ten years ago only one Brahmin woman knew how to sew; now at least a half dozen women sew.

Those Sudra women who have clothing stitched in Brahmin households might be surprised to discover that they are more frequently identified in terms of their husband's than by their own names. Indeed, Brahmin women do not know the names of many non-Brahmin women; however, the non-Brahmin reaction in many cases to the inquiry about how higher caste people were addressed when the personal name was not known was that it was inconceivable in such a small village not to know the names of all the people residing there. Indeed, not only does a Brahmin woman rarely know the names of non-Brahmin women, but the only view she usually has of non-Brahmin hamlets are those located on the road to relatives' houses. This year when a Brahmin woman went to the Divaru hamlet on her husband's business, she created a

8. This has changed and the lower castes no longer repay this debt. In reaction to this Brahmins are no longer lending marriage money.

sensation. This past year she was the only Brahmin woman to venture alone in a non-Brahmin hamlet. The social structure is such that Brahmin women have little contact with non-Brahmin women and are not likely to have reason to develop more extended contact with them in the near future.

As the Lingayat family lives in a hamlet with Potters and Vokkaligas, the Lingayat women necessarily have a lot of contact with non-Lingayats. The Lingayat women rarely go outside of the two hamlets on the northern end of town. Indeed they only go over to the Divaru hamlet for *pūja* (worship) or for other religious functions and even then rarely do they appear. In spite of the lack of mobility of Lingayat women, they are not physically isolated from women of other castes. Ritually and linguistically the Lingayat women retain strict segregation from women of other groups in the village. This separateness is demonstrated by the forms of address *amma* (mother) and *akkamma* (elder sister-mother) used to Lingayat women by all groups in the village. On the other hand, recognition of Lingayat subordinate ranking to Brahmins is illustrated by a Lingayat comment when asked how Lingayats address Brahmin women, "One cannot call members of higher castes by name."

The Harijans illustrate their position at the bottom of the ranking by calling all the women except the Lingayat *amma* (mother). Harijans indicate a special position of distance for Brahmin women and girls by occasionally calling them *ammnōru* (mother plus an honorific suffix, *-ru*). A similar suffix is used in address to Lingayat women, only the suffix is added to *akka* (elder sister), that is *akkanōru.* This serves to differentiate between Brahmins, Lingayats, and Sudras- Girijans in forms of address. Harijans tend to work for Brahmin households. In the past Brahmins provided Harijans with bride price money so there was a special bond between Harijans and Brahmins. Although marriage money is no longer provided, the terms of respect remain.

KINSHIP FORMS

The use of inter-caste kinship terms includes at some level all the non-Brahmins of Totagadde (see Chart 4). There is

Chart 4 : Use of Kinship Terminology for Inter-caste Address

Lingayat girls		**Non-Brahmins**
akka (elder sister)	←——	all non-Brahmins
Vokkaligas		**Divarus**
atte (father's sister) if married to village	←——→	personal name
attige (father's sister's daughter) if married to village	←——→	personal name
doḍḍawwa (mother's sister) if native to village	←——→	personal name
personal name+*akka* if same age or younger	←——→	*akka* (elder sister)
personal name+*akka* if elder	←——→	personal name if younger
personal name+*akka*	←——→	*amma* (mother) if much older
		Potters
personal name+*akka*	←——→	personal name
		Girijans, Harijans
personal name+*akka* if elder	←——→	personal name+*akka*
personal name if younger	←——→	personal name+*akka*[9]
Divarus		**Vokkaligas**
atte (father's sister) to old woman[10]	←——→	personal name+*akka* (elder sister)
		Vokkaligas, Potters
tangi (younger sister) if younger	←——→	personal name+*akka*
		Potters
akka, if elder	←——→	personal name+*akka*
		Girijans
akka, if elder	←——→	personal name

9. Contrary to the elicited data, Vokkaliga women were observed being addressed by personal name+*akka* by considerably older Girijans.

10. As reported by Divaru, but not practised. In practice, the Vokkaligas use *amma*.

		Harijans, Girijans
tangi, if small	←———→	*amma* (mother) if old woman
	———→	personal name+*awwa* (mother) if old woman
	———→	personal name+*akka*, if elder
attige (husband's elder sister)[12]	←———→	*attige*, if somewhat equal in age[11]

Girijans		Harijans
personal name	←———→	personal name
		Divarus, Vokkaligas, Potters
personal name	←———→	personal name+*akka*, if elder

considerable variation in usage among the castes. The Divarus are the only ones to have provided terms for extended affines as well as for metaphorical consanguineal kin. The Divaru provide this extended terminology for all non-Brahmins, with the exception of the Potters. This is curious, as the Potters of all the groups in the village are the ones whose speech patterns most closely resemble those of the Divaru. The greatest number of extended kinship forms are for the Vokkaligas who rank above the Divarus and emphatically do not reciprocate. Vokkaligas insisted that they did not use affinal forms with the Divarus, and I have also never observed such usage. The Vokkaliga and Divaru are also similarly occupied with rice paddy and vegetable growing. This extended terminology might be an upwardly mobile gesture along with the recent donning of the sacred thread by several younger Divaru men, the emulation of Brahmin cooking at Divaru ritual gatherings, a remodelling of house design to parallel Brahmin houses, and Sanskritisation in naming children.

The Vokkaligas and Girijans both reported that they use only the personal name for women younger than they. In observing Vokkaliga women talking with Girijans, however, it was clear that a Girijan would only call a Divaru child by her personal name. An older Girijan woman addresses an adult Vokkaliga woman by personal name plus *akka* (elder sister). There is an ideal of reciprocity which just does not exist.

11. In effect this is not reciprocal as reported by the Divaru, but in practice the Divaru are not called *attige* but by personal name.

12. The glosses provided are that of the basic kinship term.

Visiting patterns among all the non-Brahmins, except the Harijans, is extensive. The greatest degree of communication is Vokkaliga-Divaru, Vokkaliga-Potter, Vokkaliga Girijan. The Vokkaligas are the ones the Divaru generally visit on their way to and from the fields; the Potters visit the Vokkaligas when they have spare time. Never have I seen a Vokkaliga in a Potter house, in spite of the two castes residing in the same hamlet. The only time I have seen Vokkaligas in the Divaru hamlet have been for religious events. Girijans do not frequent the Vokkaliga hamlet, but they are visited by the Vokkaliga women whenever they pass the Girijan hamlet. Despite the considerable amount of interaction between Vokkaliga and other non-Brahmin groups, Vokkaliga speech is different from that of other groups. Vokkaliga women are quick to point out a form which they label Divaru and to deny that they use such forms. Vokkaliga children can be heard to use both Divaru-Potter forms and Vokkaliga forms; adults are rarely if ever heard using Divaru-Potter forms. Although Vokkaliga children sometimes use Divaru-Vokkaliga forms in play, they also enjoy ridiculing the forms specific to those groups. The rapidity with which Vokkaliga women point out forms belonging to other castes seems to be significant in retaining separate forms, forms which resemble colloquial Kannada. While terms of address show a close relationship among non-Brahmins, dialectal forms as maintained by women give each group its separate identity.

HIERARCHICAL STRUCTURE

Unlike kinship terms which stress an actual or fictional relationship, the use of *huḍugi* (girl) as a means of address points to a clearly hierarchical structure. The use of these terms is considered entirely appropriate by those so addressed. Basically, the structure is for the highest ranking group to address lower ranking groups in this manner when the name is not known. In case of considerable hierarchical difference, the name although known is simply not used. However, there is some change occurring in the use of *huḍugi*. Some families use personal name; others substitute *tangi* (younger sister). Still others use *huḍugi* regularly for relatively high caste help if the woman works quasi-permanently in a particular household (see Chart 5 for the use of *huḍugi*).

Chart 5 : Use of *huḍugi* (girl) in forms of address

Brahmins	——————→	*huḍugi* (girl) to all castes except Lingayat
	——————→	*muduki* (old lady) to older Vokkaliga women
	——————→	personal name if know personal name; other wise *huḍugi* to Vokkaligas, Divarus
	——————→	*huḍugi* even if know personal name to Girijans, Harijans to Harijans, Girijans
Vokkaligas	——————→	personal name; if not know personal name
Girijans	——————→	*huḍugi* to Harijans

The three different ways women have of addressing each other—*amma* (mother), kinship terms, and *huḍugi* (girl) may be viewed in terms of power. Roger Brown and Albert Gilman in their article "The Pronouns of Power and Solidarity" define power in the following manner.[13]

> One person may be said to have power over another in the degree that he is able to control the behaviour of the other. Power is a relationship between at least two persons, and it is non-reciprocal. . . .

Those exclusively addressed as *amma* (mother) have both ritual and economic power. The Lingayats and the Brahmins both provide priestly services for the entire village. The Brahmins are the only ones to hire people on a regular basis. The power ascribed to the men who are in charge of the religious well-being of the village, of most of the occupational opportunities, and a refuge in times of financial stress is also inherent in the women. Brahmin women, as well as men, frequently direct maid-servants. These maid-servants are the ones usually addressed by *huḍugi* (girl).

Non-Brahmin women follow the example of Brahmin women or their idea of Brahmin women's behaviour, of their

13. Roger Brown and Albert Gilman. *op. cit*,, reprinted in Joshua A. Fishman (ed.), *Readings in the Sociology of Language* (The Hague : Mouton, 1968), p. 254.

dress, and their cooking. Brahmin ritual control is exemplified by the observance of menstrual taboos by every group in Totagadde. Even the Lingayats, a group which does not ordinarily follow menstrual taboos, does so in Totagadde. As some non-Brahmins have become more prosperous and their women are able to stay away from work, menstrual taboos are elaborated. Those groups which use kinship terms among themselves do not emphasise the ritual distance which separate their caste groups, but instead emphasise a common relationship of being from the same village. Those who are addressed only as *huḍugi* (girl) are without economic or ritual power of any sort. It is obvious that the means of address used serves to show the basic divisions within Totagadde, as well as strong emphasis on hierarchy.

FORMS OF ADDRESS : THE FAMILY

Although family structure among the various castes of Totagadde has undergone considerable change, the greatest change has been among the Haviks. Women in the other castes have enjoyed relatively greater freedom, perhaps related to their being essential to the agricultural cycle. Havik women have in the past remained primarily at home, with the exception of going to other Brahmin's houses to husk areca nuts. In this section I will first discuss the relative positions of women in two castes, the Havik Brahmin caste and the Divaru caste, and then relate this to ways of addressing children and husband and wife.

In a model fitting the Havik family the eldest man in the family is the *ejmānru,* head of household. He has complete power to make all the decisions with regard to all matters in the running of the household and the areca plantation. He manages all the money. The *ejmānru* even dictates the dishes to be cooked. When daughters arrive at a marriageable age, he has the task of arranging the marriage. In the past he had total power even in this. However, now the daughter has a veto power and has been known to break engagements to which she had previously agreed. The *ejmānti,* the wife of the *ejmānru,* regards her husband as a personal god and does his bidding. Younger brothers and sons are in a similar position. Metaphorically speaking, the ship has one captain and all work together for a common cause, the good of the family. This system may have been more functional at a time when women were married before puberty and trained in the ways of a household from a young age. The raising of the marriage age from pre-puberty a generation ago to between eighteen and twenty-five and the education of girls have been factors in changing this structure. Two case studies follow. Case *A* provides an example of a crisis and settlement of the crisis. Case *B* is an example of a new type generally approved of by both men and women.

CASE *A*. Gange spent many years happily married. Her husband's gambling did not overly concern her until she discovered he planned to sell land to settle gambling debts. She let it be known that there would be trouble if anybody bought the land. With advice from her brothers she took over the management of the land. At the time that this land quarrel was occurring between husband and wife, her husband was pitied by the other women of the village. After she obtained control of her and her children's share of the land, her husband simply left. Gange has proven a competent land manager and has gained access to groups such as the Havik panchayat which previously were all-male. She goes to town alone, something not done by any other Havik woman. When her daughters reached marriageable ages, she handled all the negotiations: because all this is in the line of work and because of her success, she has been able to combine both management and motherly duties. Although her sons have reached an age when they could be managing land, she continues to do so. The label, 'Indira Gandhi' written on her door by a prankster aptly sums up her role in her family.

CASE *B*. Lalita and her husband are considered the happiest couple in town from the viewpoint of other women. She, as president of the village women's club, frequently goes to conferences. When the daily paper arrives, she and her husband divide the paper so both can read at the same time. Lalita does not stay in the background, but participates in conversations. The ease with which she enters conversations with men has brought her some criticism, as the old pattern was that a woman only participated in conversations with relatives. However, now people think that a woman should be able to deal with visitors; so Lalita's behaviour is regarded preferable to the older pattern where a woman stayed in the background or retired to the kitchen. Like Gange, Lalita can take over if her husband is not present. The ease with which Lalita talks with others—both men and women—and her ability to handle affairs when her husband is away provide a model of the new type of woman.

CHANGING RELATIONSHIPS

While the old model where the woman is helpless and incapable of managing of her own is true for many older women, younger women have become much more independent. As Case *A* illustrates, a woman may go to rather extreme measures to protect property and the means of livelihood for her family. At the moment such extremes are tolerated; indeed Gange (Case *A*) is not even criticised for her independence. Rather, her independence is accepted as necessary for the job she has undertaken, namely the management of family lands. Lalita (Case *B*) better fits the ideal, a complement and not a subordinate of her husband, one who can help and take over when the occasion demands.

Havik women in the past tended to view their identity in terms of their husbands. To a large extent this is still true. However, with a high school certificate now considered the minimum acceptable education for marriage, a woman is more inclined to be independent. The change from wide age differences between husband and wife to that of approximately the same age is recent. Yet this new pattern is accepted by all to the extent that an engagement which in the past would never have been broken was when a younger man appeared. Engagements are theoretically not broken among the Haviks; however, in this case a young girl was engaged to a much older man. Younger Haviks in Totagadde thought the engagement was best broken; older people also think that there should not be a wide disparity in the ages between husband and wife. However, older people think that under no circumstances should an engagement be broken.

In contrast to Brahmin women who in the past had no responsibilities outside of the household, Divaru women are important contributors to agricultural work. Some of the work is specialised. Only men do the ploughing; only women, the sowing and transplanting of rice. Although both transplant other crops such as chilies, the women are more likely to be involved in the transplanting of rice; the men, in the irrigation of newly transplanted plants. Both work side by side. Both men and women prepare the fertilizer. Only women do the cooking unless a woman is observing menstrual taboos. Women control the food that is served and the money. Upon a girl's marriage, she is given a chest with a lock which has only one key which she keeps around her neck. This is the chest where the girl keeps her money; should she become the *ejmānti* (female head of household), this is the chest where the household money will be kept. Women are as likely as men to go to town for shopping. In contrast to Brahmin women who never argue openly or criticise their husbands in public, Divaru have no such inhibitions. Consequently, it is somewhat surprising that women do not tell folktales if a man is present. The man is given precedence in this realm.

In a model fitting the Divaru family the eldest man in the family is the *ejmānru* (head of household). He is in charge of the farming and making decisions affecting the household. Unlike the Brahmins, however, the Divaru *ejmānru* does not have total power. This is shared with the *ejmānti* who has no inhibitions in expressing her opinions. As Divaru women work alongside their husbands in the fields, they have first-hand knowledge about farming. The Divaru widow rises to a position of even greater power in the household; the Brahmin widow loses her position to her son's wife. Divaru women are basically in charge of the home and child care; however, this is in addition to their other work. The women have the authority to run the household as they see fit. In effect, this means that the *ejmānti* has the authority and is responsible for supervising the work of her daughter-in-law.

Divaru marriages are arranged by the girl's and boy's male relatives. The girl does not see her husband until the wedding day. She has no veto power, but there is the possibility of divorce and remarriage.

The importance of the distinction between male and female children is clear from the forms of address. There is no merging of terms for the Brahmins; there is for the Divarus.

Brahmin boys are called either *māṇi* or *appi;* girls, *kūsu* or *ammi.* Among Divaru, on the other hand, there is a common term *eppi* for addressing either boys or girls. Although clearly sons are wanted, a number of Divaru households have only one daughter. Divaru girls, as well as boys, have a ritual first hair-cutting. In contrast to Brahmins, the Divarus have the same number of life crisis ceremonies for boys as for girls—the first hair-cutting, marriage, childbirth ritual pollution, and death. This suggests that Divarus value girls more than the Brahmins value girls.

Both Divarus and Brahmins have a taboo against saying the spouse's name. This taboo, which still applies equally to husbands and wives among the Divaru, does not apply to Brahmin men. Brahmin women in their thirties do not hesitate in saying the husband's name if the husband is not present. Older women will not say the husband's name at all. Younger women will say the husband's name in front of the husband if the situation requires that she say her husband's name. Among both groups there is the use of the plural-respectful form when speaking about or to the husband and the singular form when the husband speaks to the wife. When angry at their husbands the Divaru, will use the singular, but not Brahmin women who try to swallow their anger quietly.

CONCLUSION

Forms of address have been discussed on two levels: the village and the family. On the village level the basic three-way division in the village of Brahmin, non-Brahmin and low caste is portrayed both in terms of address, occupational patterns and ritual hierarchy. On the family level the change in the authority structure, while not indicated by terms of address, has led to an increase in the wife's use of her husband's name. Contrasted with the Divaru the relative equality of importance in terms for sons and daughters seems to be illustrated by a lack of differentiation in the most common term for addressing a child.

Etiquette in Totagadde consists of knowing the proper behaviour towards other people. Avoiding the uttering of a husband's name is as much a part of etiquette as calling a lower ranking woman by the term *huḍugi* (girl). The use of only singular forms among Haviks is as appropriate as the use of the grammatical plural is by non-Brahmins to Brahmins.

Change in the relationships may be seen on the village level by the incipient usage of *tangi* (younger sister) or personal name to those on a lower ritual level. Claims for greater status by members of non-Brahmin castes are seen in the adoption of what were Brahmin names and the adding of the suffix—*amma* (mother). That this claim is projected with some caution is obvious by the fact that when a Brahmin requests the names they are supplied without—*amma*. On the family level a decrease in the gap between husband and wife among Brahmins may be illustrated with a decline in the taboo of saying one's husband's name. All of these changes suggest a reordering in the social organisation of the village, a reordering of etiquette from what was exclusively hierarchical to what is more egalitarian.

5

J. MURICKAN

Women in Kerala: Changing Socio-Economic Status and Self-Image

Kerala women have distinguished themselves in the various sectors of public life in India and internationally. Kerala had the first woman Surgeon-General in India (Dr Mary Punnen Lukose), the first woman minister in a state cabinet (K.R. Gauri Thomas), the first woman delegate representing India at the United Nations on the status of women (Lakshmi N. Menon, a former minister of state in the Government of India), the first woman lawyer in the state and later the first judge of a High Court in the British Commonwealth (Anna Chandy), the first woman Chief Engineer (P.K. Theresia), and the only woman paraplegic surgeon in the world (Dr Mary Varghese). Nearly 30 per cent of the nurses in Indian hospitals outside Kerala are Malayalee girls. Even outside India, in the U.S.A., Canada, the Persian Gulf, and in many European countries like Germany and Italy, Kerala nurses are preferred because of their competence, spirit of service and readiness to work in new environments. In the field of Indian sports female stars from Kerala are among the record setters in several athletic events.

Kerala has the unique distinction among the states of having a sex ratio with an excess of women over men. Table 1 clearly shows how the increasing number of women in Kerala during the first five decades of the century contrasts sharply with the decreasing number of women in the Indian sex ratio.

TABLE 1

Sex Ratio in Kerala and India, 1901-1971

(Females per 1000 males)

Year	Kerala	India
1901	1004	972
1911	1003	964
1921	1011	955
1931	1022	950
1941	1027	945
1951	1028	946
1961	1022	941
1971	1016	930

Source : *Economic Review, Kerala 1973* (Trivandrum : State Planning Board, 1974), p. 25, Table 2.2; New Delhi: Registrar General and Census Commissioner, 1972.

High female infant and maternal mortality rates are commonly believed to be the main reasons for the low female sex ratio in a developing country. In this matter Kerala seems to have reversed the trend as the education of women and health services available to them are far superior in Kerala compared to the rest of the country. In fact, while female infant mortality is as high as 264 per thousand for the whole of India it is only 48 in Kerala.

Life expectancy for the Kerala females has been consistently higher than that of males while for India the trend has been constantly the reverse as seen from Table 2. Though the latest figures for Kerala and India are not yet available, it is estimated that by the turn of 1970 life expectancy for women in Kerala had exceeded 60 years while it is still below 50 for the whole of India. The average age at marriage of both males and females in Kerala has been consistently higher than in other states of India. Thus while the average age at marriage of the Kerala female has exceeded 20, it hovers around 16 years for India. In the younger age group the proportion of unmarried females is much higher in Kerala. Thus, for example, while 43 per cent of the females remain unmarried in the age group 15-24 in Kerala, the corresponding figure for India is only 10 per cent.[1] The remarkable expansion of female education in Kerala is primarily responsible for this phenomenon of a steadily rising age at marriage of the female population.

TABLE 2

Expectation of Life at Birth (in years)

Period	Kerala		India	
	Males	Females	Males	Females
1911-20	25.5	27.4	19.8	20.9
1921-30	29.5	32.7	26.9	26.6
1931-40	33.2	35.0	32.1	31.4
1941-50	38.9	42.3	32.5	31.7
1951-60	40.2	50.0	41.9	40.6
1971	—	60.9	47.1	45.6

Source : Trivandrum : Bureau of Economics and Statistics; *Economic Review, Kerala 1973*, pp. 28-29, Table 2.8

In the field of education, Kerala is ranked at the top among the states of India; Table 3 shows the remarkable progress made by the women and men of Kerala as contrasted with the bleak picture for the whole of India. If the women of Kerala have achieved three times more literacy than the female population of India in general, it clearly shows the high priority the people and government of Kerala give to the value of education. In fact education accounts for one-third of the total expenditure of the state while it is only one-fifth for India.[2]

It is remarkable that the wide disparity that exists in other states of India between male and female education is almost non-existent in Kerala. Taking the figures of enrolment for the lower primary, upper primary and high school section together during 1974-75, we find in Kerala that out of a total of 5.36 million pupils, 2.81 million are boys and 2.55 million girls. The difference is not at all significant as 47.6 per cent

1. Census of India 1971; *Kerala* (Kottayam : Southern Publishers, 1947), p. 76.

2. *Economic Review*, p. 129, 9.4.

3. *Enrolment Statistics, 1974-75* (Trivandrum ; Government of Kerala Administrative Report—Education Department), p.1.

of the seats in all the schools are filled by girls. This suggests that in Kerala there is greater equality of opportunity for

TABLE 3

Percentage of Literates in Kerala and India

	Kerala		India	
	1961	1971	1961	1971
Persons	46.85	60.16	24.03	29.35
Male	54.97	66.54	34.45	39.49
Female	38.90	53.90	12.95	18.47

Source : *General Population Tables*, Kerala, Census of India, 1971. Registrar General and Census Commissioner of India, New Delhi, 1972.

females in the field of education. Even at the level of higher education there is relatively less imbalance between male and female enrolment.

TABLE 4

Students and Teachers in Colleges Affiliated to Kerala University, 1972-1973

	Number of Students			Number of Teachers		
	Boys	Girls	Total	Men	Women	Total
Arts and Science	53748	43114	96862	3036	1368	4404
Junior Colleges	8415	6798	15213	230	98	328
Training Colleges	462	1035	1497	72	37	109
Eng. Colleges	1444	74	1518	210	22	232
Medical Colleges	1574	628	2202	312	139	451
Ayurvedic College	235	74	309	19	12	31
Law Colleges	1202	290	1492	31	3	34
Total	67080	52013	119093	3910	1679	5589

Source : *Economic Review*, Appendix 9.15

It is only in the professional colleges such as engineering, medicine and law that Kerala women show reluctance to compete with males. Engineering and law are generally considered professions for men, though there have always been some women practising law and medicine: it should be kept in mind, however, that most women who are attracted to the field of medicine enter the nursing profession and today dominate it not only in Kerala but in most of the metropolitan cities of India.

The performance of the Kerala women in the occupational arena seems to be less spectacular than in education. Apart from nursing which is almost dominated by them, the teaching profession seems to attract the largest number of women in Kerala. According to the 1971 Census, out of an estimated total of 25,700 registered medical practitioners in Kerala, only 2,400 or 9.3 per cent were women. On the other hand, women constituted 62.5 per cent in nursing and other allied medical services. The Government of India set up a National Commission for Women's Welfare in 1971 which submitted a three volume report on the status of women after a three year study in December 1974. One of their main recommendations that 50 per cent of teachers in primary schools all over India should be women, was realised in Kerala even before the report was published.

TABLE 5

Distribution of Teachers in Primary and High Schools in Kerala According to Sex 1972-1973

	Primary	Percentage	High Schools	Percentage
Men	64050	50.64	18016	57.03
Women	62439	49.36	13577	42.97
Total	126489	100.00	31589	100.00

Source: *Administrative Report : 1974-75* (Education Department, Government of Kerala), p.18.

Even at the high school level women are moving fast to equalise their position with men. It is only a matter of time before women in Kerala overtake men in the teaching profession at the secondary school level. At the college level women occupy only 30 per cent of the teaching positions as shown in Table 4. There are relatively more women teachers in the arts and science colleges than in the professional colleges of Kerala. Taking the teaching profession as a whole it was estimated, according to the 1971 census, that there were 1,95,000 teachers in Kerala of whom 86,000 or 44 per cent were women.

Between 1911 and 1971 the proportion of women in the total labour force of India fell drastically from 34.4 to 17.3 per cent. The proportion of women workers to the total female population fell by a third from 33.7 to 11.8 per cent during the same period. In the agricultural sector women have been steadily pushed into the ranks of landless labourers. According to the 1971 census women account for only 5.14 per cent of the total working population in the cultivating sector and 8.76 per cent of agricultural labourers.[4] In the organised sector, which accounts for only 6 per cent of the working women, their distribution in the various industries has shown a marked downward trend over the years.

The lot of women workers in Kerala is no better than that of the female working population of India. The percentage of workers to total population in Kerala declined from 33.71 in 1961 to 28.91 in 1971, and this was more marked in the case of female workers whose proportion fell from 19.71 per cent in 1961 to 13.68 per cent in 1971.

The following table indicates the trend in the shift of the female labour force of Kerala during the decade 1961-1971.

TABLE 6

Percentage of Working Population in Three Sectors in Kerala 1961-1971.

	Cultivation (1)		Agri. Labour (2)		Other than 1 & 2	
	1961	1971	1961	1971	1961	1971
Persons	20.92	17.95	17.38	30.68	61.70	51.37
Male	22.91	22.12	13.10	25.14	63.99	52.74
Female	16.25	4.64	27.42	48.35	56.33	47.01

Source : Census of India, Series IX, Kerala, Paper 1.

It appears that during the last decade there has been a steep fall in the proportion of women engaged in cultivation and a sharp rise in the number of female agricultural labourers. This trend conforms to the all-India pattern. The non-agricultural sectors, particularly the industrial, have registered a 10 per cent decrease in the female participation rates which is different from the pattern for male workers. A conclusion which emerges is that the women of Kerala are still deprived of equality of opportunities in agricultural as well as industrial employment.

4. General Population Table, Census of India 1971.

It is in this overall context of the distinctive characteristics of women in Kerala that one can understand the role they could play in the complex process of social change. With this in view several studies were carried out in three urban centres of Kerala—Trivandrum, Cochin and Kottayam. The preliminary findings of these exploratory research investigations will be presented in the following sections of this paper with a view to promote a better understanding of the self-image of women in Kerala and the nature of their participation in the economic, social, political and religious life of the state.

WOMEN AND POLITICAL CONSCIOUSNESS

During the independence movement, women all over India and also in Kerala took an active part in the struggle for freedom. In Kerala, women were not merely tolerated but their menfolk depended on them for the success of the civil disobedience movement and the organised Satyagraha. On the other hand, one notices a definite decline in the active participation of women in the political life of independent India. In the first general election (1951) 51 women contested seats for the Lok Sabha and 216 for State Legislative Assemblies of whom 18 and 82 were successfully elected. Once in the legislatures, they found places in parliamentary committees, government delegations, embassies and missions according to their abilities. However, in the subsequent elections there seems to have come about a steady decline in the presence of women in the political arena.

The 1962 Lok Sabha had 33 women while in 1971 their number came down to 21. In 1962, 50.6 per cent of women candidates who stood for election won whereas in 1971 only 25.9 per cent of women contestants were successful. Similar trends are noticeable in almost every state. In the State Legislative Assembly in Kerala there are at present only two women out of a total of 134 members. This almost total absence of women in the State Legislative Assembly must not too easily be ascribed to the lower level of interest of women in the political life of the state. Much more important is the perception of politics as a sphere of corruption which is best left to men who are considered to be less sensitive to moral issues. Women see themselves as helpless in changing the social evils that prevail and do not therefore appreciate their tremendous potential power to change political and social structures by capturing positions of power and influence in the political structure at the local, district and state levels.

It is to explore this aspect that a study was undertaken in Cochin in January 1975.[5] The sample consisted of 60 women, 50 per cent of whom were between 25 and 28 years of age and the remaining 50 years and above. Half of them belonged to the lower income group (Rs. 300-500) and the other half to the upper income group (Rs. 501-1000). The sample consisted of an equal number of women who had voted just once and those who could have voted in all the elections since the re-organisation of states in 1957. One of the aims of the International Women's Year is to increase participation of women in decision making and to ensure full integration of women in the total developmental effort. The study was in the nature of an exploratory one using the interview method for collecting data.

Newspapers are a powerful means of communication and help to create and sustain political awareness, yet of the 60 respondents 35 per cent did not read any newspaper at all and of the remaining 65 per cent only 35 per cent read political news. Exercise of franchise is one of the more significant expressions of political consciousness. Only 9 women had not voted at all, but 20 others failed to vote in one or more elections. No less than 35 per cent of the respondents indicated that they were not at all particular about exercising their right to vote, and 28 per cent of them said that they would not even protest if women were deprived of their constitutional right to vote. One-fourth of the respondents did not approve of the idea of women contesting for electoral office.

Since attitudinal data do not always provide a basis for the prediction of actual behaviour, an attempt was made to study the actual involvement of these women in political acti-

5. This section of the article is based on "Women and Adult Franchise: A Study of the Political Consciousness of Women in Kerala", (Ernakulam: Department of Sociology, St. Theresa's College, 1975), mimeo; "Changing Political Involvement of Indian Women with Special Reference to Kerala", (Trivandrum, Department of Sociology, Loyola College of Social Sciences, 1975), mimeo.

vities. It was found that two-thirds of the women interviewed were totally inactive, had never taken part in political meetings, discussions and study groups, demonstrations, and had never made a financial contribution to any political party. Over 90 per cent of the respondents had not approached any political party or politician for help in solving their personal or community problems. Thirty-three per cent had no political ideology nor a clear understanding of the competing ideologies of the political parties and were not concerned when the candidate they supported lost the election or his party was defeated. These women's knowledge of political affairs was extremely poor. While 57 per cent did not know when the next elections were due, 11 per cent could not identify a single political party by name and only 28 per cent could name correctly one or more political parties in Kerala. These data suggest that the widely held assumption that there is greater political awareness among women in Kerala needs to be re-examined in the context of available opportunities for participation in politics and the various social and economic constraints which restrict and discourage their involvement in local or state politics.

How do the reactions of the younger generation differ from those of the older women ? Those in the age group 25-28 who read political news in newspapers, were very particular about exercising their vote and would protest vehemently if they were to be deprived of their right to vote. About 50 per cent of these younger women thought they had a political ideology and discussed it with their friends and relatives in contrast to 25 per cent of the older group. Of the younger group, 80 per cent reported that they would be disappointed if the party they supported were defeated as against 50 per cent of the older group. While only 20 per cent of the younger generation appeared to be unaware of current political issues, nearly 40 per cent of the older women were both unaware and uninterested. Thus, on the whole, the younger generation showed much greater political awareness compared to the older group of women.

Among the more important factors which influenced the voting behaviour of these women, this study showed, were religion and caste. Victor M. Fic in his analysis of the 1957 elections in Kerala had concluded that "the politics in Kerala was merely a projection of the aspirations and strength of the communal organisations in the political arena".[6] The situation in Kerala of course is more complex than Fic has suggested but, as far as women are concerned, religious and caste considerations appear to have greater influence on their voting behaviour than party loyalty.

Even in a state like Kerala where the political consciousness of the people is known to be very high, the women are still far from being partners with men in the political decision making process. They continue to be an exploited constituency by the dominant male party politicians who value women for their vote but do not recognise them as persons who should participate in decisions affecting the social and economic well-being of society. A widespread movement organised by women to conscientise women about their personal dignity and political rights is required to liberate them from ignorance and political exploitation.

ATTITUDE TO DOWRY

The social evil of dowry persists in Kerala, in spite of the Dowry Prevention Act. From the very birth of a female child the parents begin worrying about her marriage and tend to consider her a liability because of the financial implications of dowry. For many parents raising loans by mortgaging the little property they have, is often the only way to raise the dowry demanded for the marriage of their daughter. At times parents are forced to marry their girls off to widowers, to men much older, with less education or even physically handicapped only because they have no money to pay the dowry. Today in Kerala, the fixing of the dowry has become a highly systematised machanism with each occupational category carrying a recognised price tag; a doctor, for example, will easily demand rupees one lakh and a car. Marriage brokers have long lists of available and eligible women with the price tag attached to each of them in order to improve their prospects in the marriage market, where bargaining is conducted with impersonal ruthlessness.

6. Victor M. Fic. *Kerala: Yenan of India, Rise of Communist Power; 1937-1969* (Bombay : Nachiketa Publications Ltd., 1970), pp. 6-7.

Is dowry practised only among the upper classes who can afford it or is it also prevalent among the lower middle class people? An attempt was made to investigate the practice of dowry among lower middle class groups and a study was made of class III and IV women employees in the Cochin Corporation area of central Kerala.[7] A purposive sample of 50 young women working as nurses, primary school teachers, clerks, trainees, typists, police women and attendants was selected. All the respondents were unmarried and between 17 and 28 years of age. Their educational level was relatively high with only 22 per cent not having obtained their Secondary School Leaving Certificate (SSLC), 62 per cent with SSLC and 16 per cent graduates.

All the respondents considered dowry as a serious social evil about which they were helpless to do anything. In 54 per cent of the families of the respondents a marriage had taken place in the last two years. In the vast majority of these marriages (over 90 per cent) dowry took the form of cash, ornaments, furniture, and utensils. Cash and ornaments were given or received in all the cases. Neither education nor employment of the bride reduces the incidence of dowry. It is an impersonal bargain. Among Hindus dowry included cash and jewellery, but some gave only jewellery and few paid only cash. Among Christians dowry consisted of cash and jewels, and furniture and utensils have to be provided within a year or so. Dowry is considered by most as a matter of prestige. If one is willing to marry a girl without dowry, this would be attributed to some defect in the bridegroom or his character.

The study, which also explored the attitude to dowry, found that 96 per cent of the respondents favoured the dowry system because it was the only means to get a husband, though 50 per cent of them pointed out the severe economic difficulties to which their parents were put to meet dowry requirements. The most common methods of raising the dowry money were loans, help from relatives, and mortgaging or sale of property. It was surprising to find that 44 per cent of the women in the sample

7. See for more details "Dowry, A Social Evil which Passes as a Normal Custom: A Study of Unmarried Working Women's Attitude to Dowry in Kerala" (Ernakulam: Department of Sociology, St. Theresa's College, 1975), mimeo.

were unaware of the Dowry Prevention Act. Remedies suggested by the women included agitation by women's organisations and the refusal to take dowry when brothers married. But not one in the sample was ready to denounce publicly those who demanded dowry. Yet 34 per cent expressed willingness to marry those who demanded dowry while 66 per cent honestly admitted that, whatever the hardships, if no other solution could be found, dowry would have to be paid to get a girl married.

It is the fear of remaining unmarried that made these women accept in practice the dowry system, though in principle they are opposed to it. Dowry is an institutional aspect of a traditional community that has been stubbornly resistant to change in spite of social legislation. Its abolition will require not only a change of mentality which is widely found among men and women in Kerala, but a radical change in the social structure which would support a new understanding of marriage as a partnership between two persons for the benefit of the community. It is widely known that the Prevention of Dowry Act has been completely ineffective in Kerala and in fact, both the man who receives the dowry and the woman who gives it, continue to consider dowry as a status symbol. The day when marriage in Kerala becomes a partnership in life with no dowry to demand or to give will be the real liberation for women—and men.

MARRIAGE AND HIGHER EDUCATION

It is generally believed that higher education is responsible for raising the age of women at marriage and several studies have shown a correlation between the level of education and age at marriage of women. Since Kerala has an exceptionally high literacy rate for women, an attempt was made to explore the relationship of college education with the age of women at marriage in Kerala.[8] Higher education for the purpose of this study was defined as the first degree in arts, science, education and law or a postgraduate or professional degree. A pur-

8. For the data presented here I have relied on "Marriageablity and Higher Education of Women: A Study of the Influence of Higher Education on Raising the Age of Marriage of Kerala Women"(Kottayam: Department of Sociology, C.M.S. College, 1975), mimeo.

posive sample of 100 women aged 25 and above was selected and interviewed in Kottoyam, a metropolitan town in central Kerala. Half of these women were post-graduates, 22 per cent were housewives, and the rest were employed as teachers, lecturers, doctors and secretaries.

Ninety per cent of the respondents were married and 18 per cent of them waited till the age of 29 and later to marry. Higher education of women in Kerala, as in India, is one of the factors responsible for raising the age at marriage. Unemployed women are settled earlier by their parents, but when their daughters are employed, parents become more selective and this tends to postpone marriage. Employment of the woman, her higher education and economic independence are cited as reasons for tension in the family. However, 96 per cent of the respondents were of the view that education helped them to adjust better to family life and to reduce tension in marital relations.

The higher the education of the woman, the more difficult it is to find a partner with equal or higher educational status. When 80 per cent of the respondents, who were between 25 and 35, were asked why they were still unmarried they could only say that they were waiting for the right man. They were all aware that higher education acts as a restrictive factor in the selection of a partner and results in raising the age at marriage. As we had noted earlier the enrolment of Kerala women in institutions of higher education is very high and it would appear that the motivation for higher education is linked to the new demands that are emerging in the marriage market as well as new opportunities for professional careers for women. Higher education particularly at the post-graduate and doctoral level could function as a deterrent, since it makes it difficult for a highly educated woman to find a husband of comparable educational attainment, yet it would appear that even though highly educated women have to postpone marriage, they need not remain unmarried, at least in Kerala.

FEMALE DOMESTIC SERVANTS IN COCHIN

Availability of female domestic servants is a relic of Kerala's feudal past. The system of land tenure facilitated constant supply of free labour to the land-owners. Whenever there was a large number of female children in the family it was the tradition of the very poor tenant to entrust one of them to the wife of the landowner which would mean one mouth less to be fed. The landlady may not pay the girl but when she grew up she would be settled in marriage. Then her younger sister would take her place as a domestic servant.

Casual labour and domestic service have been two acceptable forms of gainful employment for poorer class girls in Kerala. Though the conditions have changed considerably in Kerala homes, the status and salary and working conditions of domestic servants have not improved. In the past the lady of the house and may be another elderly relative were always at home. Now that women go out to work the servant has to shoulder the responsibility of looking after the young children, cooking, washing and housekeeping.

To investigate the recruitment of domestic servants in Cochin, their working conditions, job satisfaction and economic situation, a sample of fifty full-time maid servants was chosen who belonged to the Hindu, Muslim and Christian communities with three or more years of service in the residential areas of Cochin.[9] Eighty per cent of the sample took up employment as servants to support themselves, generally after the death of the father, while 16 per cent reported that they had no alternative job opportunities. Do the educated women treat their servants better and pay them a better salary? Women graduates as well as those who had little or no schooling paid their servants a more or less uniform salary—about Rs 25 per month. The concept of a just wage, or of a family wage was little understood by women employers. Given these circumstances, it is strange to find that 52 per cent of these maids were completely and 44 per cent partially satisfied with their service conditions. Rs 20 a month is considered a "good salary" since all expenses of food, clothing and medical aid are met by the employer. The question of increment arises only when the servant is likely to leave to take up a better job.

9. This section presents in summary form data from "Women in Low Grade Occupations : A Study of the Working Conditions of Domestic Servants in Kerala" (Ernakulam : Department of Sociology, St. Theresa's College, 1975), mimeo.

The working hours are long and irregular from early morning till late at night. However, 48 per cent reported that they had fixed leisure time from two to four hours per day though 4 per cent had no free time at all. The chief leisure time activities of the domestic servants were occasional movies and visiting friends. The question of going home rarely arises as many of these domestic servants have their families in distant rural areas.

The extent of exploitation becomes clear when we take into account the uncertainty regarding job tenure, wages, hours and conditions of work of the domestic servants. There is no registration of this category of workers nor legislation to protect them; they are given no compensation for injury nor any social security benefits. Yet in spite of this lack of security and job protection these women servants preferred domestic work to the hardships of agricultural labour. Domestic service has its compensations, not the least being the assurance of three meals a day.

What this study showed was that the employer is hardly aware of the changed circumstances in modern society and takes domestic service for granted. The domestic servant, on her part, is quite unaware of her personal worth and, largely because of the economic situation of her family, allows herself to be exploited as cheap labour without realising the injustice of her situation. Will the leadership to organise the domestic servants come from among themselves? It seems doubtful. In an industrial urban city like Cochin where domestic servants do make life comfortable for many a family no attempt has yet been made to organise domestic servants for the improvement of the conditions of service and to provide them with legal protection so that they may claim the same status and enjoy the same security and benefits as workers in any trade or industry.

CHANGING RELIGIOUS VALUES

The transmission of traditional religious and cultural values from one generation to the next is primarily the function of women who dominate the early socialisation of the child. In India, where women are for the most part uneducated and often illiterate the tendency has been for them to observe strictly social and ritual practices which carry religious sanctions. However, the younger women who have been exposed to education and an urban environment tend to develop new attitudes towards religious beliefs and practices so that there appears to be a real generation gap between them and their mothers.

To test this hypothesis a study was made of a sample of 50 urban women students, in their final year of graduation, from three well known colleges in Trivandrum, and their mothers.[10] All the respondents belonged to the lower and upper-middle income groups. The ratio of Christians to Hindus in the sample was 18:32 corresponding to their proportional representation in the total population of three colleges studied. Muslim women were excluded as they constituted a negligible minority of the students in the degree classes. The questionnaire method was used to explore the opinions of the daughters while the structured interview technique was used in the case of their mothers. In this section, we will present a comparative statement of the opinions of mothers and their daughters concerning religious beliefs, values and practices so as to identify some of the trends of change in this important sphere of life.

It was found that while their mothers (68 per cent) preferred vocal prayer to singing, meditation and reading of scripture, their daughters (62 per cent) showed a preference for meditation and reading of scripture. When Hindu and Christian women were considered as two distinct groups, it was found that a greater number of Christian women (71 per cent) preferred recitation of prayers and reading of scripture while Hindu women gave greater importance to meditation. This difference may perhaps be related to the fact that Christians unlike Hindus have a tradition of formal liturgical worship. The differential preference for meditation and vocal prayer between the Christian women students and their mothers may

10. The observations in this section are based on data from "Changing Religious Values of Women : A Study of the Intergenerational Difference in the Attitude towards and Practice of Religion among the Women of Kerala" (Trivandrum: Department of Sociology, Loyola College of Social Sciences, 1975), mimeo.

perhaps be attributed to the fact that their mothers have a lower level of education and also to liturgical traditions which placed almost exclusive stress on the recitation of prayers rather than on meditation or contemplation. It seems very doubtful whether the preference for meditation to vocal recitation of prayers can be attributed to a greater sense of individuality and independence among the younger women.

The notion of God is fundamental to religious belief and there is a tendency to hold that belief in God is inseparable from affiliation to a religious group. In this study it was found that 89 per cent of the younger women thought that it was possible to have belief in God without belonging to any particular religion whereas only 45 per cent of their mothers were of this view. It is interesting to note that many more Hindu women (75 per cent) accepted this idea than the Christians (59 per cent). Christianity is one of the most organised religions in the world and its hierarchical structure is characterised by the exercise of strict authority in matters of religious belief and ritual. On the other hand, a relativistic trend in religious belief has always been a strong tradition in India, particularly in Hinduism, and because of the emergence of world-wide movements towards hormony among religions there is a growing tendency among younger people to attach less importance to exclusivism in the notion of God and religious beliefs. The "Gods" of the various religions are felt to be only manifestations of the same universal power. How closely this attitude corresponds to actual changes in religious affiliation and practice needs to be studied more intensively before any firm conclusions can be reached.

There was a considerable difference in the responses of the younger women and their mothers to the question of why they followed particular religious traditions—was it out of conviction, social acceptability, parental coercion, mental satisfaction, or because they had no option as they had been born in one religion? While 62 per cent of their mothers reported adherence to a religious tradition because they had been born in it, only 19 per cent of their daughters did so. Taking Hindu and Christian women separately, it was found that 65 per cent of the Christian women in contrast to 59 per cent of Hindu women continued their allegiance to their particular religion because they had been born in it. Corresponding to this, 22 per cent of the Hindu women stated that they belonged to Hinduism out of conviction in contrast to only 12 per cent of the Christian women.

Over 60 per cent of the mothers stated that their chief source of religious knowledge was their parents in sharp contrast to their daughters (48 per cent) who stated that the chief source of their religious knowledge was outside the family such as, books and contact with religious institutions and associations. Employment seems to exercise some influence in this area since 71 per cent of employed women claimed to have derived their religious knowledge through personal effort in contrast to only 5 per cent of unemployed women who reported that they had relied mainly on their parents for their knowledge of religious beliefs and practices.

Temple and church going is much more common among mothers than their daughters. The majority of mothers visited the place of worship either daily (31 per cent), or at least once a week (45 per cent), or once a month (13 per cent). Their daughters tended to worship in the church or temple far less frequently, 39 per cent once a week, 34 per cent once a month, and 17 per cent daily. What motivated these women to go to the temple or church? This question involves a complex interplay of several factors among which are custom and obligation, personal conviction, and social interaction with friends and fellow worshippers. If Hindus and Christians are considered separately more Christian women worship in the church because of custom, obligation and social mingling with their co-religionists than Hindu women.

These data must be interpreted with caution because Christians, particularly Catholics, have an obligation to participate in liturgical worship in the church every Sunday unlike Hindus who are not under any obligation to visit the temple at prescribed times by religious authorities. Similarly, the finding that more mothers (60 per cent) derived consolation from religious observance and worship than their daughters (41 per cent), and that more mothers (83 per cent) than daughters (57 per cent) always have recourse to prayer in times of need, does not necessarily mean that the younger women find less emotional and social support in religion than their mothers. It is important to keep in mind that women's attitudes to prayer and religious worship are influenced by their position in their life cycle. The importance of this factor of age is seen even more clearly in the function which religious associations perform for these women, for most of whom membership in a religious association provides opportunities not only for worship and social service but also for social mingling.[11]

This brief comparative survey of the religious beliefs, values and attitudes of women in Kerala and their daughters appears to suggest that the older generation of women is more conservative, orthodox and faithful to religious customs and traditions. On the other hand, the younger generation of women appears to be moving away from institutionalised religion and to be less attached to traditional religious beliefs and ritual practices. There appears to be therefore in the sphere of religion a change in Kerala women's outlook from one bound by tradition and custom to one more open to experimentation and new ideas. However, it would be rash to conclude from this attitudinal survey that the younger women in Kerala have initiated patterns of behaviour in religious worship and inter-religious marriage that are substantially different from those observed by their more traditional and orthodox mothers.

SELF-CONCEPT

Women in India enjoy Constitutional protection against discrimination on the basis of sex and there is a body of social legislation which has attempted to implement the Constitutional directives regarding the elimination of discriminatory practices against women in marriage, divorce, succession, employment and so on. It is well known that social legislation has generally been ineffective because the people are still unaware of its objectives and social legislation has been imposed on "society" whose social and cultural structures are resistant to change. Since women in Kerala have a higher level of education than in other parts of India and enjoy relatively more

11. On this point see Helena Z. Lopata, "The Effect of Schooling on Social Contacts of Urban Women", *American Journal of Sociology*, 79 (November, 1973), pp. 613-614.

independence in the choice of occupations, it was thought useful to investigate the self-concept which women in Kerala have of themselves. By self-concept is meant here the perception which women have of themselves in the light of prevailing social norms and accepted modes of behaviour. It is generally agreed that over the last 25 years there has been a change in the outlook and attitudes of women. Younger women today distinguish between what they term "conservative" from "modern" or "democratic" attitudes and, in the sphere of marriage and the family education and employment, conservatism implies inequality for women in all these spheres of life.

The self-image of women in Kerala was measured by an attitude scale designed on Likert's technique of summated ratings.[12] The statements included in this scale referred to the nature of women, marriage and family, education, employment and activities outside the home. The sample consisted of 50 women students in the age group 19 to 23 and 50 working and non-working women between 40 and 65 years of age from the Cochin Corporation area. All belonged to middle class families. Students of III degree and post-graduate classes were selected by means of a table of random numbers. A woman was selected from every 5th house provided she had the minimum educational qualification of SSLC and fell in the age group.

Nature of women: The study revealed that the younger women are moving away from the attitude of submissiveness, which was traditionally expected of them; they were of the view that the traditional division between "male" and "female" jobs was no longer relevant since, given the opportunity, educated women could function as completely as men in any type of employment. The older generation, however, continues to believe that anatomy is still destiny and that the submissive nature of women is related to their biological characteristics.

12. I have relied in this section on the study, "Self-Concept of Women: An Assessment of the Intergenerational Difference in the Self-Concept of Women in Kerala" (Ernakulam: Department of Sociology, St. Theresa's College, 1975), mimeo.

As regards marriage and the family the older women tended to be conservative and insisted that parents should choose the partners for their children. On the other hand, the younger

TABLE 7

Distribution of scores of young and older women on selected indicators

	Maximum score	Young women mean (19-23) yrs.)	Older Women mean (40-65 yrs)	*t*
Nature of women	30	18.73	15.98	4.10*
Marriage and family	25	18.42	16.18	3.60
Education	20	15.48	13.08	5.30
Employment	20	10.06	8.54	2.55
Miscellaneous activities outside the home	25	18.14	15.34	5.10

*There is a significant difference at 1 per cent level between the attitudes of the younger and the older women in each of the five spheres of enquiry.

women felt that they should select their own partners and that some acquiantance before marriage was essential for adjustment in marriage. They strongly disapproved of arranged marriages as a contract between two families rather than a commitment between two individuals. The older women wanted to restrict women's activity within the home and were of the view that men should not participate in household chores. The younger women, however, held that in a marriage relationship husband and wife are partners and consequently household chores and the rearing of children should be shared by father and mother.

Education: The older women who believed that the place of women was essential in the home, preferred a system of education essentially adopted to home life, and they were of the view that higher education tended to make women more self-centred and less willing to serve others. Nevertheless, both groups of women desired an educational status for females comparable to that of males, though they accepted the fact that all problems cannot be solved by education. The younger women were of the view that education for girls should be identical with that of boys, and that intellectual cooperation with men and participation in all aspects of life will be possible only if women are educated.

Employment : The younger women were of the view that working women have opportunities for a variety of experiences that helped to develop their self-confidence and personal qualities; at the same time employment enables women to use their potentialities to make a substantial contribution to the social and economic development of the country. Nevertheless, they felt that a woman should be employed only if she could perform effectively the triple role of wife, mother and career woman. On the other hand, the older women felt that the talents and attention of a woman should be devoted to her family and the home. Experience shows, they noted, that employment of women leads to economic independence which in turn creates tensions in the home. The rising cost of living often necessitated the employment of women but, they felt, women should go out to work only when absolutely necessary.

Women's activity outside the home: The scores on this indicator revealed that the younger women believe that women should engage in activities outside the home. These activities included involvement in politics, hobbies, association with friends and other interest groups. On the other hand, the older group desired women to keep out of politics altogether, since the source of a woman's satisfaction should be the household that runs smoothly. This study revealed that employment was regarded by these women as often necessary for economic reasons as well as for the development of their personal qualities and for the enrichment of family life. A new self-image is developing among the younger women who see themselves as equal partners with men not only in education and employment but also in the family. It is almost certain that society in Kerala will not permit these younger women to express fully their self-image, nevertheless one may hope that certain compromises and adjustments will take place which will provide women with more opportunities to express concretely in society their new self-understanding.

CONCLUSION

In this paper we have reported the findings of several research studies which were conducted recently in three metropolitan centres of Kerala. What emerges most strikingly is the progress of formal education among women and the impact which education and urbanisation, among other variables, have made on the values and attitudes of the younger generation of women. Education appears to be of pivotal importance not only because it enables the woman to become economically independent but because through it she acquires the self-confidence necessary to affirm her dignity and human rights. Nevertheless, the fact remains that the mass of women in Kerala lag far behind their middle-class sisters in the urban centres of Kerala. Most women in Kerala continue to live under male dominance and to be hampered by traditional cultural and religious taboos. Education by itself is not enough to liberate women. Only a strong mass-based movement organised by enlightened female leadership will be able to provide women freedom and equality to work in partnership with men for their mutual development.

6

JOSEPH MINATTUR

Women and the Law: Constitutional Rights and Continuing Inequalities

"Our women have more rights than women of other countries, but there are large areas wherein women are suffering, where, maybe they are not conscious of their rights," said Indira Gandhi, Prime Minister of India, in April 1975.[1] Her reference here may have been to certain provisions in the Constitution of India relating to equality of the sexes and universal adult suffrage. The Preamble to the Constitution speaks of securing to all citizens of India equality of status and of opportunity as well as justice—social, economic and political. One of the directive principles of state policy prescribes that the state should direct its policy towards securing equal pay for equal work for both men and women. Although the directive principles are fundamental in the governance of the country and are to be applied in enacting legislation, they are not judicially enforceable. In this context, one of the provisions of the Constitution is of special significance. After having laid down that the state shall not discriminate against any citizen on grounds of sex, among other things, it provides that nothing in this article shall prevent the state from making any special provision for

1. Gulshan Ewing, "Indira Gandhi Talks about Women and International Women's Year," *Eve's Weekly* (May 10, 1975), p. 8.

women and children.[2] So there is a Constitutional provision in India permitting the state to discriminate in favour of women, if such discrimination is found necessary.

Women claim to be the largest minority in India with a variety of social and economic disabilities which prevent them from exercising their human rights and freedoms in society. Child marriage, especially of the female infant, was common; widow marriage was prohibited, evenif she succeeded in escaping from the funeral pyre of her deceased husband where she was expected to be burnt alive; a divorce was generally looked down upon and her remarriage was socially disapproved. If some of these attitudes still persist it is not because legislation has lagged behind, but because law has not succeeded in playing its role of social engineering and changing certain deeply rooted social attitudes. During the last two decades a number of laws were adopted with a view to ensuring equality of status and opportunity for women. But it appears that in practice this equality eludes the Indian woman's grasp.

In what follows an attempt is made to examine some of the more important legislation enacted by the Central legislature[3] in India to ameliorate certain unhappy conditions in which women, particularly Hindu women, found themselves. Occasionally, there is talk about ameliorating the conditions of Muslim women, but political considerations stand in the way of doing anything substantial towards that end. Muslim personal laws are considered to be part of the religion of Islam and government generally considers it necessary not to interfere directly in matters regarded as religious.

MARRIAGE AND DIVORCE

With a view to preventing child marriages, especially the giving away of infant girls in marriage, the Child Marriage Restraint Act was passed in 1929 declaring it an offence for a man to marry a girl under fifteen years of age. Any per-

2. Article 15 (3).

3. Various state legislatures also adopted certain legislative measures; see, for instance, prevention of prostitution enactments and suppression of immoral traffic acts passed in Bihar, Uttar Pradesh and West Bengal.

son who performs a marriage where the bridegroom is below 18 years or the bride below 15 years commits an offence, as also parents or guardians of the bridegroom or the bride. This socially motivated legislation has been made relatively ineffective by stating that a marriage celebrated in violation of the stipulation regarding age would nevertheless be valid. The same restrictions regarding marriageable age are found in the Hindu Marriage Act, 1955. There is a Dowry Prohibition Act (1961) also in the Indian statute book which prohibits the giving or taking of dowry. But this again is ineffective in practice mainly because any dowry given may be construed as "presents" which are not prohibited by law if made at the time of marriage. In the case of both these statutes the teeth of the legislation are practically blunted both by loopholes within the law and by the resistance of social structures and attitudes to change. Certain conservative sections of the community regard child marriage a good, if not a proper, thing and would prefer to pay a fine rather than keep their infant sons and daughters unmarried. A large number of young men and their parents consider dowry a legitimate stepping stone to higher rungs in the social ladder, and possibly a passport to domestic comfort, if not happiness.

Two years before the adoption of the Hindu Marriage Act, which *inter alia* provided for divorce, the Special Marriage Act, 1954 was enacted. There is a provision in the Special Marriage Act for obtaining a decree of divorce by mutual consent, provided the parties have lived separately for a year and three years have elapsed since the date of marriage. Apart from the common grounds on which either party to the marriage may obtain dissolution of a marriage performed or registered under the Act, the wife may sue the husband for divorce on the ground that he has committed rape, sodomy or bestiality. Persons married under other forms may obtain registration of their marriage under the Act with the result that they would now be governed by its provisions. Those who marry under the Act or whose marriages are registered under it are, in matters of inheritance, governed by the Indian Succession Act, 1925. When a man to whom the Indian Succession Act applies dies leaving a widow and lineal descendants, the widow is entitled to one-third of the property of the deceased and the lineal descendants to two-thirds. Under the Act, in the case of Christians other than Indian Christians, a widow in the absence of lineal descendants will get the entire property of the husband provided its value does not exceed Rs. 5,000. If it does, she will receive Rs. 5,000 and a share in what remains along with the kindred of the deceased according to the specific rules laid down in the Act. Some persons, especially women, prefer to be married under the Special Marriage Act because of its beneficial provisions regarding divorce and intestate succession. We shall advert to this later.

It may be said in general that the right of a wife to obtain a divorce in India is much more restricted than that of the husband under customary law; however, in certain Hindu communities, as also among most tribal groups, it is possible for the husband and the wife to obtain divorce without recourse to court. They are only required to follow some customary practice, like making a declaration before the elders of the community[4] or the headman of the tribe that they no longer desire their marital relationship to continue. It is well known that among Muslims, while the husband can unilaterally and without assigning any reason divorce his wife by pronouncing *talaq* (that is by uttering the words, "I divorce you") three times, the wife has to get a judicial pronouncement of divoree on specified grounds.

It is, however, possible for the wife to have the power of divorce delegated to her by the husband at the time of entering into the marriage contract. For instance, it may be stipulated that if he takes a second wife, she should have the option of repudiating her marriage. Such delegation is, however, uncommon. Considering the fact that the Constitution makes provision for equality of the sexes, it may be desirable to give judicial recognition to *fasaq* by means of which a Muslim wife may unilaterally repudiate her marriage. An opportunity for such recognition was lost when the Kerala

4. See Sujata Manohar, "Token Concessions or Legal Rights", *Eve's Weekly* (May 10, 1975), p. 12.

High Court in 1975[5] ruled that the right of Muslim women to obtain divorce is exclusively governed by the Dissolution of Muslim Marriages Act, 1939 and that it is not permissible to go beyond it.

The divorce provisions of the Hindu Marriage Act, 1955 maintain equality of the sexes in the matter of grounds for divorce. The Act applies to Hindus, Buddhists, Jains and Sikhs. In the provisions of the Indian Divorce Act which applies to Christians there is some discrimination between the sexes in the matter of grounds for divorce. A single isolated act of adultery on the part of the wife is a valid ground for granting a divorce on the petition of the husband but, if a wife has to be successful in her petition for divorce, she has generally to prove against her husband not only adultery, but also an additional ground such as desertion or cruelty. Commission of rape, sodomy or bestiality by the husband can also be ground for obtaining a decree of divorce.

This Act was modelled after English enactments for matrimonial reliefs adopted about the middle of the last century. Over a hundred years later the United Kingdom prescribed by legislation a single valid ground for divorce, that is, irretrievable breakdown of marriage. If in 1869 the idea was that Indian Christians would do well to follow in the footsteps of the British in obtaining matrimonial reliefs, is there any valid reason to assume that they should be governed by rules different from those applicable to the British after the passage of a century. If irretrievable breakdown of marriage is made the only ground for judicial declaration of divorce applicable to all communities and religious groups in India there will be equality of treatment not only between men and women but

5. Moyin *v.* Nafeesa, 1972. *Kerala Law Times*, 785. A. R. Kutty reports that in the Laccadives, under certain circumstances, a Muslim woman "enjoys the legal right to sever a marital relationship. The procedure is known as *Fasaq*; in it the woman utters the formula of divorce dictated by the Kazi." A. R. Kutty, *Marriage and Kinship in an Island Society* (Delhi: National, 1972), p. 184; Leela Dube also refers to the same legal right enjoyed by Muslim women in the islands. See Leela Dube, *Matriliny and Islam* (Delhi: Nationnl, 1969), p. 72,

also between various religious groups. Perhaps one has to wait for the adoption of a uniform civil code for such unification of laws. In the meantime the Indian Divorce Act could be amended making grounds for divorce identical for both men and women, preferably adopting the provision regarding irretrievable breakdown of marriage as the *sole* ground of divorce as laid down in the (British) Divorce Reform Act, 1969.

During the pendency of a suit under the Indian Divorce Act, a wife may apply for alimony and the court may grant an amount not exceeding one-fifth of the husband's average net income. While passing a decree for divorce or judicial separation, the court may order the husband to pay a lump sum or make periodical payments for life to the wife, taking into account her fortune, the means of the husband and the conduct of the parties. There are similar provisions for the benefit of the wife in the Parsi Marriage and Divorce Act, 1936. The spirit of equality envisaged in the Constitution finds clear expression in the Hindu Marriage Act, 1955. It makes provision for the grant of expenses of matrimonial suits and a monthly allowance for the support of either spouse during the pendency of legal proceedings, provided the spouse applying for the expenses and allowances has not sufficient income to support himself or herself. The Act also has a provision for making an order for permanent alimony or maintenance in favour of either of the spouses. On remarriage the spouse loses his or her right to maintenance. Further, if the recipient of the alimony is the wife, she is required to remain chaste; if maintenance is granted to the husband, he is enjoined from having sexual relations with any other woman.

In spite of the provisions for divorce contained in the Act of 1955, it is not often that recourse is had to them; this is because Hindu social values in general are opposed to the concept of divorce. As Kapadia puts it, "the principle of divorce is alien to the social pattern" with the result that "the norm accepted by law has not been accepted in practice".[6] Whereas prior to 1955, divorce was considered absolute

6. Quoted in A.J. Barot, "The Divorced Woman and her Options", *Eve's Weekly* (May 10, 1975), p. 31.

anathema by women of the higher castes, after the passing of the Act it is the women of the upper classes and higher castes as well as the rich and educated in urban areas who petition the courts for divorce. Probably, the illiterate women in the rural areas do not even know that there are legal provisions for divorce apart from those enshrined in the customary law of certain communities or tribes.

PROPERTY

We have already seen that marriage under the Special Marriage Act has the effect of making the provisions of the Indian Succession Act applicable to the parties. These provisions were more beneficial to women, be they Hindus, Muslims Indian Christians of Pondicherry or Indian Christians in those areas of Kerala which formerly comprised the princely states of Travancore and Cochin, provided they were not governed by matrilineal custom. Before the adoption of the Hindu Succession Act in 1956, when a woman succeeded to the divided property of a deceased Hindu male, she took only a limited interest. A woman was denied legal capacity to be a coparcener in a Hindu joint family. The Hindu Succession Act, 1956 which applies to Hindus, Buddhists, Jains and Sikhs determines the heir on the basis of consanguinity or affinity without any discrimination on the ground of sex. It gives a woman full ownership in the property inherited or acquired by her. The widow, the mother and the daughter now not only inherit property along with the son but also take an equal share with him. A Parsi woman takes only half the share that her brother gets in their father's property. A similar half share is the lot of Muslim women as well.

Though the Indian Succession Act is generally applicable to Christians there are various regions in the country where the Act is not applied. There are also certain Christian communities to which it not made applicable. Certain tribal Christian communities and those who follow matriliny are outside the purview of the Act. As the Act is not extended to the Union Territory of Pondicherry, Indian Christians in the territory are governed by traditional Hindu law (that is, Hindu law as it was in force in the region before certain changes were effected by the Indian Parliament in 1955 and 1956) in the matter of inheritance with all the disadvantages and disabilities which that law imposed on women.

In the erstwhile princely states of Travancore and Cochin, there are in operation local enactments relating to succession among Christians which appear to discriminate against women. Under the Travancore Christian Succession Regulation, 1916 the share of the widow in the estate of the husband is a life interest, terminable on her death or remarriage, except where she gets the whole estate in the absence of certain specified relatives of her deceased husband. Under the Cochin Christian Succession Act, 1921 the widow gets a share equal to two-thirds of the share of a son if the deceased is survived by a son or lineal descendants of a son. The Travancore Regulation seems to discriminate against daughters who can take only one-fourth of the value of the share of a son or Rs. 5,000 whichever is less. The Regulation does not apply to the small body of Indian Christians in the taluk of Neyyattinkara of the erstwhile princely state who follow *marumakkathayam* (matrilineal descent). The Roman Catholic Christians of the Latin rite and certain non-Catholic Christians living in a few southern taluks of Travancore follow their customary usage, and among them male and female heirs of an intestate share equally in his property. Under the Travancore Regulation, the maternal relatives are excluded from succeeding to the intestate if there are paternal relatives surviving him, whereas in the Cochin Act no maternal relatives are included among the heirs.

The areas where these two enactments are still in force are remarkable for a high female literacy rate and a large number of highly educated women. Nevertheless the fact remains that these women, if they happen to be Christians to whom these enactments apply, have a right to only a quarter of the share of a brother in the property of their deceased father. Would these educated women and their literate sisters think of reverting to matriliny which was once prevalent in these areas? At the moment they do not appear to be eager to effect any change.

ADOPTION

The Hindu Minority and Guardianship Act, 1956 also

bestowed a few additional rights on Hindu women.[7] It provides that though the father may appoint by will a guardian for his minor children, any such appointment will not take effect during the lifetime of the mother if she survives the father. It will take effect only on her death, provided she has not appointed a guardian by her own will. A Hindu mother is entitled to act as the natural guardian of her minor children if the father ceases to be a Hindu or renounces the world by becoming a hermit or ascetic. The Hindu widow and the Hindu mother, entitled to act as natural guardians of their minor children, are empowered under the Act to appoint guardians for them by will.

In 1956 substantial changes were effected in the law of adoption applicable to Hindus.[8] The Hindu Adoption and Maintenance Act, 1956 has invested the Hindu woman with certain rights of adoption which she had not enjoyed before. Previously an adoption could only be to a male but, under the Act, a woman is competent to adopt to herself a son or a daughter. Again, under the Act, a married man cannot, except under certain special circumstances, make an adoption without the consent of his wife. Under the earlier law her consent was immaterial but under the present law, her consent is unnecessary only when she has renounced the world or has ceased to be Hindu or has been judicially declared to be of unsound mind. A Hindu woman who is not of unsound mind and who is not a minor is now competent to adopt a son as well as a daughter, provided she is a spinster, divorcee, or widow or one whose husband has finally renounced the world or has ceased to be a Hindu or has been judicially declared to be of unsound mind. In general, during coverture it is only the husband who can adopt. If the woman wants to adopt a son, she should not have a Hindu son, son's son or

7. These enactments which are considered parts of a Hindu code, apply to Hindus, Buddhists, Sikhs and Jains, so that a reference to Hindu women in this context includes Buddhist, Sikh and Jain women as well.

8. Adoption as a legal institution exists only among Hindus in India. See J.D.M. Derrett, *Introduction to Modern Hindu Law* (Bombay : Oxford University Press, 1963), p. 92. Though a bill has been introduced in Parliament no general legislation relating to adoption has yet been passed into law.

son's son's son living at the time of the adoption, and the boy to be adopted should be younger to her by at least twenty-one years. If she intends adopting a daughter, an essential condition is that she should have no Hindu daughter or son's daughter living at the time of the adoption. Corresponding requirements have also to be observed by the man who wishes to adopt a son or daughter.

The wife has a right to maintenance for life. She may not forfeit this right even if she lives separately from her husband on certain specific grounds such as the husband's cruelty, desertion, keeping a concubine or having another wife, his suffering from a virulent form of leprosy, his conversion to another religion or any other cause justifying her living separately. She, however, forfeits her right to maintenance if she is unchaste or ceases to be a Hindu.

EMPLOYMENT AND EDUCATION

The Factories Act, 1948 empowers state governments to prohibit employment of women in dangerous operations. A few enactments lay down the general rule that women should not be permitted to work between 7 p.m. and 6 a.m., but this rule is relaxable in certain circumstances.[9] Provisions for maternity benefits for women have been incorporated in the Employees State Insurance Act, 1948 and a number of state enactments. While maternity benefit in coal mines is governed by the Maternity Benefit Act, 1961 women workers in factories and plantations are entitled to maternity leave according to the maternity benefit enactments of different states. Both the Factories Act, 1948 and the Plantations Labour Act, 1951 make it obligatory for factories and plantation employing not less than fifty women to provide creches.

In spite of these statutory benefits and the constitutional directive regarding equal pay for equal work, women agricultural labourers generally get 10 to 60 per cent less in wages than men for the same work. It is not infrequent that, when the husband becomes a "bonded labourer" for the landlord or the labour contractor, the wife also becomes similarly

9. See K.N. Vaid, *Labour Welfare in India* (New Delhi: Shri Ram Centre for Industrial Relations and Human Resources, 1970), p. 301.

"bonded" with the not unusual result that she is made vulnerable to exploitation including trafficking for immoral purposes.[10]

Only 13 per cent of Indian women, according to the 1971 Census, may be regarded as workers, i.e., those who are engaged in some form of economic activity. About 80 per cent of these working women are engaged in agriculture. Only 12 per cent of the total employees in central and state administrative services and public sector undertakings are women. This may not be unrelated to their education or lack of it. Only 18 per cent of Indian women are literate. Though one of the directive principles of the Constitution requires the state to provide free and compulsory education for all children under 14 years of age the directive is generally followed with callous disregard of its spirits and its significance for the country. Coupled with the general apathy to women's education, this indifference to put in practice a constitutional directive results in greater social and economic deprivation for girls than for boys.

At the primary school level while 97 out of 100 boys attend school, the corresponding figure for girls is 62. Further, out of 100 girls who enter the first grade only 26 go up to the fifth grade. It is only about 2 per cent of women who are able to benefit by the opportunities provided for higher education.[11] In 1971-72, 36 girls only were under instruction at various levels of education compared to a hundred boys.[12] If in 1971 about 18 per cent of women were literate this may appear to compare well with only 8 per cent literacy for women on the eve of independence in 1947, but an increase of 10 per cent in the not too short span of about three decades is hardly something that should make us complacent.

10. Kamla Mankekar. "Employment among Women in India", *Eve's Weekly* (May 10, 1975), p. 65. See also V. Dhagamwar, *Law, Power and Justice* (Bombay : N.M. Tripathi, 1974), p. 183 and Appendices.

11. See *Women in India : Selected Statistics* (New Delhi : Department of Social Welfare, Ministry of Education and Social Welfare, 1975). mimeo.

12. Kamla Mankekar, *op. cit.*, p. 35.

ABORTION

There are certain other types of social legislation which seek to protect interests and benefits that are of special concern to women. The Suppression of Immoral Traffic in Women and Girls Act, 1956, as its title indicates, is intended to protect helpless women and girls from a typical mode of exploitation not altogether unknown in the country. The same year saw the enactment of another piece of social legislation: the Women's and Children's Institutions (Licensing) Act, 1956. This was later on superseded by the Orphanages and Other Charitable Homes (Supervision and Control) Act, 1960. The object of the enactment was to regulate the activities of these institutions and to prescribe a proper standard to which the treatment and the training of the inmates should conform. Such a measure was found necessary because, while there are many good and properly managed charitable institutions, there are many others run with the objective of exploitation as their main and sustaining inspiration.

The Medical Termination of Pregnancy Act, 1971 may also be mentioned in the context of social legislation relative to women. The enactment seeks, among other things, to protect women's interests. It has a few provisions which, it is clear, were enacted with the sufferings of women in the legislator's mind. It provides that a pregnancy may be terminated where the length of the pregnancy does not exceed twenty weeks, if two medical practitioners are of the opinion that the continuance of the pregnancy would involve a risk to the life of the pregnant woman or of grave injury to her physical or mental health. Two explanations are offered in the enactment itself of what constitutes grave injury to the mental health of the pregnant woman. The first explanation reads:

> When any pregnancy is alleged by the pregnant woman to have been caused by rape, the anguish caused by such pregnancy shall be presumed to constitute a grave injury to the mental health of the pregnant woman.

In this case the "anguish" is perhaps palpable. The second explanation is more intriguing in that "anguish" is given an extended application. It states :

> Where a pregnancy occurs as a result of failure of any device or method used by any married woman or her husband for the purpose of limiting the number of children, the anguish caused by such unwanted pregnancy may be presumed to constitute a grave injury to the mental health of the pregnant woman.

Though the promotional slant of the government's family planning programme may be perceptible in this explanation, it is evident that Parliament cannot be blamed for any lack of solicitude for the largest minority in the country. This solicitude may be even more evident in another provision of the Act which stipulates that in determining whether the continuance of a pregnancy would involve grave risk to the health of a pregnant woman, account may be taken of her actual or reasonably foreseeable environment. This enactment has been hailed as "a major landmark in India's social legislation", and "a far-reaching measure assuring the women of India freedom from undesirable and unwanted pregnancies."[13]

It is generally assumed that the Act was envisaged by the government partly as a family planning measure and some of the rules framed by the government appear to strengthen the basis of this assumption.[14] In this context, it may be interesting to hear what the government has to say about abortion. Mrs. Gandhi said recently: "Unless the girl's life is in danger, there should be no abortion. No, I definitely think...I would not like abortion to be easy."[15] In fact, it has been made easy by legislation. If the Prime Minister's concept of social values trails quite a few steps behind the law adopted by her government could one blame the illiterate village woman if she does not take kindly to permissive legislation relating to widow marriage or divorce, or medical termination of pregnancy which is the accepted euphemism for abortion? Perhaps it is the "Indianness" of the Prime Minister that comes through in her statement.

13. S. Chandrasekhar, *Abortion in a Crowded World* (London : Allen and Unwin, 1974), p. 106.

14. See J. Minattur, "Medical Termination of Pregnancy and Conscientious Objection", *Journal of the Indian Law Institute*, 16 (October-December 1974), p. 705.

15. Gulshan Ewing, *op. cit.*, p. 11.

CONCLUSION

From a study of the ameliorative legal provisions relating to women and the actual situation in which they find themselves, it is clear that something more than legislation is required. Perhaps the first thing to be attempted is to make women aware of their rights, however this is done. It is also necessary to change the attitudes of both men and women, of society in general, to social objectives sought to be achieved by legislation. A radical change in the attitudes of women induced by an awareness of their rights which are constitutionally guaranteed and legally protected will be the first step in the complex process of transforming the social structure so that women may enjoy full equality with men in every sphere of life.

7

URSULA KING

Women and Religion : The Status and Image of Women in Some Major Religious Traditions

Religious beliefs and practices have been a universal feature of human life. Thus, it is not surprising that women have always had a place in religious activities, however much the degree of their participation may have varied. Of great importance are the explicit teachings about women which the major religious traditions have propounded. On one hand, these teachings reflect the actual position held by women in society at different times in history; on the other, the teachings have in turn contributed to determining such positions by upholding a particular image or ideal of womanhood.

What is the nature of woman? What is her particular role in the family, her position in society at large, her situation in the general scheme of salvation? All religions have to some extent provided answers to these questions, however inadequate they may be for us today. In the higher religions, we find the great philosophical and theological teaching about the essential sameness of human nature, of the intrinsic worth of all human beings as everyone, woman just as much as man, is endowed with a soul, a divine spark, or is part of the same *atman*. This lofty ideal is often of very little practical consequence, however; in actual practice, much of the ethical teaching and the religious counsels reflect the social position of women in a particular environment. As a result, we also possess many sacred texts which relegate women's place to a lower or secondary rank to man. Such texts are frequently quoted as the scriptural basis for the legitimation of women's low status through the ages; they are the sacred authority which teaches that woman's status has to be low and unequal to that of man. In addition, we have the paradoxical situation that in some religious teachings an idealised exaltation of woman in her role as mother and wife occurs; in some instances, an ideal of woman in her eternal essence is projected when in actual social life subjugation is woman's common lot.

Today, with an altogether different situation in society, the religions are faced with an entirely new challenge. Since the social, economic and political emancipation of women has become widely accepted, new pressures from the social environment are affecting all the religious traditions, and the inadequacy of their traditional teaching regarding the general status or image of woman is being fundamentally questioned. How do different religions respond to this new and challenging situation? Before discussing this important question, we have to look more closely at the situation in the past.

WOMEN AND THE HISTORY OF RELIGIONS

It has been rightly pointed out that the various attempts to write a comprehensive history of women through the ages and variety of cultures, have all proved to be failures. The conditions of life and local traditions have been too disparate, the gaps in our historical knowledge too great. Any attempt to write a continuous history of women, including their role in primitive cultures, ancient civilisations and modern societies has to be abandoned. All one can aim for is an investigation limited to a certain time and space.[1] The remark applies equally well to the relationship of women and religion. We can hope to possess a complete picture of the situation through the ages and varieties of religious teachings and practices. No uniform development can be traced through the general history of religions, nor through the history of one particular religion as great discrepancies have occurred at different times.

1. Cf. the entry "Women, Status of" in Encyclopaedia Britannica, *Macropaedia*, Vol. 19, pp. 906-916.

It may be stimulating, however, to reflect upon a few random data provided by the history of religion.[2] Women have not always and everywhere been excluded from religious rites and relegated to an inferior status. Certain writers have, in fact, maintained that early matriarchy and mother-right preceded patriarchy and male dominance in the development of human societies. However that may be, there is no doubt that the status of women in early agricultural societies was relatively high. Women were not only creators of life, providers of food, and helpmates of men, they were also the supreme symbols of fertility itself. Thus we find a widespread worship of the mother-goddess in the form of many powerful deities in the civilisations of Babylonia, Egypt, Phrygia and Phoenicia from where it spread to Greece and Rome, paradoxically coexisting there with a legal position of women's complete subordination to the authority of either father or husband. We also know of the presence of the mother-goddess in the Indus Valley Civilisation, possibly the historical source of the still important village goddess (*gramadevata*) of South India.

The Greek, Roman and Indian pantheon in particular are replete with female deities who often play a central role in the respective mythologies. But it is not so much the deification of the female form which interests us as the participation of real women in religious life. Here again we find in both primitive and ancient religions the widespread presence of women magicians, shamans, healers, visionaries and seers, prophetesses, and priestesses. Female visionaries played an important role in Germanic religion, and the women oracles of Greece were equally well-known, especially the famous oracle at Delphi (the marble base of whose tripod, by the way, ended up in a stately Yorkshire home, Castle Howard). Of great renown, too, are the sibyls, the prophetesses and fortune-tellers of old, considered to be the mouthpiece of a particular god. They were pictorially represented in Christian churches from the eleventh century onwards, the most famous example being Michelangelo's paintings in the Sistine Chapel in Rome. Female temple priests and attendants were known in many religions, for

2. Cf. the section "Die Frau" in F. Heiler, *Erscheinungsformen und Wesen der Religion* (Stuttgart, 1961), pp. 411-426.

example, in Egypt, Sumeria, Babylonia, Greece and ancient Japan. Roman religions knew the vestals, the consecrated virgins charged with the perpetual care of sacred fire in the temple of the goddess Vesta. At the other end of the spectrum, we find the phenomenon of temple prostitution in several religions.[3]

REGRESSIVE TREND

In earlier times, when religious practices were less formally organised and religious roles less institutionalised, it was easier for individual women to hold positions of religious authority. With the gradual development of the higher religions, a more definite institutionalisation of religious roles occurred. Sacred authority, like secular authority, rested with men and the exercise of religious funtions, be it sacrifice, teaching, preaching, blessing or initiation, became a male prerogative. We can observe such developments as much in ancient Mithraism and Brahmanism as in Christianity and Islam. Thus we are faced with a certain regression in the participation of women in religious life. This is not to say that in area of religion women once held a position above men. It only means that in an earlier, more undifferentiated age of development, certain areas of religious activity were open to women which later became closed.

This regressive trend can be found in many religious traditions, and it seems to express itself in two ways. First, there is the general decline of the oracular, prophetic and even priestly activity of women if one compares the situation in ancient cultures with that of more recent times. Then there is the specific regression of religious activities of women in particular religions if one compares the creative time of the founder with later practices. At the time of a religious beginning, when a charismatic personality, an enlightened being, shapes a new way of life, much is questioned and little taken for granted. In such a period of flux, women, in their support of a new move-

3. Many ancient pagan practices continued in Christianity in medieval Europe. It has been said that sometimes a kind of secret priesthood was exercised by women; this custom is thought to be one of the reasons why the witch hunt was so vigorously pursued by the Church.

ment, were often allowed greater freedom than was customary in their environment. Only later, after the newly emerged religion had became codified, were women's roles once again consigned to what they had previously been in that particular social milieu.

It is in itself a remarkable phenomenon that we do not know of any woman who was a great religious founder. Moses, Mahavira, Buddha, Jesus, Mohammed, are all men. However, this is not as extraordinary as it at first appears; the great statesmen, philosophers, writers and scientists of the past have almost invariably been men, too. Public life was, by and large, notwithstanding a few exceptions of remarkable women in history, the sphere of men. Women's sphere was not public but private life: home and family, the preparation of food and clothes, the birth and nurture of children. If one considers for a moment how much time and energy these activities required in traditional societies and keeps in mind the much shorter average span of life, it is not at all surprising that there was neither surplus leisure nor surplus energy available to women to achieve more. Only the changing patterns of life in very recent time have opened up an entirely new arenas of freedom and possibilities for women.

If one looks at the women associated with the person of a particular religious founder, or with a particularly creative period in the history of a religious tradition, one can see that women were always present and often more actively involved in religious activities than was possible later. One has only to think of some of the outstanding women in the Old Testament, their active and sometimes crucial role in the early history of the Israelites. This contrasts sharply with, for example, the passive role of women in later Jewish synagogues. Even today, only the reformed synagogues allow women active participation in their service. A similar regression can be observed in Islam: Mohammed's spouse played a decisive role in early Islam; the prophet's daughter, Fatima, occupies an eminent position for Shia Muslims. Yet, women's activities in Islam are generally restricted to the private sphere. The use of the mosque on Friday is denied to them. Women may read the *Koran* but not preach it. Perhaps among the Sufis alone the distinction between the male and female tends to disappear. Thus a woman may reach the highest ranks in the hierarchy of Muslim saints. This greater equality of status may well be due to the fact that the mystic path, perhaps more than any other religious orientation, strives to realise the lofty teaching about the divine in all human beings on a practical level.

In early Christianity too, we find women making an important contribution. Their activities are associated with preaching, teaching, social work and even liturgical service. Yet, later, many of these activities became impossible through a retrograde development, often linked to a strong emphasis on male asceticism. Such a pattern of retrogression can also be shown in the development of Hinduism, and it is to the closer examination of the Indian religious traditions that we now turn.

WOMEN AND INDIAN RELIGIONS

In the well known book, *The Position of Women in Hindu Civilisation*, A. S. Altekar[4] argues that Indian women in the distant past had a higher status than in more recent times. Women once enjoyed considerable freedom and privileges in the spheres of family, religion and pubilc life; yet, over the centuries, their situation changed adversely. This better position applies more specifically to the Vedic age when women played a more active economic role and participated more in ritual. For example, for a long time girls in higher society were allowed to undergo the *upanayana* rite. During that time asceticism was far less prominent than subsequently. As far as we have any evidence, there was also no seclusion of women.

Later, when the ascetic *sannyasa* ideal became very dominant, the status of women deteriorated. Furthermore, just as the introduction of slavery revolutionised the position of women in the classical period of Greece, the emergence of the semi-servile Sudra Caste within Hindu society deprived women of many of the economically productive functions. Altekar sees the period of 500 A.D. to 1800 A.D. as one of progressive deterioration in the position of women in society; only the

4. A.S. Altekar, *The Position of Women in Hindu Civilisation: From Prehistoric Times to the Present Day* (Delhi: Motilal Banarsidas, reprinted 1973).

recognition of certain proprietary rights developed for the better. The *upanayana* rite for girls was completely abandoned; marriage was seen to be its main substitute. At the same time the marriage age was increasingly lowered; child marriage became a common practice, precluding any formal education for girls, whilst the remarriage of widows was taboo. Through the influence of the Islamic custom of *purdah*, more strictly enforced in India than elsewhere, North Indian women in particular lived in great seclusion. Theologically speaking, women were classed in the same category as Sudras. They were not allowed to recite the *Vedas* nor to perform the Vedic sacrificial ritual. This right was extended to women only by the Arya Samaj, a Hindu reformist movement founded by Swami Dayanand Sarswati in the nineteenth century, which attempted to free Hinduism from later accretions by going back to the original customs of Vedic times. Traditionally, women had only a subsidiary role in worship, being associated with it at home and through their husband.

The great traditional ways to salvation were normally not open to women. However, the *bhakti* and *puranic* schools, which came to prominence by 500 A.D. and stressed devotion and faith, amply provided for women's emotional and religious needs. Thus women became the followers, custodians and patrons of devotional worship in Hinduism. Altekar stresses that women in the past were largely educated through the stories of *puranic* literature which inculcate blind faith rather than rational behaviour; with more time on their hands, women could visit temples, perform vows and submit to fasts with greater regularity than their menfolk who were preoccupied with other work. "Thus the very women whom religion had once considered as outcasts...were the most faithful custodians of its spirit and traditions."[5]

Orthodox Hinduism as we know it today associates woman mainly with the family but everything here is defined in relation to the husband. A modern Hindu writer[6] has stated this in the following words :

5. *Ibid.*

6. R.N. Dandekar, "The Role of Man in Hinduism", in K.W. Morgan (ed.), *The Religion of the Hindus Interpreted by Hindus* (New York : The Ronald Press Company, 1953), pp. 140-141.

> A man's religious life is considered to be essentially deficient without his wife's active participation in it....Without a wife...the psychological and moral personality of man remains imperfect. She is his constant companion in his religious life, preparing for him the sacred articles used in worship, accompanying him on pilgrimages, present at all ceremonies....And finally, in her role as the mother, woman is regarded as divine, respected many times more than the father and the teacher.

Yet, at the same time, some of the special sacraments of Hinduism do not apply to women, especially not the important rite of initiation:

> The most important sacrament for a woman is marriage. After marriage a woman is generally considered to have no existence apart from her husband, especially so far as religious practices are concerned. Her husband is her proper spiritual preceptor, or guru, and in all spiritual matters she is dependent on him. The conscientious performance of household duties constitutes her proper ritual.[7]

This is the traditional Brahminical position. The author concedes, however, that in popular Hinduism women are allowed greater freedom in worship and other religious practices. But granted the different levels at which Hinduism operates in practice, it nevertheless seems paradoxical that women are given such a low, dependent status in all practical religious matters when the mythological and theological formulations of Hinduism express the motherhood of God and the female aspects of the divine, the *Shakti*, with greater force and beauty than those of any other world religion.

PATH OF RENUNCIATION

Hinduism also declared women ineligible for the path of renunciation (*sannyasa*). Not renunciation but the discharge of her family responsibilities is woman's specific *dharma*, her

7. *Ibid.*

most sacred duty. This general injunction notwithstanding, we know of famous Hindu women saints—Lalla, Mirabai, Sarada Devi, to name only a few, and, in our own age, Anandamayi. As in Christianity, asceticism appears to have had important repercussions on the status of women in Hinduism; and the fact that women were normally altogether excluded from the path of renunciation, must have had graver consequences still. The early *Dharmasutra* writers still regarded renunciation as an anti-Vedic custom. A hero of the *Mahabharata* epic has even been quoted as saying that renunciation appeals only to those who are unsuccessful in life. However this may be, it would be far too simplistic to merely accept that in the distant past, before the advent of renouncers in large numbers, all was well with women in Indian society. They may have had greater freedom of movement and a greater share in important economic, social and religious functions; yet, anti-feminine views may have been more widely spread than one likes to admit in an egalitarian age.

Both Buddhism and Jainism, dating from the sixth century B.C. or earlier, do express such views in their writings. Buddha was initially opposed to the admission of women into the *Sangha* but he eventually gave way. Thus we find Buddhist nuns from the beginning, and the Jains have nuns too. However, the stricter *Digambara* Jains hold that women can never gain salvation unless they are reborn as men. Yet in spite of certain discriminatory practices, Buddhism and Jainism have both produced some distinguished women preachers. For Buddhism, the service of the *upasika*, the laywoman, is also very important; many such women lay followers are well known and have exercised an influential patronage in the past history of Buddhism.

It would be quite inadmissible to explain the status of women in a particular society as being exclusively due to the dominant religious views held by that society. The image of women in a religious tradition is an important variable affecting the status of women, especially in a religiously oriented culture, yet it is not the only variable. A well-known Indian anthropologist[8] is of the opinion that

8. D.N. Majumdar, *Races and Culture of India* (New Delhi: Asia Publishing House, 1961), p. 206

> the status of woman in India can be more understood in the context of Indian ethnology than in that of religion or Brahmanism. . . . Brahmanic influence appears to have been overestimated, and the rigid mores of woman's conduct have been read in the context of the doctrines of *Karma* and *Dharma*, but if Brahmanism had such a great influence, how is it that the majority of social groups, castes and tribes escaped it or did not conform to such a . . . system?

This brings us back to a point made earlier: religious teachings and attitudes to women are closely related to specific groups and the mores of a given society. Often enough, religious teaching underwrites the *status quo* but in certain instances, it may also contain the anticipatory capacity for a change of state. In a secular society, such a change of state is already occurring in the position of women; in the last fifty years or so, it has changed almost beyond recognition. Yet traditional attitudes die hard and, sad though it may be, these traditional attitudes towards women are sometimes both sanctioned and further reinforced by Christian tradition.

WOMEN AND CHRISTIANITY

The historical and theological background of the Christian image of woman has been most comprehensively studied in the recent book *Woman in Christian Tradition*.[9] As this topic is of great relevance to our present discussion, it seems best to examine some of its main arguments. The book provides a much-needed balance to contemporary studies on women which are often too exclusively focused on present problems and questions without seeing how these are rooted in a past tradition. The image of woman in one particular religion, in this case Christianity, is far from being uniform; it always includes several aspects, possibly exclusive of each other. At certain times, some traits may become more prominent than others due to extraneous reasons. As the earlier views on women seem to be more differentiated than later ones when positions have become more fixed and rigid, we tend to react

9. G.H. Tavard, *Woman in Christian Tradition* (Indiana: University of Notre Dame Press, 1973).

strongly against the image of the most immediate past, the image of woman closest to us.

Two quite different images of the nature and status of woman can already be inferred from the two accounts of creation in the Old Testament (Genesis, chapter two, being the earlier version and chapter one, the later). The two divergent traditions can be followed right through Biblical literature. Social conditions assigned an inferior position to women but

> Jesus's behaviour, as recorded in the Gospels, does not follow traditional Jewish reserve. To his companions' surprise, he speaks with the Samaritan woman at the well. He heals women as well as men, entertains relations of friendship with Martha and Mary. The group of his followers includes both married and unmarried women. His teaching on marriage implies the equality of man and woman. This will be of great importance for the concept of womanhood in the early Church; it was at variance with the mainstream of the rabbinic tradition.[10]

However, the ambiguity of the status of women comes out strongest in the writings of St. Paul. There are those texts which clearly express the subordination of women. For centuries, Pauline teaching that woman is the glory of man[11] and that women are not allowed to speak in Church[12] was taken as the scriptural justification of woman's subjugation to man and the exclusion of women from liturgical activity in Christian Churches.

> The married woman stands at the bottom of a hierarchy at the top of which is God. Christ and husband mediate in between, so that the woman seems further removed from Christ and from God than her husband.[13]

Then, there are other texts which express the principles of equality or identity operating through Christian baptism: all

10. *Ibid.*, p. 20.
11. First letter to the Corinthians, 11, 7.
12. *Ibid.*, 14, 34.
13. Tavard, *op. cit.*, p. 28.

Christians, whether male or female, slave or free, enjoy the same freedom based on their identity in Christ.[14] In him Christian men and women are raised beyond the distinction of the sexes. A new spiritual freedom was experienced which led to much heavenly daring and experiment in the early Church and to a flouting of conventions.

Yet at the same time people remained subject to the law of the flesh which made them male and female. Accordingly,

> Paul's injunctions to his communities waver between a vision of heavenly identity of male and female, to whichthe faithful bave been elevated by the Lord, and the earthly reality of sexual life. Indeed. . . much of the difficulties that troubled the Church at Corinth stemmed from the inherent dilemma of belonging to two worlds. Some of the Corinthians attempted to translate their eschatological freedom into their everyday experience.[15]

This striving for an acting out of spiritual freedom found in baptism, and for a realisation of the kingdom of God on earth in tension with the given social environment, characterises much of the history of early Christianity. In principle, there was the equality of women with men found through baptism; in practice, however, the living out of this spiritual freedom could only be realised through strong asceticism and lived by an ascetic elite. Logically, the spiritual freedom given to woman in baptism should have been followed by her complete emancipation in the world. This consequence, however, is only coming into force today.

IDEALS OF ASCETICISM

Historically, the freedom of venture and new experiment was soon curtailed when the immediacy of the coming of the kingdom of God receded into the background as only a remote possibility. Christians became settled; the Church had to accommodate itself to the world at large. Injunctions for the behaviour and status of women were modelled on the example

14. Letter to the Galatians, 3, 23-28.
15. Tavard, *op. cit.*, p. 32.

of the Hellenistic and Roman environment; women were assigned to their customary, subordinate position. Liberation, found in the New Testament through the experience of baptism, was now only possible through the strictest asceticism, a path theoretically open to both men and women. However, many ascetic writings also reflect a strong anti-feminist character. The view of woman as an embodiment of evil and, at the root of all, sexual evil, gained strong support. Woman was seen as a creature of imperfection and congenital weakness.

It is not necessary to mention here the many Christian writers who through the ages, gave vent to their anti-feminist feelings. One reason for this is that the ideals of asceticism, contemplation and monastic life became closely associated with virginity. This is by no means always the case in other religious traditions; suffice it to mention the married Sufis in Islam and the married monks in certain forms of Buddhism. In Christianity, virginity was ranked higher than married life. There is no doubt that, apart from the Biblical sources, neo-Platonic thought with its contempt for the body, had a strong influence on these developments.

It is equally important to remember that only relatively late in the early history of Christian thought did marriage come to be considered a sacrament. In the first centuries, marriage was mainly a family and civic affair. The ordinary Christian woman had the status assigned to her by society. Only the consecrated virgin could claim equality with men as a member of an ascetic elite; as Tavard notes, "the life of virginity was a prophetic anticipation of restored incorruptibility, a manifestation of the fullness of deification, of the final integrity of the image of God in man and in woman."[16] Both Western and Eastern Christianity promoted the life of consecrated virginity but the Western Church tended to separate, much more than was ever the case in the East, the liturgical service of the Lord from contact with women. In the West, the marriage of priests was abolished by the decision of a Council in the twelfth century; instead of the custom dying out, however, we find much clerical concubinage in the fourteenth and fifteenth cen-

16. *Ibid.*, p. 87.

turies when the desire of priests to marry reappeared. The Protestant Churches of the reformation all allowed their ministers to marry whilst the Council of Trent reiterated the prohibition of clerical marriage in the Catholic Church, this time with a great deal of success. New questioning of this decision is only recurring in our own day.[17]

NO ADEQUATE MODEL OF WOMAN

The double typology of womanhood—subordination or equality—is reflected in many contemporary Christian writings, both Catholic and Protestant. Referring to various Catholic models of womanhood, Tavard perceives as their central problem the open schizophrenia they imply. There is the presence of

> contradictory streams of thought to see woman as weak and as a symbol of temptation, and to idealise her as a symbol of transcendent goodness. . . . Encomiums of the feminine ideal and praises of the Virgin Mary notwithstanding, the position of woman reflects the idea of her debility rather than any other of the elements of the total Catholic tradition. . . . Thus it happens that Catholics who wish to promote the rights of women today confront us with the humanistic tradition of Simone de Beauvoir, with Freudian reconstructions or, at a lower level of sophistication, with statistical data on women in and out of wedlock.[18]

17. *Ibid.*, p. 119. Tavard points out the important relationship which obtains between women and those who build theological systems. In the West, theology has always been the speciality of a section of the clergy; thus, the history of both asceticism and celibacy has its bearing on the image and status of woman. He states emphatically that "the separation between priests and women is bound to entail a one-sided theology of womanhood, to which woman remains alien and from which she is likely to find herself alienated".

18. *Ibid.*, p. 149; But how do we discover the adequate categories of thought within which to envisage the role of woman? The author examines different orthodox models (the Greek Church Fathers; Soloviev; Bulgakov; Evdokomov) and Protestant examples (Luther, Calvin, Barth, Brunner) yet all of them fall short of an acceptable anthropology for today.

The conclusion to be drawn from a survey of the Christian tradition is that there exists no fully adequate Christian model of woman which would meet modern women's requirements—and this can be said of the traditional image of woman in all religious traditions. Nor is there any model which would adequately express the spiritual freedom of the central Christian message. The Christian theological stance concerning woman, her function in society, and her place in the Church, was originally dominated by Jewish, Greek, and Roman patterns of thought and behaviour into which the Christian revelation

> wedged an element of newness, of fermentation, perhaps we may even say of revolution. Yet this element could only take shape in the context of the prevailing cultural forms which to a great extent contradicted it. And so forms of thought or behaviour essentially alien to the Christian message have carried through the centuries the seeds of transformation which this message entailed. As I see it, the task of a theological reflection on womanhood lies here: we should disentangle the inner message and its containers.[19]

To achieve this disentanglement, to develop a comprehensive theological anthropology for both women and men, one also has to recognise the need of competent women theologians who can participate in this task. Who else can adequately express the self-understanding of women and create a richer, more balanced image of woman if not women themselves? Under different social and economic conditions, women today have come to claim a new position in society; they have acquired a new status of equality. Any outdated image which may still regard them, due to the one-sided idealisation or denigration, as either semi-divine or sub-human, cannot answer the needs of a new situation where women claim and fight to be persons in their own right.

WOMEN AND THE MODERN WORLD

Let us briefly examine the reasons why the status of women is changing in modern society.

19. *Ibid.*, p. 188.

The largest single factor affecting the status of women to-today is the changing family pattern coupled with the increased access to formal education, even though the percentage of women in higher education is still considerably lower than that of men. In all countries where data are available, there is evidence of a strong correlation between educational level and the employment rate of women. The more highly educated married women are the more they are motivated to continue in or return to their careers, irrespective of their husbands' social status or income group. Earlier it was feared that a girl's prolonged education might diminish her marital prospects; now we have a development whereby education provides additional prestige and represents an important asset for marriage. This can be witnessed in contemporary India; it also accounts for the rapid increase of women students in countries as different as Argentina, Italy and Japan.

It is erroneous to believe that the employment of women, especially married women, is a new phenomenon. Women have at all times and in all types of economy made a substantial contribution to the production and distribution of their communities' resources. But whilst the economic unit in pre-industrial society was the family itself, industrialised society introduced a strict separation of the home from the place of work. What is new, therefore, is the fact that women are employed outside the home, as independent individuals, receiving monetary rewards. Thus the emphasis is more on *going out* to work than simply on work.

The changed position of women in society together with an increasing emphasis on the nuclear rather than the joint family pattern and other social changes affecting the contemporary family, make the husband-wife relationship of crucial importance. Marriage nowadays is increasingly seen as a partnership where family life becomes a cooperative venture. Thus, the compatibility of marriage partners is of the utmost importance; the leading role in a family may depend more on temperament than on accepted conventions. In the process of mutual adjustment towards a situation of equal status, women are increasingly stretching their interests beyond the home whilst men, in turn, are becoming more home-centred than in the past. This new situation also affects the relationship between parents and children which, due to the smaller number of children and the nuclear family structure, allows for a more intensive but less authoritarian pattern. The most revolutionary factor affecting women's lives today is certainly the availability of birth control and family planning.

These changes deserve closer scrutiny than is possible here since many of them may have an inherently ambivalent character. This brief survey is only intended to bring out the deep changes which have revolutionised the status of women in industrialised societies. Of great additional importance is the increased expectation of life together with a drastic reduction in the years a woman devotes to the bearing and rearing of children. All these changes will increasingly affect the entire female population of the globe, whatever their religious traditions may teach about the status of women.

At present, no religion can offer an adequate model for contemporary women's self-understanding. The newness of the situation has to be matched by a corresponding new creative effort on the part of religious leaders and thinkers male and female alike. Otherwise, women, the most faithful devotees and upholders of religious traditions through the centuries, may well have to abandon religion itself as being an instrument of their subjection.

WOMEN AND RELIGION TODAY

Whilst women have reached a crititical stage of self-reflection and a new status in the contemporary world, religion itself is undergoing a crisis at present. None of the religious traditions has so far been able to offer and adequate spirituality for the needs of men and women today although many religions contain excellent counsels and models of holiness. But what was adequate for the past may not be so for today. Even when the position of women at the earliest period in religion can be seen as a relatively better one, it is far from being comparable to the contemporary situation. It was usually in her social role as wife and mother that woman's position was assessed. In the past, women's status has always been closely dependent on her child-bearing role. This can be seen especially from the stigma traditionally attached to barrenness, and the tremendous importance placed on male offspring.

The new social and economic conditions which, at last, have given women the freedom to be persons in their own right (whilst not precluding their roles as wife and mother), require a corresponding theological elaboration of the image of woman. Perhaps the time has come, during a period of religious crisis and renewal, to work out in practical terms the basic religious teaching about the essential equality of human nature Wherever the ascetic ideal has been too prominent in religion women were denigrated. The counsels of ascetic spirituality have in the past been largely addressed to men only, to the exclusion and detriment of women. What about women's own spirituality? Women's views have rarely been heard or asked for in religion, and women's 'nature', so well projected by men, needed little on its own account. All too often the faults of men have been blamed on women. The ascetic ideal which has often had a nefarious influence on the status of women, needs to be replaced by a richer and more balanced spiritual ideal which both men and women can share. Women who still care for religion and see the importance of religious values today, can only plead with religion to give them a fuller share in all religious activities.[20]

In India, too, the traditional ideal of womanhood is often strongly modified in practice. Many outstanding women leaders were deeply involved with the struggle for national independence. The successful contribution of women to the independence movement accounts for the fact that in India there are, relatively speaking, more women active in politics than in Western countries. Theoretically, however, the supreme ideal of Indian womanhood is still modelled on the Brahmanical tradition and linked to a strongly patriarchal

20. This is now increasingly happening. The World Council of Churches has promoted the collaboration of men and women for many years. Certain Christian denominations have had women ministers for quite some time. Today, there are strong movements for the ordination of women in both the Anglican and Roman Catholic Churches.

structure of society.[21] In religion, too, women still occupy the traditional place.

It is most interesting to note that recently a woman of the Lingayat sect in Mysore has begun to propagate the religious equality of women by fighting for women's right to become a guru and to initiate disciples. This is just one example which shows that if women want to improve their status in the sphere of religious belief and practice, it is up to women themselves to assert their right and presence. Today, in a time of much religious transformation and renewal, women themselves have to make sure that their voice will be heard and listened to. The religions of the past have not been able to offer an adequate model for the image of woman, but all religions in the future will be under greater pressure to be more just in representing, and responding to, the aspirations of *all* members of the human community. The challenge presented by the modern world and the status of women in it has to be taken up in a creative way. Women alone cannot achieve this task; the status of women in religion may be worked out more satisfactorily if both women and men have an equal share in influencing the development of religious thought and practice.

21. This paradoxical situation between Indian theory and practice is well brought out in the detailed sociological study on Indian women by Maria Mies, *Indische Frauen zwischen Patriarchat und Chacengleichheit : Rollenkonflikte studierender und berufstaetiger Frauen* (Meisenheim am Glan: Verlag Anton Hain, 1973).

8

VICTOR S. D'SOUZA

Family Status and Female Work Participation

The study of participation of women in the working force is beset with many difficulties. First of all the problems of measuring the extent of their participation in gainful employment has not yet been solved. Attempts at refining the definition of the working force affected the measures of female work participation the most as in the 1961 and 1971 censuses. However, distortions brought about in the rate of female work participation by changes in the definition of the working force apart, there are certain clearly discernible trends about female work participation which are quite puzzling.

A careful examination of the census figures shows that while the rate of male work participation is more or less uniform that of female work participation fluctuates very highly from region to region. The percentage of women workers in the total working force as well as their percentage in the total female population have been declining. Underlying the overall trend there are certain structural features and the changes in these features which can be gleaned from the census data as well as the various city surveys conducted recently. While the majority of both male and female workers are illiterate, the percentage of illiterate workers among females is much larger than among males. When occupations are divided into different prestige grades the proportion of workers in the lower prestige grades is much larger among females than among males. The rate of female work participation declines from rural to urban and from smaller to larger communities.[1]

TWO HYPOTHESES

It is possible to explain these trends with the help of a theoretical model using generalisations of an economic nature, as I did in my earlier study.[2] The model is based on two hypotheses. First, the main reason why most women work is the low income of their menfolk. When the husband's income is not adequate for the support of the family, the wife also is compelled to work. This hypothesis agrees with the fact that the vast majority of women are employed at lower occupational prestige levels and it can be presumed that their husbands also are employed in correspondingly lower prestige occupations with very low incomes. The hypothesis is further corroborated by the data pertaining to rural agricultural labour families which show that the higher the wage rate for men the lower is the number of women per family in the working force.[3]

The second hypothesis of the model is that with the socio-economic growth of a society the proportions of occupations of higher prestige are, on the whole, increasing at the cost of occupations of lower prestige. This has been clearly demonstrated in the case of the U.S.A.[4] and I have indicated that a similar trend is visible in our country also.

By relating these two hypotheses it is possible to derive some implications for trends in female work participation. It is obvious that the occupational structures of rural and urban communities are different. In the urban communities there

1. Victor S. D'Souza, *Social Structure of a Planned City: Chandigarh* (New Delhi: Orient Longman Ltd., 1968), pp. 241-242; Kamla Nath, "Women in the Work Force in India," *Economic and Political Weekly*, III (August 3, 1968), pp. 1205-1213.

2. Victor S. D'Souza, "Implications of Occupational Prestige for Employment Policy in India, "*Artha Vijnana,* I (No. 3, 1959), pp. 233-274.

3. *Ibid.*, pp. 239-240.

4. Nelson N. Foote and Paul K. Hatt, "Social Mobility and Economic Advancement", *American Economic Review*, XLII (1953).

are relatively lower proportions of occupations in the lower prestige levels. So also there are lower proportions of occupations of lower prestige in larger communities as compared to smaller ones. Since in the urban areas as compared to the rural ones and in larger communities as compared to smaller ones, there are higher proportions of men in higher prestige and hence higher income occupations, lesser proportions of women will have need for employment. Hence the differential female work participation rate. In the country as a whole it is evident that the proportion of urban population has been increasing in the recent decades and so is the proportion of people living in larger cities. There is also continuous socio-economic growth. These trends account for a diminution in the rate of female work participation.

It is on the basis of this analysis that I predicted that the proportion of women workers in the working force would come down so long as the proportion of occupations at the lower prestige level keep on diminishing as a result of socio-economic growth.[5] Nath's analysis of the female working force in the 1961 census lends support to my prediction.[6]

But there is another important trend in female work participation which, although I noticed in my study referred to above, I did not take into account in the analysis because it was then of a small magnitude. The trend is that while at the lower levels of education, say below Matriculation, with increasing education of women the rate of female work participation declines (which is consistent with my theoretical framework), at higher educational levels the rate goes on increasing (which is inconsistent). This trend was relatively more prominent in the 1961 census.[7] If it is assumed that at higher educational levels the husbands or fathers of working women are also working in higher prestige and higher income occupations, there is no ostensible economic reason for the women to work. Therefore, the hypothesis that the low income of their menfolk is the main reason why some women work, which is an important assumption of my theoretical

5. D'Souza, see n. 2
6. Nath, see n. 1
7. Nath, *ibid.*, pp. 1206-1207.

framework, stands unsupported. It has, therefore, become necessary for me to re-examine the model.

The contradictory evidence shows that I had given too narrow an interpretation to the factor of economic motive by regarding it as the need to make both ends meet—for mere subsistence. It would, however, appear that the economic motive is almost universal; if one has enough income for subsistence one would desire more income for raising one's standard of living; and even if one has enough wealth for a comfortable living one would still desire more money for the power and prestige which wealth brings. If the economic motive for women to work is a universal one, it obviously cannot account for the fact that some women work while others do not.

CURVILINEAR RELATIONSHIP

The revised theoretical framework has to reconcile two apparently irreconcilable trends: (a) in the lower educational levels the rate of female work participation declines with the increase in education, and (b) in higher educational levels the rate increases with increase in education. The two trends together represent a curvilinear relationship between the rate of female work participation and the education of women. It would appear that the change from the linear to the curvilinear relationship between these variables is a relatively recent one which has been brought about by the growth of education.

One of the important assumptions of the earlier theoretical framework is that work participation on the part of women is related to the type of employment of their male relatives like husbands and fathers. A major dimension of occupations which is relevant for studying the relationship between the occupations of women and their male relatives, say, husbands, is their prestige. But the earlier observation was that with the increase in the occupational prestige of husbands the rate of work participation on the part of wives declined in a linear relationship.

The observation of the more recent trend of the curvilinear relationship between the education of women and their work participation led to a re-examination of the relationship between the rate of work participation of women and the occupational prestige of their husbands with reference to more recent information. That relevant data from the study of Chandigarh[8] are presented in Table 1 according to the percentage of working wives in the various occupational prestige categories of husbands who are heads of households. The occupations are classified into seven prestige categories, from the highest to the lowest, according to an objective scale of occupational prestige devised for that study.[9] It can be seen that in the lower prestige levels of husbands, i.e., from category VII to category V the percentage of working wives goes on diminishing with the increase in prestige. But from category V onwards, by and large, it goes on increasing. Thus the variation in the rate of participation in work by wives at different prestige levels of husbands' occupations is more or less similar to the rate of female work participation at different educational levels. As in the case of educational levels we have two contradictory trends: (1) at lower prestige levels of husbands' occupations the rate of work participation by wives goes on diminishing with increase in occupational prestige and (2) at higher prestige levels the rate goes on increasing with increase in occupational prestige.

TABLE 1

Percentage of Working Wives in the Occupational Prestige Categories of Husbands

Occupational Prestige categories of husbands	No. of working wives	Total No. of wives	Percentage of working wives to total
I	3	65	4.6
II	12	185	6.5
III	8	307	2.6
IV	24	644	3.7
V	0	143	0
VI	5	213	2.4
VII	11	45	24.4
Total	63	1602	3.9

Source: Victor S. D'Souza, *Social Structure of a Planned City : Chandigarh* (New Delhi : Orient Longman Limited, 1968).

8. D'Souza, see n. 1
9. D'Souza, *ibid.*, pp. 379-383.

OCCUPATIONAL PRESTIGE OF WIVES AND HUSBANDS

Another important element in the relationship between the employment of wives and their husbands is the relationship between their occupational prestige. This is given in Table 2 in respect of a sample of married working women in Chandigarh taken from a field study conducted by Kulwant Anand.[10] As in the case of the Chandigarh study referred to above the occupations in this case are also classified into seven prestige categories in a descending order using the same occupational prestige scale.

There is a remarkable association between the occupational prestige of wives and husbands. Out of 168 cases for which complete information is available 79 women (47 per cent) are in the same occupational categories as those of their husbands. In another 45 cases (27 per cent) the occupational prestige categories of the wives are just one step lower than those of their husbands. The general trend is for wives to have occupations either of the same prestige levels or of levels one step lower than those of their husbands. It may, however, be pointed out that in the occupational prestige category III of wives quite a substantial number of women have occupations one step higher in prestige as compared to that of their husbands. This apparent discrepancy is due to the coarseness of the scale for occupational classification. The women in question are mostly primary school teachers who, along with secondary school teachers, are included in prestige category III, whereas their husbands who are mainly clerical workers are included in prestige category IV. If primary school teachers are equated in prestige with clerical workers, these women would mostly have the same occupational prestige as that of their husbands. Thus the evidence on the whole confirms the statement that when both husband and wife work, the wife follows an occupation either of the same or slightly lower prestige as compared to the occupational prestige of her husband. The prevalence of wide disparity between the occupational prestige of husband and wife, and also cases in which the wife has higher

10. Kulwant Anand, "Impact of Changing Status of Women on Population Growth" (Chandigarh: Unpublished Ph.D. dissertation, Punjab University, 1970).

occupational prestige. are very rare. These findings are supported by the evidence reported in another study of the same community but using a different sample.[11]

TABLE 2

Occupational Prestige of Wives and Husbands

Occupational prestige categories of husbands → Occupational prestige categories of wives ↓	I	II	III	IV	V	VI	VII		Total
I	*15*	4	2	2					23
II	5	*12*						1	18
III	3	25	*5*	15				3	51
IV		1	3	*5*				2	11
V			1	8	*8*	4		3	19
VI					3	*4*		6	14
VII			1			1	*35*	2	39
Total	23	42	12	30	6	9	36	17	175

Source : Kulwant Anand, "Impact of Changing Status of Women on Population Growth" (Unpublished Ph.D. dissertation, Panjab University, 1970)

In addition to the two empirical generalisations noted above this evidence provides a third generalisation stemming from the relationship between the employment of husbands and wives. This may be stated as follows: There is an association between the occupational prestige of husbands and wives, the wives' occupational prestige on the whole being slightly lower than that of their husbands.

While the first two generalisations indicate contrary trends in the work participation of women at different prestige levels, the third generalisation points to a uniform pattern in the association between the occupational prestige of husbands and wives at all levels. It therefore, suggests the possibility of finding a larger generalisation which can explain all the three different trends.

11. D' Souza, *Social Structure of a Planned City: Chandigarh*, p. 80.

FAMILY STATUS CONSISTENCY

In the three empirical generalisations just discussed the unit of analysis is the husband and wife pair and the major variable considered is occupational prestige. It would, therefore, occur to one that for a logical explanation of the phenomena under study one should consider the family and its status as important elements in one's analytical framework. In sociological literature the family is usually taken as a status unit meaning thereby that the husband and wife who constitute integral members of a family have the same status. To be more specific, in most of the societies including that of India which are male dominated, the wife occupies a slightly lower status in the family as compared to the husband. Therefore, for consistency in family status husband and wife should have near equal status, the husband being slightly superior to his wife. Family status consistency is necessary for an efficient functioning of the family, and since the family is an integral unit of society it can be assumed that there is always a tendency for the family to maintain a consistent status system.

On the other hand the status of a person is usually derived from his occupational prestige. Generally, it is the man who is considered to be the natural breadwinner in the family, and the various members of the family including his wife derive their status from his occupational prestige. So long as only the man in the family is working there is no ambiguity about the status of different members in the family. If the wife is also working, this raises problems for family status consistency. For consistency the wife should follow an occupation which is almost equal in prestige to the husband's occupation or slightly inferior to it. If the wife is not able to fulfil this condition she does not participate in work.

THREE FACTORS

The above reasoning gives rise to a fourth more general hypothesis, namely, the work participation of wives or female work participation is a function of family status consistency. This hypothesis is in conformity with the third generalisation above that the occupational prestige of women is either the same or slighly less than that of their husbands, which provides positive evidence of concomitant variation in

TABLE 3

Sample of Working (N=169) and Non-Working (N=150) Married Women in Chandigarh Classified According to Education of the Subjects and their Husbands

Education of Husbands ——→ / Education of Wives ↓	Working Women						Non-Working Women					
	Illiterate	Below Matric	Matric	Graduates	Post Graduate & Professional	Total	Illiterate	Below Matric	Matric	Graduate	Post-Graduate & Professional	Total
Illiterate	*43*	6	1			50	3	6	4	7		20
Below Matric	2	*10*	9			21		*3*	26	19	7	55
Matric	1		*9*	11	3	24		2	*10*	20	16	48
Graduates			1	*13*	11	25				*2*	15	17
Post-Graduates & Professional	1		1	5	*42*	49				2	*8*	10
Total	47	16	21	29	56	169	3	11	40	50	46	150

SOURCE: Kulwant Anand *op. cit.*

support of the former. To substantiate the fourth generalisation more fully it is also necessary to adduce negative evidence of concomitant variation. It would consist in showing that if the wife is not working it is because she is unable to secure an occupation at the level of family status consistency. Since occupational prestige and educational level are interrelated, it would mean that in the case of working wives their education is almost equal to that of their husbands, as a consequence of which they have succeeded in securing occupations at consistent levels; on the other hand, in the case of non-working wives there is a wider disparity between their education and that of their husbands because of which they are unable to secure occupations at consistent levels.

The above hypothesis can be tested from data taken from the study of Kulwant Anand, referred to already, which consists of two samples, one of working married women and the other of non-working married women, but derived from the same community, namely, Chandigarh. In Table 3 the samples of working and non-working women are classified according to their own educational levels and those of their husbands. It can be seen that in the case of working wives there is a great similarity between their levels of education and those of their husbands, whereas in the case of non-working wives there are wide disparities; while 117 out of 169 (67 per cent) working wives are at the same educational levels the corresponding number among the non-working wives is only 26 out of 150 (17 per cent). This confirms the hypothesis that if the wives are not working, it is because they are unable to secure occupations at consistent levels.

Now it can be explained why at the lower educational levels of women and at the lower prestige levels of husbands the rate of female work participation decreases and at higher levels it increases. The explanation has to take into account several factors: (a) first of all, for participation in work a woman's education should be more or less equal to that of her husband; (b) a second factor is the requirement that the wife should be subordinate to the husband. Because of this a man usually marries a woman younger to him in age and also less educated than he. If we look at Table 3 we find that it is only rarely that the wife's education is higher than that of the husband. Among working women such cases are only 11 out of 169 and among non-working women they are 4 out of 150. Then again in 12 out of the total of 15 aberrant cases the difference between the wife's and husband's educational levels is only one step. It is also possible that in such cases what is lacking in the quantity of the education of the husband is made up by its quality, as, for instance, in the case of a husband who is a first class graduate married to a third class postgraduate wife. (c) A third factor in the explanation is that hitherto the education of women has been more neglected than that of men so that at every level of education there are relatively more men than women.

From an analysis of these three factors it becomes evident why the variation in the rate of female work participation in different educational categories follows a curvilinear pattern. According to factor (b) at one extreme, all illiterate men have to marry only illiterate women and at the opposite extreme all highly educated women have to marry only highly educated men. Therefore, because of factor (c) the chances of husbands and wives having equal educational background are the greatest in the case of wives who are either illiterate or highly educated. Hence by factor (a) the rate of work participation on the part of women is greater when they are illiterate or when they are highly educated.

SOME APPLICATIONS

Because of the intimate relationship between educational levels and occupational prestige, the above reasoning can also be employed to explain the curvilinear relationship between the variation in the rate of female work participation and occupational prestige levels of husbands.

The preceding analytical framework can also be used to show why there is a marked decline in the rate of female work participation from the rural to urban communities and from smaller to larger communities. In the rural areas the overwhelming majority of men and women are illiterate and, consequently, most of the husband-wife pairs have equal education making it possible for relatively more women to take to gainful employment. In the urban communities, because of the growth of education the disparity in the education of husband and wife occurs in a greater proportion of husband-wife pairs and, consequently, a relatively lower proportion of women is able to secure occupations at consistent levels. Larger the community, the greater the development of education, the greater the proportion of husband-wife pairs with educational imbalance and so smaller the rate of female work participation.

The tendency for the rate of female work participation to decline in the urban communities, however, is not an indefinite one. In these communities, while the chances for husbands and wives to have equal education at lower levels diminish, such chances increase at higher levels. The net decrease or increase in the rate would depend upon the magnitudes of these two opposite trends. To begin with, the decline in the rate at the lower educational level would be greater than its increase at the higher level, but eventually, its increase at the higher level would more than offset the decrease at the lower level and on the whole the rate would increase. I have discussed this phenomenon elsewhere.[12]

Thus, I have demonstrated in this paper that through a system of logically interrelated propositions it is possible to explain the different features of the female work participation. It may be pointed out that social causation is a highly complex phenomenon involving a large number of factors making up the causal nexus. For a satisfactory solution of a problem all the relevant factors have to be identified and the nature of their relationship should be specified and this has to be accomplished in a theoretical framework. I should admit that in the present case I have not taken into account all the factors, but indicated some of the important ones.

For instance, while the consistent educational background is an important factor in a wife's participation in work, by itself it may not be sufficient; in addition, it is necessary that suitable occupation should be available and also that it should

12. Victor S. D'Souza, "Changing Socio-Economic Conditions and Employment of Women", in *Trends of Socio-Economic Change in India 1871-1961* (Transactions, Vol. 7; Simla : Indian Institute of Advanced Study, 1969), pp. 443-457.

be conveniently located so that her customary residence with her husband is not disturbed. The type of occupational structure of the community is also an important variable. Factors like these should be taken into account in formulating a theoretical framework for the actual solution of a given problem about female work participation. It should also be borne in mind that the propositions put forward may not be adequate for explaining problems of all kinds in the field under consideration. For instance, one may use the generalisation that female work participation is determined by family status consistency to explain changes in the rate of female work participation in a given region and over a period of time, but it cannot provide an explanation of the variation in the rate among different regions, without taking into account important historical and cultural factors.

In discussions about the economic independence of women and their right to work, the economic and legal issues, such as, equal employment opportunities and equal wages for equal work at par with men, usually come to the fore. Such issues can also be legislated upon. One may, therefore, get away with the impression that the constitutional right of women to work could be secured through legal means alone. This paper, however, has focused attention upon some important social structural factors which also underlie the participation of women in work. Not all these factors are susceptible to legal manipulation but can only respond to broad social changes and social movements.

9

SYLVIA VATUK

The Aging Woman in India : Self-Perceptions and Changing Roles

This is a preliminary report on one aspect of an on-going research project concerning the social and cultural framework of aging in Indian society. The project is an anthropological field study being carried out in the city of Delhi in one of the so-called "urbanised villages", former agricultural settlements which have been caught in the path of the expansion of the city in recent years. Their fields have been acquired by the municipality for the building of roads, residential colonies, and commercial and public edifices, and their economic base removed, to be replaced by earnings from rents, salaried jobs or wage labour, or interest from bank accounts and investments, in the now-surrounding city. There are many such urbanised villages within metropolitan Delhi—the one in which the present research is being undertaken (and which I will call Rayāpur) has been gradually incorporated into the growing city over the past 40 years, the last remnants of land having been lost to agriculture about 12 years ago. The Rayā or Ravā Rājpūt caste was the dominant caste of this village.[1] Because all but

1. This is a localised and relatively small agricultural caste found in Meerut, Muzaffarnagar and Bijnor Districts, as well as occupying six villages of substantial size in the Delhi urban area. Formerly known as Ravās or Rayās, they have since the 1930s preferred the designation of Rājpūt.

an insignificant amount of the village land had formerly been under the ownership of members of this caste, they have profited greatly from the acquisition of its territory for urban construction. While at present the financial status of the Rayā families still resident in Rayāpur varies widely (depending upon the amount of land originally owned and their success in keeping or augmenting the money paid in compensation), all of the local inhabitants of the caste are at least relatively well-off: all own their own homes and most have other real estate which they give on rent; all have the basic necessities of life and certain luxuries as well, while some are wealthy even by Indian urban standards.

SCOPE

The focus of this research is the life-cycle and social roles of the aged within the local caste community of Rayā Rājpūts. In this paper I will discuss these issues as they concern the life of Rayā women. The indigenous definition of old age (*buṛhāppā*) has been treated from the beginning as one of the empirical questions to be researched, and therefore it was decided not to establish any *a priori* chronological age as a cut-off point for delimiting the universe of study. Indeed, to do so would have been to come up against a serious difficulty in the widespread ignorance of precise chronological age, epecially among the elderly. While various devices, such as the making of a time-events table, can be used to get at a fairly close approximation of chronological age in such situations, it was felt that for our purposes it was more appropriate to select for study those who consider themselves and are considered by others as "old" in the context of their own society, regardless of actual age.

While the self-perception and the perception of others as old obviously differs from one individual to another, and tends to depend to an important degree on such variable external signs of aging as tooth-loss and graying hair, the general consensus seems to place primary stress on life-cycle criteria. Thus the marriage of one's children—particularly of one's sons—marks the beginning of old age in this society far more clearly than does the passing of a specified number of years. We have, therefore, included in our "aging" sample all persons with effectively married sons or adopted sons[2]. In case of son-less or childless persons, we have included them on the basis of their contemporaneity with those already in the sample. There are so few of these, almost all of a clearly advanced age, that ambiguities about proper assignment to the sample have been negligible.

The women of the elderly sample[3] are all either married or widowed—a significant number have been remarried after the death of a first husband, usually to his younger or elder brother.[4] None of the women was born in Rayāpur: because of the practice of village exogamy, all local "wives" come from other villages and those of this older group come for the most part from villages in Meerut and Muzaffarnagar Districts in Uttar Pradesh. A few were born in Rayā Rājpūt villages located elswhere in the Delhi area. While it sometimes happens in this region that a separated woman or a widow will return to live in her natal village, or that a man without sons will invite a daughter and her husband to remain with him in her natal village (as *ghar jamāī*), there are no such cases within this caste in Rayāpur among the elderly group.

The background of almost all of the women is rural—before and after marriage—and in some cases, until fairly recently, they were actively engaged in agricultural pursuits as well as in housekeeping, cooking and child care, for in this caste it was (and still is in the rural areas) customary for women to work in the family fields, to cut fodder for cattle, to fetch water from the well for all the household needs, and so on. Because of the

2. By "effective marriage" I refer to the coming of a wife to live with her husband after their *gaunā* or consummation rite. In earlier time this rite took place some 3 to 7 years after the wedding ceremony, commonly performed for girls before puberty. Today, however, most Rayāpur girls (and the in-coming wives of Rayāpur boys) are at least 16 by the time of marriage, and no more than a few months normally intervene between marriage and its consummation.

3. Because this research is still in progress and the collection and analysis of the data has not been completed, I will avoid presenting here any absolute figures percentages which might have to be altered in subsequent publications.

4. Among Rayā Rājpūts and some other castes of this region it is customary to remarry widows of child-bearing age, preferably to a brother or other close agnatic kinsman of the deceased. Failing this, a widow is sometimes remarried to an outsider.

fortuitous location of Rayāpur, these women now rather suddenly find themselves in a position to enjoy almost total leisure (if they so wish) and an urban middle-class life-style, and some have such comforts in their homes as hot running water, gas stoves, refrigerators, air-coolers and Saturday night television. While they are almost universally illiterate, their younger daughters and their granddaughters are graduating from college, and they are observing, and even fostering by their tolerance, new standards for the relationship of husbands and wives as they marry their sons and grandsons to educated girls of their caste from the other Delhi villages.[5]

While similar changes are affecting the lives of millions of other older Indian women who at some point in their lives have migrated from a rural to an urban environment (and even in a lesser degree the lives of millions who remain in the also changing rural milieu), the situation of these Rayāpur women, and of others in villages similarly "swallowed" by the relentless march of urbanism, is unique in many respects.

RESIDENCE PATTERNS OF THE ELDERLY

The old women of Rayāpur live, with negligible exceptions, in "joint" households of three and sometimes four generations.[6] The most frequent type of household includes an older married couple, one or more married sons and their wives and children, and unmarried children of the older couple as well. Many such households also have additional members, a widowed or separated daughter, a daughter's child or other young relative come to attend school in Delhi. A few also include the elderly father or mother of the older couple, making a four

5. Because of their new prosperity and urban character, the Delhi area Rayās have begun to restrict marital unions as much as possible to among themselves, rather than continuing their previous pattern of alliances with the more distant and still-rural U.P. settlements of their caste. Rayāpur is in a peculiarly advantageous position in this respect, not only because of its wealth (it is known within the caste nowadays as *Amrikā* ["America"], but because the two exogamous *gotras* present in the village are not found in the other major Rayā settlements of Delhi, while several of the latter are inhabited by members of a single *gotra*, preventing intermarriage between them.

6. This is not to say that the majority of all Rayā households in the village are "joint" in structure, as they are not.

generation family group. There are very few widows in the older sample, no doubt partly because of the custom of widow remarriage. The bulk of the "older" women are in the 55-65 age range (based on reported ages and other means of estimation) and there are very few over 70.

While the residential norm is thus for the aging woman to hold the position of mother-in-law and wife in a lineal extended household, there are some exceptions : those who have no sons or whose sons are young despite their own advancing age. A small number of married couples in this category live with adopted "sons" (usually a husband's brother's son or a daughters's son) or with their own unmarried young children. One couple in their late fifties lives alone with only a young granddaughter (a SoDa), their only son having died and his wife remarried out of the family. A widow in her mid-seventies lives with her teenage granddaughter (DaDa), who has come to stay in Rayāpur from her village home in order to look after her grandmother and attend high school. This woman never had a son and is on bad terms with her closest relatives in the village, her former co-wife and the latter's son, with whom she might otherwise reasonably expect to be able to make her home.

PREPARATION FOR OLD AGE

As the extended family residence pattern is the universally desired one by and for old people, it is not surprising that preparation for old age security begins early in terms of assuring that there will be such a family in which to live when the time comes. This preparation manifests itself first in the attempt to have at least one son. While in the literature on Indian society the need for a son is typically given a religious, other-worldly rationale, for these villagers it is pre-eminently and most practically a matter of providing for someone to take care of one's needs in old age. Childless couples, and those who have managed to produce only female children, begin at some point to consider the alternatives: remarriage, adoption (formal or informal), or the taking of a *ghar jamāī*. While men sometimes take a second wife during the lifetime of the first in order to have a son, women may remarry only after the death of their husbands. Remarriage is almost routine in this caste if the woman is still in her child-bearing years and does not already have growing sons on whom she can begin to rely for support. Although the custom is justified in a number of ways, one important reason given by the Rayās themselves is to ensure that the woman will not be destitute in old age.

Adoption is always of a male relative, a daughter's son or the brother's son of either husband or wife. Occasionally, a sister's son may be adopted. The adoptee is usually a child, but there are instances of the adoption of boys in their late adolescence, done with the explicit understanding that the arrangement is being made to ensure that there will be someone to "serve" the adopter (*sevā karnā*) when the need arises. In some cases land or money is signed over to the adoptee at this time. Widowed women rarely adopt, although widowed and unmarried men do so not infrequently. There are, however, some widowed women now living with adopted sons who were taken in during the lifetime of their late husbands.

Taking a *ghar jamāī* seems to be a less attractive solution to the problem of care in old age, even though many women may be heard to maintain that "only a daughter can really serve her parents with all her heart". There is a certain awkwardness in the living arrangements of a couple with the wife's parents, not least for the live-in son-in-law himself, who tends to be looked down upon by others as a young man with little to offer, reduced to living off his wife's family. In other ways also the situation reverses or makes impossible of maintenance many of the accepted kinship role behaviour patterns. While there are at least two cases of village sons who are living as *ghar jamāīs* elsewhere, there are no such cases among Rayās in the village itself, although there are a few village "daughters" living with their employed husbands in quarters separate from those of their parents.

Whether an old couple or a widow has a son of their own, or has made arrangements to adopt a substitute, it is expected (and almost always followed in practice), that this boy when married will live on in the family home with his new wife and subsequent children. No other alternative is even considered initially, except in the rare case of a family with several sons where one is asked to marry as *ghar jamāī*. However, this arrangement does not always last indefinitely. When a man has had two wives, it is unusual for married sons of the first to live for long in a joint household with the second. And even in the case of a woman's own son, it often happens that after a number of years he and his wife will set up separate cooking arrangements and even cease contributing to the joint family budget (although he usually continues in joint ownership with his father and brothers of any family property). When a couple's sons are beginning to think about arranging their own children's marriages, it is common, at least nowadays, for a formal division of even this joint property to be undertaken, although for the "prestige" (*izzat*) of the family, it is still considered best to marry one's grandchildren while the family is still "together" (*ikaṭṭe*).

However, in spite of the desire and need for some degree of partition of the joint family over the years, one thing that is considered quite out of the question is to separate off the old couple—or a widowed parent—leaving them to fend for themselves in the preparation of meals. If the elder son's wife wants to cook separately, she will begin to do so only after her husband's younger brother has married. And if full partition among the brothers takes place while one or both parents is still living, arrangements will be made to have them live and eat with one of them. More rarely, all the *bahūs* will feed them together or in turn.

Even in such circumstances, sons remain in the family home. It should be stressed that the number of sons in Rayāpur who have actually moved out of the parental residence in the course of a partial or complete partition of the joint family while either of their parents was still living is negligible. At most, some have moved by mutual agreement to another house owned by their family in the village. In fact, there has been very little movement out of the village by any men of this caste, with the exception of several families who have bought rural land elsewhere with the proceeds of their own land compensation and have left to farm it. More typically, even these families maintain one or more of a set of brothers on the farm, while the main part of the family remains in Rayāpur. Even leaving the parental home because of the demands of employment is extremely rare for young Rayāpur couples. Because Delhi as a large metropolitan city provides employment opportunities of all kinds and at all levels, and because few Rayāpur boys have obtained the kind of high-level position or highly specialised advanced training that might make it difficult to insist on remaining in the city if the most favourable job opportunities are to be availed of, the kind of mobility that is becoming typical of much of the educated middle and upper classes in urban India has not yet affected Rayāpur household structures appreciably.

It is evident that this lack of mobility is not accidental: parents consciously want to keep their sons at home and consider it a defeat and a cause of much unhappiness if the joint household dissolves during their lifetime—so much greater their distress if a son actually moves away from the village. Up to the present the very few cases of the latter have been the result of severe family dissension (either between the young couple and a parent or parents or between brothers and/or brothers' wives). Because of the view that such a breakup is something for the family to be ashamed of, they are usually presented to outsiders as cases in which the couple had to move because the son's place of work was on the other side of Delhi and it took too long to commute, or because the young family was very large and the son's employer provided living quarters free of charge, and so on. It remains to be seen if this pattern of joint residence can be maintained in the next generation, for aside from the pressure of space which is already becoming severe in some homes, village young men are increasingly aiming higher than the B.A. or LL.B. that only five years ago was a rare attainment for Rayā boys, and a few are even making plans for postgraduate education abroad. But because of the persistence of the traditional residence pattern for the aged at present living in the urbanised village of Rayāpur, we must still look at the elderly woman's life and earlier life-history within the framework of this type of household structure.

STAGES OF A WOMAN'S LIFE

Rayā women tend to think about their own lives, and those of women in general, in terms of three main stages or periods, each having its own character and characteristics, its own appropriate set of activities, its own duties and rewards. The first of these is childhood (*bacpan*), a time that from the perspective of the end of life is viewed as having been generally pleasant, carefree, without much responsibility and few demands for hard work or restraint of freedom. During this period a woman is felt to have received the only unqualified love and nurturance she will ever have, and the warm and pleasant associations of childhood, of life "in the mother's kingdom" (*mā ke rāj mẽ*) colour a woman's perception of her natal home and village (*pīhar*) forever afterwards. Women in their sixties still look forward to frequent periodic visits "home", even when parents have long since died and other familiar faces are rapidly dropping out of sight as well. One of the most often heard laments in this age group concerns the inevitable loss of touch with the *pīhar* as the years go on, and with few exceptions, these women do manage to make such a visit at least once every year or two. Similarly, Rayāpur households receive periodic visits from elderly village "daughters" married 40 or more miles away.

For most of these women, childhood ended abruptly with the onset of puberty or shortly thereafter. Although there are a few examples of women of this age-group who married in their late teens, the majority were married before the age of 12 or 13 and went to take up married life in their husbands' households and villages (*sasurāl*) within two or three years. Some women claim to have been so young at the time of the wedding that they were unaware of what was going on. These, who may have been as young as 7 or 8 years old, did not, of course, join their husbands' households until they were physically mature, many years later.

The second major period of these women's lives (ironically referred to in contrast to the earlier period as "mother-in-law's kingdom" (*sās kā rāj*) began for almost all in the position of junior member of a large joint farm family, where the contrast with the natal home in terms of workload and the ability to move about and speak freely with household members and others was sharp and often traumatic. There was little time and less privacy in the first months and even years to develop a close relationship with the new husband ("those were 'simple' times", as one such woman put it), and frequent lengthy visits to their natal villages were a welcome respite from the physically and often emotionally trying atmosphere of the *sasurāl*. The first pregnancy was eagerly awaited, and those who had difficulty conceiving or who aborted easily or whose first children died in infancy report trying various measures, spiritual, magical and medical, to help them become pregnant or to ensure that their children would live beyond the perilous first year. Most did succeed in this, although some were never able to have a son, seen as so necessary for a worry-free old age. They spent the succeeding years rearing their children (although in many instances this task was mainly pre-empted by their mothers-in-law), and gradually, as in-laws died and brothers and cousins separated, succeeded to the position of senior woman of their own household, making the transition into old age with the marriage of sons and the coming of their wives and later of grandchildren— "the kingdom of the daughter-in-law" (*bahū kā rāj*).[7]

SELF-PERCEPTION OF WOMAN'S LIFE

Since the purpose of this research has been to look at old age in the context of the entire life-cycle, considerable attention has been given, in eliciting life-histories and in interviews, as well as in observing interaction and listening to spontaneous conversation involving the elderly, to obtaining an overview of their perception of the total life experience (in the present case, of the female experience), both in specific, personal, individual terms, and in the broad, generalised aspect. What emerges from the data is often contradictory—there seems to be a marked discrepancy between the largely pessimistic, discontented, and resigned verbal utturances about "woman's lot" and the sad fate of the aged, and the observed high level of good-humoured and extraordinarily active participation and interest in social, work and family activities.

7. It is interesting to compare this feminine version of the woman's life cycle with that of the well-known injunction of Manu which advises keeping a woman under the successive protection (and control) of father, husband, and son.

Women's life has been described to us time after time as being "nothing but hard work, trouble, and pain from beginning to end". Our queries often receive such responses. "How can you ask about the best time of a woman's life? There is no good time." A typical answer to the enquiry "How are you?" (particularly if the greeter is another old lady) goes something like "I can only wish that God would take me right now, but I suppose I will somehow have to get through the days that are allotted to me, although I would rather be dead."

Detachment from worldly concerns is espoused as a necessary and desirable part of successful aging, while those who recommend it most vocally are on the go from dawn to late at night managing the affairs of their family, visiting sick relatives, helping to arrange the marriages of neighbours' children, attending wedding and funerals, buying clothes for festival presents for their married daughters, grinding two kilos of wheat by hand in the morning before breakfast, and similarly demonstrating considerable attachment to the practicalities of life on this earth. Even taking into account the fact of individual variability—which is considerable despite a high degree of cultural homogeneity and general similarity of life experiences among the women of this one caste in a single village—there remains a good deal to be sorted out from these apparently conflicting impressions.

We may try to do this by discussing these women's perception of the period of life in which they are presently living at three levels. First, there is the level of ideals : how a woman's old age ought to be spent, how she should occupy herself and how she should be treated by others. Second, there is the way that these women perceive their old age, and the old age of other women they know, to be in actuality. Usually, the issue here is the degree to which their life as they see it approaches or deviates from the ideal. And third is the "objective" observer's view of their lives and her interpretation of it. This is made up partly from direct observation and questioning, and partly from clues provided by the women's own (or their family members' and relatives' and neighbours') verbal reports of incidents in which they have been involved.

REST AND SERVICE IN OLD AGE

In ideal terms, old age is supposed to be a time of rest and leisure, a time when work responsibilities should cease, and one should be "served" by the sons one has raised for the purpose and by their wives. Elderly women describe a fortunate one among their peers as one whose *bahū-beṭe* ("daughters-in-law and sons") give them much "rest" (*arām*) and "service" (*sevā*). The stereotyped manner of praising a daughter-in-law is to say that she is hard-working and serves one well. The concept of *sevā* is a broad one, and implied in it is not only the performance of all necessary tasks for the comfort of the older person, but love, consideration, thoughtfulness, and devotion as well. However, this latter aspect is implicit rather than verbalised; when asked to explain the meaning of *sevā* women almost always do so largely in terms of physical care : "I have very hard-working (*bahut kamerī*) and serving (*sevā karnevāli*) *bahū*. She gives me my meals, washes my clothes, prepares my bed at night. In all things, she serves me well."

Certain more personal services are also included in the concept of *sevā*, such as scrubbing the older woman's back when she bathes, combing and braiding her hair and, most importantly and symbolically, massaging her legs at night and when she is ill or tired. Young women often relate how their *sās* makes them press her legs (*pāo dabvānā*) for hours at a stretch each night, until they drop off to sleep from exhaustion, at which point the old woman is perversely brought back to wakefulness, demanding that the massaging continue. The older women, on the other hand, maintain that in *their* day they *really* served *their* mothers-in-law, not like the *bahūs* of today : "In those days, when one of us massaged my *sās's* legs, the others would be massaging her hands. But now!" They claim that the custom is unfortunately dying, that the old are no longer in a position to demand this kind of service, and they shrug off questions about the practice in their own homes with a cynical laugh.

Sevā also means care in time of illness. It is a common complaint among the old that members of the younger generation are not sufficiently sympathetic when an old person is not feeling well. "Here I have been coughing like this for so many days, I can't get my breath, yet no one has asked 'Mother, what is the matter?' I keep my sorrows and sufferings to myself." Yet, although modern medicine is widely accepted and utilised by persons of all ages it is rare for an elderly person to agree to go for a stay in the hospital, even in the case of serious illness. In fact, one might say that they are especially reluctant to go in case of serious illness, because of the fear of dying away from home and family. Therefore, it is not unusual for an old and helpless person to be nursed for months or even years by a daughter-in-law. There is no thought given in this kind of situation to the possibility of hiring a nurse or other outsider to take over the less pleasant or physically exhausting tasks involved in caring for an invalid, even though for many of these families there are no financial constraints to their doing so. And I know of no instance in which an old person has been sent away to a hospital against his will, no matter how difficult the circumstances. Yet, despite the fact that no fear of being sent to die among strangers hangs over these women, they are unanimous in expressing the wish to die "while my hands and feet are still able". The worst thing that can happen to someone, they say, is to become helpless in old age and to live on, a burden to others and to oneself. Indeed, whatever their private fears of death may be, they speak of it openly, cheerfully, and with matter-of-factness. Typical is the statement of a healthy woman in her late fifties, a widow and mother of three sons, of whom the eldest is married : "I have sons, a daughter-in-law has come, there are son's children (*pote-potī*) and daughter's children (*dhevte-dhevtī*). What more do I need ? I am ready to go at any time."

While the actual work involved in doing *sevā* mainly falls upon a woman's daughter-in-law, the son himself tends to share the credit—and the blame—for the quality of its performance. Some women are of the opinion that it depends mainly upon the son whether his parents are well taken care of in old age, and there is a dominant tone of pessimism when they discuss this problem in general terms. It seems to be felt that hard as one may try to ensure that one has a son to provide for one in old age, and as much as one may do for him in bringing him up, nursing him through illnesses, educating him, and so on, it is in the end an unpredictable matter "how he will turn out". They explain that, "If the son is good, then everything will be fine. But there are very few sons like that nowadays—at the most one in a hundred can be found who will really care for his parents in their old age." Some maintain that a really "good" son will make sure that his wife serves her in-laws well, but others feel that one's fate really lies in the hands of the stranger one has brought into the family: "The son may be good, but if his wife is of that kind she will turn his head (*isko sikhaegī*) against his parents,and then he will also neglect them." There is a definite feeling that social change is having an adverse effect on the position of old people, and as evidence of this they point to the increasing tendency of young married men to separate from their parents shortly after marriage. Although this has not yet become an important trend within the village or in the caste as a whole, they see it as a real threat for the future, and claim that it is being learned from the Punjabis (a very visible out-group in the neighbourhood to whom all unwelcome social deviance is credited), among whom it has become (according to them) the expected norm.

WORK ACTIVITIES OF OLDER WOMEN

It is the minimum duty of a *bahū* to relieve her mother-in-law (*sās*) of such household jobs as cooking the meals and washing the utensils and clothes. It is said that "it doesn't look nice" (*acchā nahī lagtā*) to have an older woman cooking if there are one or more daughters-in-law in the house, and although some mothers-in-law continue to share the cooking if they have only one married son (usually in this case one woman will cook the morning meal, the other the evening meal), it is the more common and expected practice for her to cease cooking shortly after her son's marriage, except in emergencies such as the sickness or absence of the *bahū*. The appropriate feminine division of labour as described by Rayāpur women has the mother-in-law doing the "outside work" (*bāhar kā kām*), while the *bahū* takes care of the work inside the house (*ghar kā kām*). This coincides with the traditional rural expectation that a young married woman should stay within the house as much as possible, and although young wives in Rayāpur are by no means completely confined to the home (or when outside it to the chaperonage of their *sās* or other older woman) to the degree that these elderly women were in their youth, the standard is still recognised as legitimate and desirable, although perhaps not very practical of execution under present day circumstances. There are many families in the village whose young married women leave the home only occasionally, and then only for such things as an excursion to the movies with their husbands (itself a serious departure from the kind of behaviour suitable for young married women in the youth and middle-age of the present-day elderly).

"Outside work" in this urbanised village includes shopping for staple provisions and vegetables and doing other errands involving contact with tradesmen and artisan specialists, such as the weavers to whom hand-spun cotton is entrusted each summer for weaving into blankets, or the cot-makers who may be called from time to time to renew the string webbing on the family cots. In all households some of these "outside jobs" may be taken care of by the men—either the old woman's husband or son—but a large part of this work, and particularly its organisation, is considered the province of the senior woman of the house. Although financial arrangements vary greatly from one household to another, it is also usual for the senior woman to keep the money for running the household, so that her daughters-in-law and grandchildren must come to her for money when they want to make any routine purchase. This household budget may be apart from money which her earning sons keep back for their own and their wives' personal use (so that it does not mean total control over all purchases by family members), but it is nevertheless an important element in her day-to-day managerial authority.

Care of animals is also in most families the province of older women. More than half of the households in which old people are present own at least one buffalo for milk and *ghī* and some own more than one and occasionally a cow as well. The symbolic significance of having one's milk own (*ghar kā dūdh*) is probably as great as its contribution to the family diet. For the older generation, to have to purchase milk is one of the signs of changing times that is most to be deprecated. Although in the rural past of this village, men took a large share in the care of milch animals, this task in most Rayāpur households is now relegated mainly to women, and among them mainly to the old, for the young wives increasingly come to marriage unfamiliar with the intricacies of milking and the care and feeding of buffaloes. This job takes a great deal of a woman's time, and necessitates her being available in the home at almost all times. A buffalo must be fed and watered three times a day, washed down at least once a day, milked twice a day (and the milk churned and *ghī* made), and her stall must be cleaned and the manure patted into dung cakes which are dried in the sun and later stacked and used for fuel. The latter job is one to which the older village women are so accustomed from their earlier days—and the savings so substantial when compared to the cost of wood, coal, or kerosene, not to mention bottled gas—that many who do not own an animal buy manure from one of the local dairies and make their own dung cakes.

Other household tasks that are typically taken care of by older women—although young women may also do them—are those which are fairly sedentary, such as spinning into thread the old cotton from the family quilts each spring, tacking new cotton into the quilts before winter sets in, and making such household staples in the appropriate seasons as pickles and hand-rolled noodles.

A major responsibility of the older women in most households is the care of young children, particularly toddlers. A grandmother will take charge of a young baby while its mother is busy with the cooking and washing, but when a baby is very small her contribution will usually be limited to holding it and perhaps feeding it sugared water while its mother is otherwise occupied. Later, however, and particularly after it is weaned or another baby is born, she may take over almost all of its care, having it sleep beside her at night, feeding it, and taking it along with her on errands or when she goes to visit neighbours or to any social or religious event. Grandmothers say "the interest is dearer than the capital" (*mūl se pyārī byāj*) to explain their fondness for their grandchildren, and their exceptional leniency and patience with the antics and whining of children whom they have hopelessly spoiled and to whom they allow liberties that they never permitted their own children. It is not unusual for grandmothers in this way to attempt—and often succeed—in weaning a child's affection from his mother. But, young mothers, by and large, seem to accept the special relationship of grandmother and grandchild—perhaps partly because it relieves them of a significant burden of work—and are more apt to resent a mother-in-law who does not show special affection for their child or who shows favouritism to one of his cousins.

While the classical Indian four stages of life (*āshramas*) are not clearly articulated in reference to the female life-cycle, either in the traditional literature or in the folk conception, Rayā women do frequently use the classical terminology to refer to the second and major stage of life, that of the householder, *gṛhastha.* Ideally, they express the view that in old age a woman should leave *gṛhastha,* should detach herself from concern with the day-to-day running of the household. To leave *gṛhastha* involves two aspects: first, a readiness on the part of the *bahū* to take over the onerous household tasks formerly performed by the *sās* (with the indifferent assistance of her daughters), and second, a readiness on the part of the older woman to give up her managerial role and her feeling that she alone is responsible for and capable of managing household affairs. These two rarely coincide. While the former is generally more or less accomplished within a week or two of the new daughter-in law's arrival, the latter is typically a very gradual process of withdrawal that may take many years and may never be completed before the senior woman's death. The symbolic act of "handing over the keys" to the daughter-in-law is often resisted up to the end. In fact, although elderly women are often chided—and chide one another—for being "too much bound up in *gṛhastha*", it is actually rare in this community for any woman to voluntarily cease taking some responsibility for the work of the household and its organisation until she is either mentally or physically quite incapable of doing so.

RELIGIOUS PARTICIPATION OF THE AGING WOMAN

It has long been a tradition in Indian society—and in other societies as well—to regard religious activities as particularly appropriate to the aged. To spend one's declining years in contemplation, to prepare oneself for the imminent departure from this world by devoting oneself to the purification of the inner self and the worship of a God for whom one had perhaps too little time to spare in one's younger days, is regarded not only as a virtue in itself but also as the better part of wisdom as the time of reckoning draws near. Consistent with this ideal, we note that the religiosity of the elderly woman in Rayāpur is markedly greater than that of their younger relatives and neighbours, if we measure this in terms of proportions of women at various stages of life and proportion of time spent in solitary and group worship. The majority of elderly women rise between four and five in the morning (often before their daughters-in-law awaken, contrary to the traditional rural pattern) and after going to the toilet and bathing spend one-half to one hour in prayer. Some go each morning to one of the village temples, others sit in front of their household shrine and "take God's name", either alone or in the company of their husbands or other family members. Only after this do they take any refreshment.

The other major form of religious participation is group hymn (*bhajan*) singing. There are regular weekly sessions at one of the village temples, organised by a women's *satsang* group. The leader of this group is a Punjabi woman who lives outside the village, but almost all of the regular members are Rayā women and on any given occasion more than half of those in attendance are over 50 years of age. There is a regular active core of such older women with a few middle-aged and young women, most of the latter being women of nuclear households. The *bahūs* of the older women rarely if ever attend. In addition to this regular hymn meeting, there are others held irregularly in private homes in the village, usually to celebrate some happy family event such as a child's birthday. A woman who enjoys such gatherings can easily spend several afternoons a week singing religious songs with her peers and exchanging gossip in the intervals.

When queried, very few of the older women admit to having had a serious concern with religion in their youth, and in general they attribute their present preoccupation with such activities to their newly acquired leisure and to its appropriateness to their present stage of life. "When did I have time for it before?" they say, or "Now that it is my time of rest I can do this". There are a number of older women who have attached themselves as disciples of a *gurū* whose main *āshram* is in a city several hundred miles away, but who spends much of the year in Delhi. He comes for several weeks each year to the village itself, where he is hosted by one of the wealthiest local Rayā families.

Despite the popularity of religious pursuits among older Rayā women, there are a significant number in the sample who seldom or never gather to sing *bhajans* (except perhaps when they are invited to a private hymn-singing in the home of a close relative or neighbour). One such woman put it this way: "I don't have time for such things—I have to take care of my buffalo. Taking care of animals is a kind of worship (*pūjā*) too, you know".

SEXUAL ACTIVITY IN OLD AGE

One manifestation of the perception of old age as a time of detachment from the concerns of early adulthood is the tendency among aging married persons to voluntarily and deliberately cease having an active sex life once their children—and particularly their sons—are married. While there are some exceptions, as a rule cohabitation is stopped when the first son's wife comes to live in the household, if not before. There are some cases of older couples maintaining an active sex life or at least sharing a sleeping room after this, but such is neither the ideal nor the statistical norm. Those who do continue to sleep together in old age typically have no married sons, or are couples in which the woman is a younger second wife and the son the offspring of the first wife. Actually, in such cases, a joint household is rarely maintained for long after the son's marriage.

The cessation of sexual relations between a couple may be gradual and unspoken, but often it is a decision discussed and deliberately entered upon. One woman, for example, described the way that her husband had come to her on the day of their eldest son's wedding saying: "From now on we will live together as brother and sister". Since that day they have not shared a bed. This practice is rationalised in terms of older people not "needing" sex, and in terms of the "shame" or "embarrassment" (*sharam*) that would result if parents were to engage in sex while their son and his wife are also doing so in the same house: "It is a matter of *sharam*. When the *bahū-beṭe* are doing that, how would it look for the *sās-sasur* to be doing it too?" Public opinion seems to be a significant factor in this sense of *sharam*, for without the custom of married couples having a private bedroom or a double bed (an innovative piece of furniture nowadays routinely included in the dowry but provocative of much amusement among the older generation), it rapidly becomes general family and later, neighbourhood knowledge if an older couple continues to sleep together: "People would make all kinds of comments. They would say, 'Imagine, their *bahū* has come and still they are carrying on like that'. After all, we had our time, now it is the time of the *bahū-beṭe*."

In earlier times, when the village had a farming economy, it was usual for the men of the family to sleep in an outbuilding (*gher*) and to spend most of their leisure time there as well, coming to the main house only for meals, and for occasional surreptitious visits to their wives at night. Even today many families maintain a separate *gher* where animals are tied and where the older men sit and entertain their guests and carry on interminable card games. Many of these older men also sleep in their *gher*—if they do not have one, they are generally assigned a downstairs sitting room, usually the front room of the house, which serves the same general function. The older woman will then sleep in another room with the children, while each young married couple, and sometimes young unmarried men, are given a bedroom to themselves.

It is interesting in this connection, particularly to observers of the aging process among women in Western societies, that awareness of the menopause as a period of physical or psychological stress seems to be quite absent among Rayā women. Considerable questioning on this subject from both pre and post-menopausal women has failed to elicit any notion that the cessation of the menstrual cycle should cause distress in women or that it should be accompanied either by marked physical symptoms or tempermental and emotional difficulties. It is generally felt that if the menstrual periods stop when a woman is still relatively young (i.e., in her thirties) she may become weakened "because of the heat that goes from there to the head at this time". The chief problem otherwise is considered to be the danger to eyesight, which is observed to become poor at around the time of (normal) menopause, and again is attributed to "heat" (*garmī*) rising to the head. However, cooling foods are recommended as a sufficient antidote.

Many women express relief at the cessation of menstruation, because it is "messy" and a "bother", and (for those who have sufficient sons and daughters) because it means the end of childbearing. Of course, for many women sexual relations have already ceased by this time, for the first son is often already married by the time the mother is forty-five. The emotional upheavals that are associated with menopause in West seem puzzling to my informants, as does the idea that a woman should feel at this time that she is "no longer a woman", that she is no longer desirable to her husband, and so on. My inquiries on the latter point were met with hilarity: "Well, he certainly isn't going to go off and get somebody else at this point, is he?" or, "He's an old man too, after all, what would he expect?"

This is not to say that what in the West are recognised as menopausal symptoms are totally absent for these women as they experience the physiological changes that are taking place in their bodies. But whatever symptoms these women may have, they are not associated by them with the decline in their reproductive capacity and are not even regarded as forming a complex, as being related to one another. It would be difficult indeed to entangle "menopausal" symptoms from others which flow directly from the social-structural circumstances in which women typically find themselves during this time of life. For example, the menopause would tend to coincide roughly for most women with the time during which her children are marrying and new wives are being incorporated into the family. A woman does not need to look for physiological explanations for the tensions and stresses of these years. And as for the physical symptoms, a person's health is expected to decline gradually as he gets older. Discomforts of the kind that a doctor would associate with menopause are probably taken in their stride as part of this general process of aging. Thus whatever physical or emotional symptoms of the menopause may be present among these women, they are given no cultural elaboration nor considered unique or peculiar to the period we characterise as the "change of life".

I have tried in this paper to present some observations on the lives and self-perceptions on one group of aging women in an Indian city. These observations are based on data that are still in the process of being collected, and are meant to be tentative and suggestive of the directions their analysis will take, rather than conclusive and definitive. The study of aging in India is in its infancy and whatever empirical research has been done has taken the form of sociological surveys with formal interview schedules probing for quantifiable facts about the living conditions and problems of the aged, their interests and activities, their needs and attitudes.[8] Such studies serve an important purpose and are necessary in order to gain one kind of perspective on the life and social roles of older persons in India. The aims of the present study have been somewhat different, however. Hopefully, what our sample lacks in size and representativeness may be made up by what it can reveal about the cultural and social framework without which no rounded picture of the aging woman in India would be complete.*

8. See, for example, W. H. Harlan, "Social Status of the Aged in Three Indian Villages", *Vita Humana*, 7 (1964), pp. 239-252; B. Raj and B. G. Prasad, "A Study of Rural Aged Persons in Social Profile", *The Indian Journal of Social Work*, 32 (1971), pp. 155-162; K. S. Soodan, *Aging in India* (Calcutta: Minerva Associates, 1975); and the recently completed but still unpublished study by the Delhi School of Social Work on old persons in the Greater Delhi area.

*I have based this report on partial data from field research being carried out currently in the Delhi area in collaboration with my husband, Ved Prakash Vatuk. This project, entitled "Social and Cultural Dimensions of Aging in India," has been supported by the National Institute of Mental Health and the American Institute of Indian Studies.

10

VERITY SAIFULLAH KHAN

Asian Women in Britain : Strategies of Adjustment of Indian and Pakistani Migrants

Asian women in Britain are as diverse in life-styles and attitudes as the indigenous British population, and manifest a far wider variety of cultures and languages.[1] Any discussion or statement about their situation in Britain involves making broad generalisations, a frequent but perhaps inevitable failing which has proved detrimental to interethnic relations in Britain.

Accepting the limitations of this tendency, there are, however, certain justifications for treating Asian women as a specific group. Firstly, the majority of Asian women do manifest significant similarities in their life-style and values *in comparison* with the white indigenous population of Britain. These include some of the distinctive characteristics of Asian culture as compared to Western culture, and the factor of skin colour with its acquired, not inherent, social significance which Asians share with certain other ethnic minorities.[2] Secondly,

1. In this article the terms Asia and Asian refer to the Indian subcontinent and its peoples, most notably Indians, Pakistanis and Bangladeshis.

2. In Britain there is a large minority of people from the Islands of the West Indies and a far smaller group of Africans. In general parlance the terms "coloured" and "black" are used to refer to these two minorities and the Asian population.

Asian women, like British women, are subject to different conditions and different problems compared to their men and these are particularly evident in the migrant situation. And thirdly, Asian women are a relevant category because the white indigenous population perceives them as such. Whether through indifference, ignorance or prejudice the indigenous population remains basically unaware of the internal diversity among Asians and, consciously or unconsciously, stresses the similarities by utilising generalisations and stereotypes to maintain or justify the lack of, or limited, social interaction with them. A further justification is related to the fact that to concentrate on any particular Asian population,—Gujarati, Sikh, or Bangladeshi,—will not be typical of the whole.

This paper restricts itself to the more general level but hopes to explain some of the specific and fundamental factors relating to the position of Asian women in Britain. The immense variation of background and degree of adjustment found among the Asian population will be hinted at by incidental reference to particular groups.

It is easy to discuss the position of Asian women in Britain in the context of the clash or meeting of two cultures and this has been the main perspective of the very limited amount of material on the subject.[3] It is argued here, however, that it is important to start an analysis of the position of Asian women in Britain within a far wider perspective. The nature and quality of the Asian women's life in Britain is dependent on a multitude of interrelated factors beyond the control of the

3. The dearth of material on Asian women in Britain and of the woman's world in other societies, particularly those with a marked segregation of the sexes is due to the predominance of men in the field of social science research and the tremendous difficulties associated with fieldwork. In such a society a male researcher cannot hope to gain entry and acceptance into the woman's world. A female researcher does so by adopting the life expected of a woman and thus restricting her movement in the man's world and even in certain other sections of the community. As an outsider she may assume a certain role flexibility which can be manipulated to her advantage but this involves a careful management of impressions to maintain a consistent picture of herself. See Verity J. Saifullah Khan, "Pakistani Villagers in a British City: The World of the Mirpuri Villager in Bradford and in his Village of Origin" (Bradford University, unpublished Ph. D. thesis, 1974), Appendix II, pp. 748-800.

individual. The structure of British society, the economic and political conditions in Britain and the Indian subcontinent are of fundamental relevance besides the more specific factors of the life she had led back home, the number of years she has been in Britain, the place in which she is living and her personal family circumstances and particularly the attitude and prospects of her husband.

After a brief outline of the typical daily routine and conditions of life for Asians in Britain, past and present socio-economic and political conditions in Britain and the Indian subcontinent will be outlined. Some of the major determinants of the nature and quality of the life of Asian women in Britain will be underestimated without this perspective and the related importance of the dynamics of migration. The significance of the cultural variable can then be judged within this framework.

In 1971 there were 652,800 persons of Asian origin in Britain and of these 268,200 were born in Britain. There were 483,100 persons of Indian origin and 169,700 persons of Pakistani origin (including at that time Bangladeshis), those born in Britain numbering 226,800 and 41,400 respectively. There were 254,300 males and 228,800 females of Indian origin and 114,300 males and 55,400 females of Pakistani and Bangladeshi origin. Thus in 1971 there were approximately 284,200 females of Asian origin in Britain of whom 137,500 were born in Britain in comparison to 368,600 men of Asian origin of whom 130,700 were born in Britain. The number of Asian women born in India, Pakistan or Bangladesh and now living in Britain has increased considerably faster than the number of their male counterparts because immigration since 1965 and particularly 1971 has been restricted almost wholly to dependents (i.e., women and children). Therefore, the sex ratio is more balanced, particularly among Pakistanis, than it was in 1971 (124 Indian males to 100 females and 295 Pakistani and Bangladeshi males to 100 females).[4]

4. All figures are from the 1971 Populalion Census of Great Britain. For details see G. B. Gillian Lomas, *Census 1971. The Coloured Population of Great Britain* (London, The Runnymede Trust, 1973).

DAILY ROUTINE AND CONDITIONS OF LIFE

The majority of Asian women in Britain are from rural areas of India, Pakistan and Bangladesh and have a limited, or no command of the English language. Like the poorer socio-economic strata of British society they live in terraced or semi-detached houses[5] which are concentrated in the "inner-city" area of the towns and cities (particularly the large industrial cities of the Midlands and the North). These areas consist of a zone between the central shopping and commercial centre and the public housing estates and the smarter newer suburbs on the edge of the city where the more prosperous inhabitants of the inner-city areas have moved with the advent of slum clearance, the influx of immigrants and available higher standard housing. The housing is usually the oldest in the city, often subject to short-term leases but in some areas undergoing re-development schemes if not eventually marked for slum clearance. Asian settlers in Britain have shown a marked preference for ownership of their own houses and it was in this area of the city that the cheapest housing was available and there was the least organised resistance (from neighbours, estate agents and local authorities) to the influx perceived as undesirably by many local inhabitants. By the time the larger influxes of migrants arrived in Britain the original population of these areas was dispersing, leaving a high proportion of the old, single students or workers in rented accommodation, the poorest and general "down-and-outs" of British society.

The houses in these and other parts of the cities of England frequently consist of two living rooms on the ground floor and a kitchen on the same floor or in the basement. The front door of the house leads into a small corridor or, in the smallest of Victorian houses, directly into the "front" room and then the stairs to the first floor are between the two downstairs rooms. On the first floor there are two or three bedrooms and a bathroom and sometimes there are one or two bedrooms in the attic. At the back of the house there is often a small yard or garden. The variation in size, quality and comfort of

5. Terraced houses have common sidewalls, i.e., you cannot walk down the side of the house. Semi-detached houses have one wall attached to another house and one open, i.e., they are built in pairs.

these houses differs considerably from area to area, city to city and according to the priorities, preferences and finances of the owners.

Similar to the British neighbours' utilisation of rooms the "front" room is invariably used and decoracted as the "best" room where visitors are received and children are under more careful surveillance. The "back" room is the heart of the household where young children spend much of their day. This division is convenient for households that are permanently or, on occasion, functioning as *purdah* households. Women and children remain in the family quarters when visitors arrive and the men occupy the front room. Other distinctively Asian features are found in many houses: brightly coloured furnishings, a *tawa,* and *koonda langree* in the kitchens and plastic buckets and jugs standing in the bath.[6] In some areas Asian households are distinguishable from the streets by the colourful exterior decoration and (to the disgust of the proverbially garden-conscious Englishman) the unkept garden.

Except for a few religious men the majority of Asian men wear Western dress. Many of the earliest Sikhs in Britain cut their hair in order to get work and a certain number of teenagers do so voluntarily but this trend seems to have slowed down and it is usual for Sikh children entering school to have uncut hair. Asian women, however, have maintained their traditional clothes, whether *sari* or *shalwar-kameez*. The popularity of the trouser suit is no doubt partly due to prevailing fashions in urban India and Pakistan, partly due to practicality in the British climate and partly a gesture of assimilation. The fact that the *burqa* has rarely been seen in Britain is not so much an indication of change but an acknowledgement that in Britain it defeats its purpose bringing attention to, rather than hiding its wearer. Many Asian girls are still wearing *shalwar* or trousers to school despite initial hostility from some educational departments, and there remain parental objections to girls wearing gym-slips at school, and in many instances to their daughters attending co-educational schools.

6. Most British bathrooms contain baths, not showers. Rather than adopt the Englishman's seemingly dirty habit Asians stand in the bath and wash themselves in traditional style.

The majority of Asian men in Britain belong to the categories of unskilled or semi-skilled workers and there are obvious concentrations in certain fields of employment.[7] The same trend is evident and possibly more marked for those Asian women who are working. Many men work long hours to supplement their relatively low pay and/or maximise their savings. Asian women rise early in the morning to prepare a meal for their husbands before they leave for work, or on their return from a night shift. The children leave for school between eight and eight-thirty and return between three and four o'clock in the afternoon. In the evening the husbands are either returning from work or getting up from a day-time sleep. The majority of Asian women stay at home with their young children for most of the day except for visiting nearby shops or friends. Some women, who have no young children or arrange to leave them with friends or relatives, go out to work and some others do not venture beyond the house alone, leaving the shopping to husbands or sons and visiting only when chaperoned. Most family visiting takes place at the week-ends when families may travel long distances to visit close relatives and friends.

The majority of Asian men and women live almost exclusively among their own people and have minimum contact with the British world around them.[8] The majority of primary and most meaningful relationships are with relatives and friends from the same regional and socio-economic background in Asia, whether they live near-at-hand or some distance away in the British context. The majority of other relationships are with their own countrymen, either as workmates or neighbours. Most relationships with the white indigenous population or other ethnic minorities are restricted to formal, impersonal rela-

7. There is a high percentage of Asian men in the textile, transport and engineering industries. See DeWitt John, *Indian Workers' Associations in Britain* (London: Oxford University Press, 1969); S. Allen, J. Bornat and S. Bentley, *Work, Race and Immigration* (London: Oxford University Press for the Institute of Race Relations, 1975).

8. B. Dahya, "The Nature of Pakistani Ethnicity in Industrial Cities in Britain", in A. Cohen (ed.), *Urban Ethnicity* (A.S.A. Monograph 12; London: Tavistock Publications, 1974).

tionships with, for example, superiors at work and officials in offices, hospitals, clinics and schools.

THE WIDER PERSPECTIVE

The very presence of a large number of Asians in Britain, rather than in any other European country is of course, due to the historical fact of British Imperialism. In order to achieve her essentially economic motive for colonisation Britain established a political, administrative, judicial and educational system to support it, whose influence is still evident today in the structure and values of the society. Imperialism in India, as elsewhere, has increased the ever widening gap between the rich and the poor nations of the world, the major prerequisite of such mass international migrations. It has carved the routes for such migrations by facilitating or forcing movement of labour and fostering rising expectations, and has influenced the structural development of British Society and formulated its prevailing values and stereotypes relating to itself and other peoples of the world.

> To the customary British distrust of strangers was added the traditional disparagement of colour. Sociologists investigating the character of prejudice against the new immigrants discovered a sediment of racial conceit among whites of all classes, produced by relics of imperial myth in school textbook and story; the acquired arrogance of many who had served in the empire as soldiers, technicians or minor administrators . . . [9]

Until recently the villager's conceptualisation of life in Britain was similarly influenced by past and present effects of the British Raj. Britain, or *vilayat*, is believed by the majority to be a rich, advanced and desirable place to live where everyone is wealthy, well-educated and happy. The remittances and inevitably one-sided feedback received from migrants in Britain tended to confirm this view. But at the same time, often held by the same individual is another more critical conception of

9. R. Segal, *The Race War* (Harmondsworth, Middlesex: Pelican Books, 1967), p. 307.

the West; its totally different standards and values in relation to loyalty to the family, marriage, social interaction, etc., means the villager has very little respect for the 'morality' (in the widest sense) of the West. This view is also confirmed by the British and American films shown in urban areas and on television, and by these migrants who do not conform to the expectations of their family.[10]

The composition of Asian population in Britain is similarly explained by economic, political and historical factors. The main emigration areas in the Indian subcontinent are invariably areas that have had a tradition of migration due to over-population (e.g., the Punjab of India) and/or infertile agricultural land (e.g., Mirpur in Azad Kashmir, Campbellpur in the Punjab of Pakistan, Sylhet in Bangladesh) and/or political disturbances (e.g., at partition in the Punjab and Kashmir). Gujarat in India has a fifteen-centuries old trade route with East Africa and Sikhs have settled abroad prior to this century (e.g., in British Columbia, the Fiji Islands), and there have always been the internal migrations from the northern mountain areas to the plains, rural-urban migration and the settlement of newly irrigated tracts of land.

In the early decades of this century hundreds of Indian doctors and students came to Britain, few taking up permanent residence. But small members of unskilled Asians came to Britain by way of merchant navy or British army and small groups of Sikhs settled as craftsmen or pedlars. Subjects of British rule as citizens of the empire were entitled to free entry into Britain. Some stayed, others returned and some encouraged relatives to join them by the same means or by sending finances. Men from the areas mentioned above were often anxious to seek alternative sources of employment and when there was a demand for labour in post-war Britain (which coincided with political upheavals in the Indian subcontinent) chains or networks developed between settlers in Britain and potential emigrants. The majority of the subsequent influx of migrants were not the poorest of villagers but small landowners joining kin or fellow villagers in Britain. The poorer landless tenant farmers and artisans depended even more on

10. Verity J. Saifullah Khan, *op, cit.*, pp. 376-381.

the migrant chains, for financial support from the kin group as well as emotional and organisational support.

It is these factors which explain the amazing selectivity in in the Asian migration to Britain—a large percentage of migrants coming from specific regions and within the regions' specific districts, *tehsils* and villages. And this selectivity, and its influence on settlement patterns in Britain, has contributed to the degree of separatism manifest in the different populations, and the perpetuation of existing prejudices and stereotypes (which is no doubt exacerbated by the tendency of the British population to categorise all Asians as one, or persume there is a coherent and organised Pakistani, Indian, Bangladeshi "community"). Concentrated areas of emigration and settlement facilitated the maximum feedback to encourage further emigration and, in the long-run, has proved a major impetus to socio-economic change in the emigration areas and a major breakthrough to social change in the settlement areas in Britain. The mechnics of such selective migrations also promote the establishment of "institutions" of migration facilitating movement between the sending and receiving areas (e.g., travel agents, banks, new air routes) and providing facilities to soften the initial difficulties of life in an alien situation (e.g., estate agents, doctors, *hallal* butchers, and shops and restaurants run by Asians). The establishment of a large Asian population with its own facilities and institutions in the short-run helps, in the long-run hinders, and in the meantime restrains individuals branching out and facing the new conditions in which they are to live.

The small but noticeable percentage of Asians from an urban-educated background was less dependent on the migration chains which so greatly facilitated the movement of villagers. They were less restricted by the imposition of successive immigration controls[11] and more able and willing to communicate with the indigenous population and other middle-class Asians of different ethnic and linguistic backgrounds.

11. Successive immigration controls in 1962, 1965, 1968 and 1971 have changed the pattern of immigration from one of mainly unskilled workers to one of professional and skilled workers.

MIGRATION OF WOMEN

It is only within this background of the processes of migration and the present economic and political situation in both countries that the position of Asians in Britain can be clearly appreciated. It is often wrongly assumed, for example, that migrants are atypical in character and/or background of the majority of their home population. This is frequently true of the earlier migrants who established footholds for subsequent migrants and who have often adopted relatively quickly a new life-style and values. These men are likely to have been of adventurous spirit, social outcasts or driven by economic necessity. But once the migration chains develop this no longer holds true; the element of individual choice is considerably reduced. The new alternative becomes a natural, less drastic choice as time passes. A Punjabi or pathan family thinking of sending their son to find lucrative employment with the help of a cousin in Karachi might now have the alternative of sending him (six times the distance but for greater financial reward) to a brother or uncle in Britain.

In the late 1950s and 1960s the preponderance of men in the migration indicated the essentially economic motive for migration and the migrant's belief in its temporary nature. The gradual increase in women migrants reflected an acknowledgement of the need or desire for an extended stay, partly due to economic pressure (the increasing cost of living, the relatively higher wages and lower unemployment in Britain) and partly due to the uncertainty caused by Britain immigration laws.

The migration of women is significant in several, often unrecognised ways. Firstly, if the close family and kin ties among Asians are acknowldged the migration of women can be seen as a force strengthening, not severing, ties with home. A migrant now has to consider his expected role in relation to his affines, and in the case of Muslims a further bond with their kin group. Secondly, the different Asian populations have reflected different trends and priorities in the migration pattern. Indians, on the whole, settled in larger numbers earlier than Pakistanis but they also indicated a greater swiftness in calling their wives,[12] reflecting their wives' earning power, less concern

12. 34 per cent of the total female immigrants from India arrived before the end of 1961 (compared with 41 per cent of males) and 35 per cent came

for the restrictions of *purdah,* and a greater acceptance of their intention to stay for an extended period. Pakistanis have, in general, felt more threatened by the infiltration of Western values and Pakistanis and Bangladeshis from particularly poor backgrounds felt a greater insecurity, manifest in their retention and strengthening of ties back home.[13] Only in the home locality and among a significant few in Britain will their financial achievements be socially acknowledged and a great obligation remains to help these significant persons back home (i.e., family and friends).

Thirdly, it is those women who expect or hope to return home in the near future who are less likely to take account of or accept the Western elements affecting their children which, if they do not speak English or go out to work, they are little equipped to understand. Such women are a particularly traditional force in the British situation where the mother is the main socialising agent at least before school-going age.

Fourthly, the present marriage preferences are bound to reinforce this and other constraints against change. Among all Asians in Britain there is a preference for sons to have an arranged marriage with a girl from home. This preference for a less independently-minded, domestically-orientated and submissive girl is, however, likely to alter, as boys brought up in Britain demand different qualities of their brides (notably those of companionship and comparable education) and possibly conditions of living (i.e., as a nuclear household). Then the limited marriage market for British-educated Asian girls may expand correspondingly. Where there are more specific marriage preferences relating to family, kin or caste, the number of eligible individuals in Britain will be small, and in the case of marriage with kin, especially cousins, pressures to maintain the tradition will be strong (because it will guarantee another member of the kin group entering Britain).

after the beginning of 1961 (23 per cent of males). Only 7 per cent of the Pakistani females (including Bangladeshi) arrived before the end of 1961 and nearly 70 per cent came after the beginning of 1967. See footnote 4.

13. On this point see B. Dahya, "Pakistanis in Britain: Transients or Settlers", *Race,* XIV (January, 1973).

DEPENDENT STATUS

Finally, it is important to remember that all the first generation Asian women migrants to Britain have come as dependents; that is their actual and legal status. In subsequent generations an increasing number of Asian women will be legally and economically independent. Loyalty to the family and the maintenance of other Asian values must not be underestimated but at the same time the existence of an alternative, whether utilised or not, is bound to affect the Asian woman's appreciation of her own situation. The pressures to conformity from family and kin ties, the reflection of the honour or shame of an individual onto the group and the, at times ferocious, gossip networks tend to restrain deviants, as do the lack of satisfactory alternatives for someone initially socialised into an Asian world[14] and perceived as non-desirable or easily exploited in the wider community.

It is the Asian woman's status as a dependent which makes her movement a reliable indicator of the future intentions of her husband or group. When the Pakistan Act was passed in 1973 the rush to call wives to Britain or to get British nationals for wives for those already resident in Britain reflected the suspicion of a complete halt in immigration, even of dependents. The problems such wives and children face before they eventually reach Britain are yet another indication of their dependent status and the vulnerability of migrants in general.[15] But it also showed that many husbands who spoke of returning to Pakistan in the near future would not do so or had hopes of returning in the more distant future. The movement of first generation Pakistani women migrants will also indicate the degree of stability of the Pakistani population in Britain. At present it seems likely that rather disparate alternatives will develop together in response to the increasing cost of living; either Pakistani women will start to go out to work

14. This is particularly evident in the case of an Asian girl who wants to marry an English boy or an Asian boy of the "wrong" religious affiliation. Usually rejected by her own and her parent's family she not only faces a sudden separation from them but a new existences in which one relationship—that of her husband—monopolises her time and emotions.

15. The law, its interpretation and the interview procedures, etc., have recently been under considerable criticism in Britain. For details see *Where do you keep your string beds*? (London : The Runnymede Trust, 1974).

(which will have considerable consequences for their future and that of their children) or they will return to Pakistan with some or all of their children to increase the saving power of their husband who will eventually join them.[16]

If the economic and political situation in the sending countries and receiving country, and the development of the migration process and its significance for women migrants are taken into account, it is possible to understand the constraints and incentives acting on a migrant once he or she has settled in Britain. The constraints against change include the tie with the homeland, loyalty to family and kin back home, the need for security in a 'hostile' world, limited qualifications and limited opportunities in the housing and labour markets, the pressure for conformity from the local population of fellow countrymen and the commitment and desire to return home. Incentives to change for the Asian woman in Britain are an acknowledgement of her homeland's uncertain economical and political future, and the limited opportunities in her home locality, the influences of urban and Western life-styles and education on her and particularly her children, an increased network specialisation and the new experiences and changing values which are inevitably felt over time and with frequent visits to and from the homeland.

The degree to which these potential incentives and constraints are felt depends on the resources of the migrant and, in the case of women, those also felt by their husbands and their reaction to them. Although many Asian migrants to Britain came with limited educational and financial resources the majority had access to a valuable resource underestimated by British society, i.e., the financial, emotional and physical support of the kin group. It is this fact that explains the

16. Some women who left apparently for this reason found it hard to settle back home and returned to Britain. If their permanent return became an obvious trend these might be a re-emergence of some of the social problems experienced during the early stages of the migration, notably, young boys without adequate maternal or family care. Many mothers would leave their sons in Britain and return to Asia with their daughters reflecting the emphasis on education for boys rather than girls, and the concern to shield girls rather than boys from the corrupting influences of Western culture. Verity J. Saifullah Khan *op. cit.*, pp., 99 and 720.

Asian's ability to purchase a house, start a business and return at short notice to his homeland when his British counterpart could do none of these. And it is this fact which has helped many Asian women to cope with otherwise insurmountable problems on their arrival.

PROBLEMS OF ADJUSTMENT

Many of the initial problems of adjustment for Asian women in Britain are common to all Asians and many other migrant groups. These are the immediate physical problems of adapting to new living conditions and a new climate which may themselves contribute to other social and psychological problems of adjustment.

The new climate demands thicker, and many more, layers of clothing, and nappies for children. Particular reticence to change is evident in relation to footwear; the practical tights or socks and closed shoes are still not worn by some Asian women of village origin even in the coldest weather. The new climate, its lack of sunshine and restricted outdoor activity can be detrimental to health, particularly for women restricted by custom or necessity to the house. The climate and type of housing in Britain combine to impose an indoor life-style restricted in space and frequency of social interactions which markedly contrasts with the outdoor sociability of the family courtyard and village or *mohalla*. Rain and cold weather force children to play in restricted space indoors. Mothers get no help from other female family members to supervise the children, give them company and relieve the monotony, and help with the larger amounts of washing.

Coupled with the natural homesickness for family and friends the impersonality and large scale of city life is striking, particularly for men and women who have never lived in a city in their own country. An indoor-orientated life-style and the traditional reserve of the privacy-conscious British limit the opportunities for communicating with neighbours and other contacts made in the daily routine. Frequently, the lack of facility in English and the mutual belief or prejudice that language and culture are a serious barrier to communication, perpetuate the tendency to ethnic exclusiveness. Even in the more formal interactions or situations, the complex bureaucracy, demand for punctuality and the faster pace demanded of inhabitants in the industrial urban West bring added pressure to those who are initially concerned to gain some support and familiarity in their new surroundings.

Such external factors often exacerbate the natural human emotions and reactions of uncertainty and anxiety arising from adaptation to a new social world and the increased self-awareness and reappraisal it demands. For many Asians in Britain it has been their first move from their 'ancestral' home and for the majority (of women in particular), it has been their first experience of urban life and of another culture, i.e., the first marked comparison with the known and valued. The degree of adjustment in life-style and values has, from the earliest stage of the migration, been gradually reduced at least in the short-term perspective. Newly arrived migrants could depend on the experience and expertise of their already settled countrymen and utilise the institutions of migration and ethnic institutions providing many of the facilities once only available through contact with the indigenous population.

Some of the more fundamental adjustments to life in Britain are noticably greater for Asian women than men. At home in India or Pakistan men were used, in differing degrees, to a physical mobility beyond the home and its immediate neighbourhood. For women, journeys beyond the home locality were restricted to occasional visits to a local bazaar or visiting relatives. In Britain many men of village background have to adjust to the new demands of industrial wage-labour and often working on night-shifts. This work is separated from the family unit but they frequently work and travel with fellow villagers or countrymen. In certain industries and certain fields of employment ethnic work gangs or complete shifts are the norm,[17] but it still remains more likely that Asian men will interact with work-mates or superiors of the indigenous population. This movement beyond the home,

17. Many Asians explain this as a preference to work with their countrymen and/or an acknowledgement of the pressures of a multi-ethnic workforce. More fundamentally, it is due to the lack of promotion possibilities (due to discrimination) and potential (due to limited facility of expected linguistic and cultural attributes) and the advantages of instant recruitment (through kin and village networks) and greater control for the management.

contact with others, and an opportunity to learn and practice English facilitates a person's adjustment to, and understanding of, the wider community.

But the Asian woman is even further restricted by her new situation. It is often assumed by British community workers and professionals in contact with Asian women that they are restricted in mobility by religion and/or custom as they were presumed to have been in India or Pakistan. This truth is limited by the dangerous tendency of comparing aspects of two cultures without reference to the contexts and complete systems in which they are a meaningful part. Most Indian and Pakistani women in Asia are restricted to some degree by specific kin or non-kin avoidances and segregation of the sexes and yet they also participate in other interactions which have less meaning or consequence in the British situation.

The Asian family system and the social life of the city, *mohalla* or village society mean that Indian and Pakistani women invariably spend their day in the company of other women. It is this "women's world" and the encumbent emotional and physical support which is abruptly ended when Asian women move to Britain.[18] The strength of village kin ties in the alien situation enables a substitute system to develop, the most meaningful relationship being with other women of the same family, kin and home village and other relationships newly formed in Britain which are usually with women from the same region and socio-economic background. Distant relatives may establish a more binding relationship and newly acquired friends may assume features of a kin retionship, thus filling a vacuum in the traditional scheme of relationships, but this social network is geographically far more dispersed.

EMPLOYMENT

Before some of the potentially positive factors arising from their new situation are discussed, an important distinction must be made between women who work outside the home and

18. Overcrowding, of several families in one house, and the residential concentration of Asians in "ghettos" are, therefore, an actual advantage for Asians women at least in the short-term concern of settling down in her new environment.

those who do not. The danger of generalising about Asian women is clearly evident without such a breakdown and yet within each category there are great variations according to particular background, present circumstances and the personalities involved. The majority of Asian women who work are Indians, Sikh or Hindu, because custom and/or religion restricts all but the urban-educated Pakistani and Bangladeshi from taking employment beyond the home (i.e., where contact with unrelated men is inevitable). But features of the stricter *purdah* system are evident in the general employment situation of all Asian women in part due to the character of the labour market and in part due to a preference to work with other women of the same ethnic group. Like British women, Asian women are found in the lowest strata of working class jobs, those that require little or no training, provide low economic rewards and possess no career structure. Some women who do not go out to work take "home" work such as sewing or making Christmas crackers for small firms which may suit their circumstance but is notoriously badly paid. Other women with young children do short shifts, for example, in the early evening and will be among the first to lose their jobs if production is reduced. Many women who work full-time do so in all-female, often mainly Asian, settings and working with English men is more acceptable than working with Asian men.

Asian women who go out to work do have some opportunity to befriend others, learn a little English and something of the British world about them. They are likely to be more aware and understanding of the pressures and influences experienced by their children, and some variety and stimulation in an otherwise claustrophobic domestic routine may compensate for the inevitable physical exhaustion. It is conceivable that, over time, Asian husbands will assume a greater responsibility in domestic affairs and caring for children to relieve their wives at present coping with the two full-time jobs of home and outside work. But, equally important is a marked improvement in child-care facilities (the training and registration of child-minders, the increase in nurseries, play-grounds, factory creches, etc). The Equal Pay Act which comes fully into operation, and Protection of Employment Bill, which is due to be passed in 1975, may do something to change attitudes and eliminate blatant discrimination against women but it does not tackle the question of equal opportunity. Without adequate child-care facilities, a reallocation of household duties, control over their own fertility and a fundamental change in the conditioning of traditional male and female roles at home and at school, the position of women will not change significantly. Added to the discrimination against their sex Asian women face is that experienced by all their countrymen and the handicaps inherent in the migration process.

It is evident that many of these problems of adjustment are not specifically due to migration to the West. A Punjabi villager moving to Karachi or Delhi would experience similar problems due to the nature of urban living, the physical separation of the family unit and the transition to a wage-based economy. The wife can no longer work on the land or beyond the home with those known to her, and if her husband finds work, the necessity to work is reduced and the family's status raised accordingly. This move for a village woman, whether in Britain or the Indian subcontinent, may be a step up the status hierarchy but it is also a step away from the relatively greater physical and economic freedom of the village woman. In a subsistence economy the woman's contribution to the family's economic situation is valued and she has a greater control over the products of their labour. In a cash economy the woman is economically dependent on her husband and the restricted physical activity can be detrimental to her health and mental state. No longer an economic advantage to the household, she becomes a status symbol.

It is important to add here that some of the new features of life experienced by Asian women in Britain are seen by some women as positive, rather than problematic features. The smaller family unit contributes to a woman's loneliness, loss of physical and emotional support and the acquisition of new responsibilities. While bewailing these factors many women admit the advantages. If a newly arrived woman finds help and support in the initial period and then establishes a circle of friends she may overcome the anxieties of, and begin to enjoy, her new freedom and responsibilities. The absence of elders is bemoaned in a country where babysitters are so valued and yet may be outweighed by the absence of a particularly unpleasant mother-in-law, a greater influence over the socialisation of one's own children and the great privacy available to a husband and wife. The early years of separation due to the migration process, and the husband working at a long distance from home may produce tensions between husband and wife resulting from their different aspirations and experiences and yet the couple's earlier acquisition of household and parental responsibilities, their relative freedom from elders and particularly the loss of alternative support (in the "woman's world" and "man's world") allows and encourages a closer companionship between husband and wife.

THE CULTURAL VARIABLE

The importance of cultural differences between the indigenous British population and the Asian minority has been indicated in the discussion of the changed family composition. Viewing the question of "culture-conflict" in highly abstract terms, certain fundamental characteristics of Asian culture do appear to be in direct contradiction to fundamental characteristics of Western culture. Western society values and fosters individualism which is in marked contract with Asian society's stress on the group, its subordination of the individual and hierarchy of status and authority. In the British situation the values inculcated by the British system of education, therefore, tend to undermine or conflict with the values taught to Asian children by their parents. The generation gap, inevitable in a fast changing society, is exacerbated by the differential influence of a second culture and value system. The older generation itself is in transition, coping with structural and emotional alterations of its traditional frame of reference which is also undermining or confusing traditional values.

To explain the position of Asian women solely in terms of culture conflict denies the importance of the other determining factors outlined in this article and ignores the elasticity of human nature. Just as all members of a highly differentiated society are used to playing different roles in differing circumstances and contexts, so many young Asians in Britain become very adept in 'switching' their behaviour and values according to context. Their adoption of Western dress and the existence of more nuclear families in Britain does not necessarily imply the loss of other underlying values. Many of the changes the observer notices in the Asian population may be changes forced by circumstance or adopted for convenience, to be abandoned in certain contexts or on return to Asia.

Many everyday issues and some of great consequence can be understood, if not easily solved, by reference to the cultural background of Asian migrants. The Asian parents' lack of involvement in parent-teacher meetings, their concern that their children are not being taught 'properly' and their high aspirations for their children's future can be simply explained to teachers. Until recently in India and Pakistan the school was totally separate from the home, teachers had total responsibility for the formal education of children, and mutual cooperation in, and understanding of, teacher and parent roles were not considered important. In Britain, this feeling is strengthened by the Asian parents' feeling of inadequacy due to language difficulties, unfamiliarity with the new school system and the lack of adequate facilities provided by the school (i.e., translators, etc.). The Asian parents' understanding of the educative process relates to that in India and Pakistan where it is more formal and disciplinarian and where young children are less likely to return from school each day with paintings and models and talk in a personal way about their teacher. The stress on child-centred education apparent in some primary education learning through activities and developing self-discipline and a friendly rapport with the teacher is unknown to the Asian parents. It is also difficult for illiterate or semi-literate parents to appreciate that their children are unlikely to become doctors, lawyers and teachers because of the different standards of teachers and schools within Britain and the discrimination they are likely to face in the future in the labour market as well as the lack of stimulation and help at home.

Similarly, an understanding of Asian culture (the taboo on open discussion of topics relating to sex, the pride associated with a large family, etc.) and conditions of life back home (the need for sons in a farming economy, high infant mortality and a shorter life-span) is essential to an appreciation of their reluctance to accept family planning just as the higher standard and yet rapidly increasing cost of living must explain its gradual spread even among orthodox Muslims.

SOME CONCLUSIONS, PREDICTIONS AND QUESTIONS

Many of the problems faced by Asian women, and often Asian men, in Britain are those experienced by any migrant group or ethnic minority, parctiularly if they are moving from a rural to an urban area.

Asian migrants in Britain clearly highlight the fact that migrants are usually a highly exploited group, vulnerable pawns in an international exchange of labour. As mentioned earlier, there would not be so many Asians in Britain without the Imperial connection and the marked contrasts between the standards of living in both countries. This, and many other migrations have benefited the receiving country (through the influx of foreign labour in times of labour shortage and to support declining industries and jobs no longer acceptable to the indigenous population) and the country of emigration (by the influx of foreign capital to the emigration areas and foreign exchange for the country as a whole). And yet there is rarely any recognition or acceptance of this contribution by alleviating or facilitating the human conditions and dilemmas it invariably causes.

The migrant finds that his status is dependent on both worlds. In one he achieves economic advancement and in the other he is accorded recognition of his success. But he is restricted physically to one world at any one time and thus he lives totally in neither. Life in Britain, and the migration itself, is meaningful only in terms of life back home. Having left the village and become associated with *vilayat* a return to village life as he originally knew it is a rejection of opportunities not only beneficial to him personally but also to his family and kin. The changing aspirations and awareness which the migration process involves makes such a return far more difficult than the migrant could have foreseen. The migrants' service to both societies, and the absence of its recognition, has tended to strengthen the *status quo* within and between both societies which was the fundamental cause of their migration in the first place and will continue to constrain their opportunities for economic and social advancement.

The instability and insecurity of such a transitional society is also, in the case of Asians in Britain, related to their lack of representation in the wider society. Like women in general, Asians in Britain are not found in positions of power in accordance with their numerical spread. In both cases this results from individual and institutionalised discrimination and particular handicaps relating to their past and present condition. One reason for the under-representation of Asians in Britain, their lack of grass-roots organisation and representative leaders is the differentiation within the Asian population based on ethnic, regional, religious and socio-economic backgrounds.

Communication between each population (Sikh, Gujarati, Mirpuri, Chhachhi, etc.) is restricted by the internal organisation based on village and kin ties, by the diversity of languages and the maintenance of prejudices, and within each population there is the marked distinction between the urban-educated Asians and the majority of less educated villagers. Most of the leaders or spokesmen of the Asian populations come from the former category and have no mandate for representing the majority to the British world. Their desire for a wider social standing has led consciously or unconsciously to their disassociating themselves from the majority with whom, they are all too well aware, they are classified by the indigenous population. These so-called leaders do not have any control over the community and are not directly interested in its cohesion or preservation except as the foundation of their power. The majority of Asians value their existence for one reason: their ability to communicate to the wider society on important issues relating to external threats to their nationality or religious affiliations. Traditional leaders, often elders or long-established migrants, do wield authority over smaller sections of the communities. In the case of the Sikh community, official representatives of the Indian Workers' Association are democratically elected and their organisation has a wider support from and great involvement in the welfare of the whole community.

FUNDAMENTAL DILEMMAS

The Asian population's lack of power and of any foundation on which organisation and cooperation between its different communities could be based is evident and severe in consequence for its women. Sikh women may pray and eat together at the local *Gurdwara* on Sundays but the majority of Asian women have no meeting point or social life beyond that of the home. This is a worsening of their previous position due to the new context and conditions of life. To compensate for this and to tackle new problems associated with life in Britain, Asian women as much as their men folk, need to cooperate and establish mutual support systems. This is hindered by lack of any focal meeting place and lack of time due to the demands of bringing up a family with one or both parents working outside the home. An increasing number of working Asian men and women are realising that their future lies with the future of the rest of the indigenous working class. An increasing number are joining unions with the hope they will pay more attention to their particular situation but many Asians, particularly women, are in areas of employment known for their weak unions or remaining non-unionised. The fact that there have been several recent cases of Asian women striking in demand for better conditions illustrates the great variations within the population and perhaps its latent potential for action.[19]

The local and national Pakistani, Bangladeshi and Indian women's associations are usually small in number and influence and organised and supported by women from an urban-educated background. Few have tackled the fundamental problems experienced by village women, the majority concentrating on arranging cultural shows and *meena* bazaars to raise funds.

Although the children of today's adult Asians will face other problems (due to the world-wide rate of social change and their specific position in British society) they are likely to break down some of these barriers, based on ethnic and class origin, and will be able to choose whether they will participate in the wider society. Their future depends on the degree of rejection or acceptance they feel from British society, the opportunities available in the alternative world back home and of

19. Well-know strikes which Asian women initiated or supported include those at the Imperial Typewriters factory in Leicester, and Yarnolds, a small textile factory in Wolverhampton.

course their parent's plans and attitudes and the nature of socialisation. It is inevitably the young Asian girls who are going to experience the greater problems, and particularly those with strict Muslim parents (Pakistani, Indian Gujarati, and Bangladeshi).

It is still usual to hear general debates about the future of Britain's ethnic minorities discussed in terms of integration and assimilation. As true integration can only take place between equals and is essentially a two-way process, it remains a non-question while power remains guarded in the hands of one side who imply it should be a one way-process. British society, which itself is not integrated into one life-style or set of values, has yet to accept the responsibilities it accumulated in past centuries and, by accepting the fact that it is a multi-ethnic society, help to eradicate the prejudices which have sunk deep into its structure.

Related to the question of integration is the equally problematic question of the influence of Westernisation or simply modern, urban living upon values and social structures which give less priority and importance to the individual. Do the demands of urban life, the increased mobility of labour and smaller family units, for example, stimulate this spread of individualism and a greater independence from the group? There are evident advantages for the quality of human life and yet some of the consequences are far from desirable. The position of old people in the West is a constant reminder. Asian old people in Britain and in cities in India and Pakistan are already experiencing the tensions and pressures of modern life-styles and values. Asians in Britain and professional and community workers who are in contact with them want to know how people in India and Pakistan are resolving or tackling such questions. The question of arranged marriages is but one example. Few villagers in Britain have lived in urban areas in their homeland and are thus particularly unprepared to consider the fundamental issues and practicalities involved in the love-versus-arranged marriage debate. British community workers are limited by their allegiance to one set of values and are not in contact with prevailing conditions in Asia.

Similarly those involved in the women's movement in Britain who are often supporters of minority rights, find inherent contradictions or gaps in their reasoning. How, they and no doubt many British Asians ask, is the liberation of Asian women compatible with retention of the fundamentals of Asian culture and values, some of which they find sadly lacking in Western society. How can they avoid cultural imperialism? Without a fundamental change in the values or structure of Asian society and British society the sexual and social freedom of women and men will mean an increase in their use as sexual objects. Asian women in Britain are, therefore, in danger of further alienation from their real potential, their parental generation and their cultural heritage. The majority of Asian women in Britain do not come from the same socio-economic and educational background as their sisters in urban India and Pakistan but the fact that they are facing the same fundamental dilemmas is reason enough to open a dialogue and to establish mutual support and understanding in International Women's Year and beyond.

11

ANDREA MENEFEE SINGH

The Study of Women in India : Some Problems in Methodology

International Women's Year has seen in India, as elsewhere, a new wave of research projects and studies which focus on the position of women in society. There is a sudden awareness that women comprise nearly half the society, that they have long been discriminated against in nearly every sphere of life and that they have 'special' problems to face in a changing society. But while the *focus* on women is new, our approach to the study of women in society this year has no doubt been heavily, if not crucially, influenced by the treatment women have received by researchers in the past.

It is important to take stock of problems in methodology since the scholar's research design sets the basic form in which data are collected and the way in which data are to be interpreted and, therefore, the kinds of conclusions and generalisations the research will generate. It is the purpose of this paper to review some of the methodological problems which have been inherent in many of these studies in the past and, in so doing, to help to delineate ways in which these problems can be eliminated, or at least accommodated, in studies of women in the future.

WHO STUDIES WOMEN?

The study of women in South Asia, as elsewhere, has generally been a subject reserved for women. Men have rarely taken an interest in the study of women or related subjects like child rearing practices. In American anthropology Ruth Benedict and Margaret Mead pioneered the subject, establishing themselves as role models for other women interested in entering anthropology as professionals; in India Irawati Karve and Leela Dube performed a similar pioneering role. Thereafter, studies of these types tended to be reserved almost exclusively for women. This had its advantages since the role of women in anthropology as a discipline was legitimised and women were perhaps more widely accepted into universities and the teaching profession than in other academic disciplines. Nonetheless, until recently, studies of women and child rearing practices tended to take a back seat to other types of studies in anthropology in terms of status because these topics were considered female topics. Women anthropologists who wished to compete directly with male anthropologists often took up more general topics on the assumption that studies of women would not further their professional ambitions to the same extent.

In India and South Asia another factor was relevant. Women researchers, due to cultural constraints, found it difficult to pursue research topics which required them to mix freely with both males and females. Unmarried women are restricted in their movements outside their homes and universities by their parents; married women are perhaps even more restrained because of their own child rearing responsibilities and household duties combined with their husbands' reluctance to allow them freedom of movement outside the home. Many women have tended, therefore, to concentrate either on theoretical problems where their research can be carried out in the library, or on field projects which require contact only with women and children. Those who do try to go beyondt his limited realm of study may also find their research hampered by the attitudes of their subjects who seem to find it more acceptable for a foreign woman to move freely in their midst than an Indian woman whom they constantly try to fit into their own cultural mould.[1]

1. Leela Dube, "Woman's Worlds—Three Encounters", in Andre Beteille and T.N. Madan (eds.), *Encounter and Experience* (Delhi: Vikas Publishing House, 1975), pp. 157-177.

One of the consequences of this tendency has been that studies of women in South Asia tend to reflect the female point of view, not to mention the very special point of view of women who have themselves broken with tradition in pursuing professional careers. Another and perhaps the more serious consequence has been that the more general studies done by men (and those women competing with men in their approach) have tended either to leave women out or to assign to them an inconsequential rôle in society since these societies have been observed wholly from the male point of view. They assume that male roles, activities and ideals are representative of the society as a whole. It is significant that one can pick up almost any well known ethnography and find in the index a reference to women (with very few entries included), but no comparable reference to men. And it is not at all unusual to read an article or book on some aspect of South Asian society where the male author points out that as a male it was impossible for him to gain entrance into the female sphere of activities. In some cases he acknowledges the help of his wife in collecting this type of information; in other cases, we find that the exclusion of women from his research and observation does not hinder him in the least from going on to make generalisations regarding the society as a whole.[2]

While it is true that there are genuine problems for male researchers in participating in female spheres of activity in the highly sex-segregated societies of South Asia, this problem has probably been exaggerated and is not insurmountable. One of the problems has been the reluctance of the male researcher, once he has been accepted by the males of the seciety he is studying, to show an interest in things or exhibit behaviour which would threaten his male role. Laura Nader, in writing about her field experiences in an isolated Mexican village, found that because she moved in an uninhibited way among both males and females and wore pants and tennis shoes rather than the traditional female dress of the village a myth

2. See Hanna Papanek, "Men, Women and Work: Reflections on the Two-Person Career", in Joan Huber (ed.), *Changing Women in a Changing Society* (Chicago: University of Chicago Press, 1973), pp. 90-110, for a discussion of the problem of studying societies which are highly sex segregated.

eventually developed that she was neither male nor female but was capable of transforming herself from one to the other at will.[3] Such movement, it seems, requires that the researcher should not concentrate too carefully on acceptance into the society's sex roles, but should attempt to assume a neuter gender, or at least not to be too sensitive about being considered feminine or masculine. It would seem that if women like Nader are able to move freely in both male and female spheres, it would not be impossible for male researchers to achieve a similar freedom of movement. This is not to say that men should wear skirts or saris in the field, but that they should show a greater interest and ingenuity in including women in their studies. We could benefit greatly by a greater awareness and effort or the part of researchers, both male and female, to include both sexes fully in their studies. Such an integrated approach in fact could possibly change much of the theory that has evolved from studies which are based largely on the male-oriented point of view.

THE STUDY OF WOMEN AS A "CATEGORY"

This brings us to a question, "to what extent can women be studied as a separate category?" There are many who argue that women cannot be studied in isolation but should always be studied in relation to men. The underlying thesis is that 'women' exist as a category, whether biological or social, only when considered in relation to its natural counterpart 'man'. Otherwise, there is no justification for selecting sex as a category of analysis.

In a passage written more than 25 years ago, Margaret Mead argues for the integrated approach in words that seem relevant to the debate today:

> ...we are passing through a period of discrepancies in sex roles which are so conspicuous that efforts to disguise the price that both sexes pay are increasingly unsuccessful. Only if we perpetuate the habit of speaking about "the position of

3. Laura Nader, "From Anguish to Exultation," in P. Golde (ed.), *Women in the Field: Anthropological Experiences* (Chicago: Aldine Publishing Co., 1970), pp. 97-116.

> women" in a vacuum will we fail to recognise that where one sex suffers, the other sex suffers also. As surely as we believe that the present troublesome problems of sex adjustment are due to the position of women alone, we commit ourselves to a long series of false moves...
> adding mounting confusion to the difficulties born of a changing world-climate of opinion, a shifting technology, and an increasing rate and violence of the cultural change.[4]

In the same set of essays Mead demonstrates that there are hardly any sex-linked aptitudes or abilities which are universally acknowledged. In all societies, there are certain aptitudes and abilities which are considered typically male and others which are considered typically female, but these vary from culture to culture and what may be considered an innate ability of females in one culture may be considered an innate ability of males in another. Devaki Jain has approached the same problem, arguing, in essence, that one's approach to the formulation of a problem depends on one's belief regarding the natural relationship between men and women in society.[5] She goes on to contrast feminists who deny that biological differences can be extended to aptitudes with those persons who hold that they can be; research formulations thus depends, she argues, on whether women are considered similar to or different from men.[6]

There is certainly a need for a more integrated approach to the study of women in India, as elsewhere. Nonetheless, the most popular approach to the study of women in India has been to isolate categories of women for study on the basis of certain shared characteristics. The advantages and disadvantages of this approach deserve some mention.

The most widespread sampling technique among sociologists is to select a random or stratified sample of women from certain offices, professions or universities in order to measure the changing roles and attitudes of women. The reason for select-

4. Margaret Mead, *Male and Female* (New York: Dell Publishing Co., 1948), pp. 288-289.

5. Devaki Jain (ed.), *Indian Women* (New Delhi: Ministry of Information and Broadcasting, Government of India, 1975), p. xiii.

6. *Ibid.*

ing women from offices, professions or universities is that it is assumed that these are the women who are in the forefront of changing roles and attitudes within the wider society and who are or will be leaders of public opinion. Thus women who pursue higher education and/or modern occupations are considered both an index of change and predictors of trends among women in the wider society.

Unfortunately, the authors rarely present evidence in support of these underlying assumptions. It is interesting to note, for example, that employment of women in nearly all fields has registered a downward trend for more than a decade.[7] Thus it would seem that increases in the general level of education among women have not led to greater employment among women. The question also arises, to what extent educated women, especially those with higher education, are leaders of public opinion and, therefore, just what impact their attitudes and opinions have on the rest of the society. In this regard one might point to the responses of married students in Goldstein's study, most of whom claim to keep their educated opinions to themselves in order to avoid conflict with their husbands and their husbands' families.[8]

Another shortcoming is a failure to delineate carefully the traditional attitudes and practices against which change is presumably measured. As will be argued below, these may vary from region to region, and within a region from caste to caste. While some studies report the general caste and income level of the respondents or the respondents' fathers, little attempt is made to analyse the relevance of these factors to attitudes. Regional variation may actually be more important than caste variation within a particular region in the statistical prevalence of the joint family, according to Kolenda.[9] This she suggests in due to regional differrences in the institutionalised sanctions women may exercise over

7. *Towards Equality* : *Report of the Committee on the Status of Women in India* (New Delhi: Department of Social Welfare, Ministry of Education and Social Welfare, Government of India, 1974).

8. Rhoda L. Goldstein, "Tradition and Change in the Roles of Educated Indian Women," in Dhirendra Narain (ed.), *Explorations in the Family and Other Essays* (Bombay : Thacker and Company, 1975), pp. 268-287.

9. Pauline M. Kolenda, "Regional Differences in Indian Family Structure," in Robert I. Crane (ed.), *Regions and Regionalism in South Asian*

their husbands.[10] Thus the study of attitudes towards the joint family are likely to differ according to region of origin, and education is not necessarily the only factor related to a high incidence of negative attitudes, especially if the study is done in a region where the joint family is relatively unstable. Furthermore, there is plenty of evidence to show that the joint family, whatever the ideal, was never the predominant form, if only due to natural pressures of the domestic cycle. Thus one must be careful not to assume that the ideal was in fact the prevalent form, or that marked differences of opinion or attitudes did not exist among people in the past.

Changing attitudes and social behaviour: One of the techniques used to assess changing attitudes is to compare the attitudes of students to those of their parents. Parents, it is assumed, are representative of the previous generations' beliefs and practices and students are representative of the present generation's attitudes and future practices. Differences between generations are assumed to represent diachronic change within the wider society. There are a number of problems with this approach that would seem obvious. First, assessment of the attitudes of parents are often based on the students' assessment of their parents' attitudes, and one might question the reliability of this kind of data. (This criticism would also apply to Kapur's assessment of the attitudes of husbands towards working wives which is based on the women's description of their husbands' attitudes.)[11] Second, it would seem that an individual's position in the life cycle would be important to his or her perspective on such things as joint family living, religion or marriage. Differences in attitudes between generations are not necessarily indicative of historical social change. The student who says she would prefer to live in a nuclear family may very well end up living in a joint family, and by the time she has college-age children of her own be convinced that the advantages of joint family living far outweigh the disadvantages. Thus we may question the extent to which

Studies: An Exploratory Study (Monograph and Occasional Paper Series, Monograph No. 5 ; Duke University Press, 1967), pp. 147-226.

10. *Ibid.*, pp. 172.

11. Promilla Kapur, *Love, Marriage and Sex* (Delhi : Vikas Publishing House, 1973).

attitudes are accurate indicators of social behaviour. It would be illuminating, indeed, to follow up these studies of attitudes among students with a study of what the same students actually do and how their attitudes change because of this. Studies of attitudes too often stop short of relating attitudes to actual behaviour. Observation techniques, when combined with interview techniques, could greatly enhance the value and meaning of such studies. Attitudes towards caste could be contrasted with the caste composition of actual friendship groups, for example, and attitudes towards arranged marriage could be set against the existing conditions and practices (such as dating) which enhance or limit the possibility of unarranged marriages.

Another problem in studies of changing attitudes and roles is the lack of a clear-cut time dimension. In only one study—a study by Kapur[12] comparing the attitudes of working women towards love, marriage and sex—do we get an idea of the changing attitudes of women over a period of time. In 1959 and again in 1969, Kapur selected a random sample of women from the same offices in Delhi and Agra. Using the same interview structure with both samples, she finds considerable change has occurred over the last decade. Unfortunately, however, a number of methodological problems lead one to question whether the changes she perceives are reflections of processive changes in the wider society, or just differences between her two samples. The two samples of women, for example, come from very different backgrounds and one wonders if perhaps the growth of the institutions themselves has led to different standards of recruitment or if changes in the cities in which the offices and institutions are located have led to a different base population from which women are recruited. And since so few of the women in the original sample are included in the 1969 sample one is left wondering what has happened to these women who are no longer employed by these institutions—have they been promoted, have they changed jobs, have they been transferred to another city, or have they left the labour force altogether?

12. *Ibid.*

It is unfortunate that studies of women as a category rarely include comparisons with male students, husbands of female students or working women, or males in similar occupations. A notable exception to this trend is the study of working mothers in white collar occupations in Madras where interviews with husbands of working and non-working mothers were held regarding both attitudes and actual practices.[13] In most studies, however, one is left without a clear sense of the differences and similarities between the male and the female world view, or of the mutual adjustments necessary between men and women in situations where women go beyond their traditional roles.

Survey research: Finally, a word should be said about survey research which includes reports based on census data and other large-scale socio-economic surveys where females are contrasted with males in terms of basic demographic characteristics. First of all we find the basic problem of the inadequacy of existing categories arising, in part, from the tendency to adopt categories used in the more urban industrialised societies of the West. Such categories are not necessarily relevant to the Indian situation. For women, the catch-all category of housewife or non-worker seems inadequate for meaningful analysis or even for an accurate description of the status of women in any society. As Jain points out, whether or not a woman works outside her home or is directly renumerated for her activity are factors not necessarily related to the developmental productive work of Indian women.[14] There is a need to take greater notice of indigenous categories of work participation rates with regard to both males and females.

Studies based on this type of data are also conspicuous for their lack of qualitative data. Where correlations and trends are found to exist, caution must be exercised in accepting explanations which are general in form and based more on guess work than on solid empirical evidence. Correlations, after all, do not necessarily imply a causal relationship between two or

13. Madras School of Social Work, *Working Mothers in White-Collar Occupations* (Madras: 1970).

14. Devaki Jain, "Women's Status: Projects and Investigations," *Eve's Weekly*, 29 (n. 19, 1975), p. 53.

more factors. Explanations must be based on more intensive research techniques. To give an example, it is widely known that females in India have an abnormally high mortality rate compared to males. The most common explanation for this discrepancy is that females in India, due to their lower status, are often more undernourished than males (therefore being more likely to die when ill), and that they are less likely to receive health care when ill.[15] While these explanations may be correct it is possible that the explanation is far more complicated than this, especially if one considers the tremendous variation between male and female mortality rates in different regions of India, and even between different castes in the same region.[16]

I would not wish to be wholly critical of these approaches or of the works that have been cited above. After all, one needs to start somewhere in making up for the lack of attention that has been paid to the position of women in the past. Despite the many methodological problems which researchers have encountered in doing survey research and studies of changing attitudes, they have served a useful purpose. Attitudinal studies give us a qualitative view of society which is difficult to achieve through other techniques. Survey research, of course, is tremendously useful in describing trends, in suggesting possible relationships between various factors and in generating hypotheses for further testing. But there is a real need at this stage to refine and redefine categories used. This will lead to the generation of important data that do not exist. There is also a tremendous need for more indepth studies using qualitative techniques to test hypotheses that have already been generated. The multiplication of studies of women in India should lead naturally to the deeper consideration of these issues, and, as more comparative data become available, there is little doubt that scholars will become more cautious in trying to generalise for all of the society on the basis of such limited data.

15. Ashish Bose, "A Demographic Profile of Indian Women," in Devaki Jain (ed.), *op. cit.*

16. Rural Health Research Centre, *Interactions of Nutrition and Infection*; Final Report to I.C.M.R. (Punjab: Narangwal, April 1972).

FACTORS OF SPECIAL RELEVANCE

One of the issues which has received special attention in public forums and the popular press this year is whether the Women's Liberation Movement of the West is relevant to the Indian situation.

Romila Thapar writes:

> "Women's Lib does not have immediate relevance to the Indian social situation. It is the product of an urbanised middle-class with a large number of women trained in professions as a result of expanding educational opportunities whose professional skills are wasted by having to limit themselves to domestic work."[17]

Without being drawn into the wider debate of the appropriateness of the feminist movement in India, it would seem worthwhile here to take stock of some of the social and cultural factors which make the position of women in South Asia somewhat different from their Western counterparts. Whereas the goals of equality, justice and peace in human development may be the same for all people, the fundamental problems and solutions are bound to be different in different societies.

While it is difficult, if not impossible, to isolate all of the variables which directly or indirectly affect the status of women in South Asia, it is possible to point to a few well-known factors which are of special importance to the position of women in the South Asian situation and which should be taken into consideration when trying to generalise about women in India. These include region, caste, religion, family structure and systems of kinship and marriage. One of the problems in studying any aspect of South Asian society, of course is the complex interrelationship of all of these factors, and it might be expected that this problem would be of some importance in the study of women as well. Although I shall discuss each of these factors separately it should be remembered that none of these factors should be taken singly as the primary factor in

17. Romila Thapar, "Looking Back in History," in Devaki Jain (ed.), *op. cit.*

determining the status of women, and that these are not necessarily the only factors which should be considered.

REGION

One of the usual ways of organising material on India when discussing the society and culture is on the basis of regions—geographic, cultural, or historical.[18]

These categories often overlap to a great extent and are used for different purposes and levels of explanation. For anthropologists, language is usually considered the most important variable in delineating cultural regions since language is the primary means of transmitting culture, especially where low rates of literacy and a well developed oral tradition exist. In India there are four major language families distributed over quite distinct geographic regions. Each of these linguistic areas have been shown to be somewhat unique in terms of the values and myths associated with women, as well as systems of caste, family structure, kinship and marriage—all of which affect the status of women in a fundamental way. Karve writes:

> The linguistic regions possess a certain homogeneity of culture, traits and kinship organisation. The common language makes communication easy, sets the limits of marital connections and confines kinship mostly within the language region. Common folk songs and common literature characterise such an area.[19]

Thus one might argue that the Bengali-speaking women of India have more in common with the Bengali-speaking women of Bangladesh than with women in other linguistic regions of India.[20] Yalman has argued that basic structural

18. See Robert I. Crane (ed.), *Regions and Regionalism in South Asian Studies : An Exploratory Study* (Monograph and Occasional Papers Series, Monograph No. 5; Durham: Duke University Press, 1967), for a discussion of how regions may be defined according to different variables and for different research purposes.

19. Irawati Karve, *Kinship Organisation in India* (Bombay : Asia Publishing House, 1965), p. 4.

20. See T.N. Madan, "The Dialectic of Ethnic and National Boundaries in the Evolution of Bangladesh," in *Studies in Asian Social Development*, No. 2, (ed.) Suren Navlakha, (Delhi: Vikas Publishing House, 1974).

similarities exist between the people of Ceylon and the people of South India in their beliefs regarding women, and this he attributes to the similarities in language and the accompanying similarities in structure of thought.[21] Kolenda, in a survey of literature on family structure, finds distinct differences in the statistical occurrence of joint family households in different regions of India which she attributes to the regional differences in woman's control over certain means of rewarding or punishing her husband for his compliance or non-compliance with her wishes.[22]

There are many more studies which trace the social and cultural similarities and differences in regions of South Asia. I just wish to point out here that one must be careful to take regional differences into account when generalising about women in South Asian society. One might be able to generalise about women in Bengal and Bangladesh, and women in South India and Ceylon, more accurately than about Indian women generally. Not to oversimplify the situation, one should also remember that most languages in India are part of a pan-regional cultural complex in some respects, but there are numerous cross-cutting factors which sometimes complicate the influence of regional and linguistic factors. Smartha Brahmins of Tamil Nadu and Karnataka, for example, might have more in common with each other in some respects than with Harijans from their own village, but Brahmins of the South might have more in common in other respects with non-Brahmins of their own region than with Brahmins of Uttar Pradesh. Thus the importance of regionalism depends very much on the purpose of the research, but it should certainly be taken into account when making generalisations about women based on studies of women in particular regions.

RELIGION

Religion in India, as has been widely acknowledged, plays an important role in defining the status of women, especially

21. Nur Yalman, *Under the Bo Tree : Studies in Caste, Kinship and Marriage in the Interior of Ceylon* (Berkeley : University of California Press, 1967).

22. Pauline M. Kolenda, *op. cit.*

regarding beliefs about their inherent character structure, natural strengths and weaknesses and their rights and obligations towards men, society and God. The fact that India hosts several major religions, each with very different myths, ideologies, beliefs and ritual practices, suggests that the status of women would vary tremendously according to religion. These religions include Hinduism, Jainism, Buddhism, Sikhism, Christianity, Islam, Zoroastrianism and Judaism. Of these, Hinduism, Buddhism, Jainism and Sikhism originated in India, the latter three representing major breaks with Hindu ideology. As Thapar points out, Buddhism and Jainism both supported greater freedom for women than did Brahminism.[23] One might also add Sikhism to her list.

In an interesting variation on this theme, Furer-Haimendorf suggests that the Buddhists' "tolerant attitude to sexual laxity" might be related to the occurrence of polyandry among the Buddhists of Ceylon and the Himalayan regions.[24] He stops short of suggesting that Buddhist ideology is a causative factor in the development of polyandry, although he considers Buddhist morality to be "permissive of a type of sexual arrangements unacceptable to the more puritan Hindu moralist."[25]

In addition to ideological differences between the major religions regarding the position of women in society, there have been different religious streams within the major religions which should be taken into account. The *Bhakti* movement in Hinduism, for example, offered women a larger role in Hindu worship and greater freedom and equality than they had enjoyed previously. Unfortunately, however, we have very little empirical evidence to suggest how widely the effects of such movements were felt in society, or how they affected the status of women in their secular roles. In a study of South Indian migrants in a neighbourhood of Delhi, I found that four out of nine women who participated individually in

23. Romila Thapar, *op. cit.*, p. 13.

24. Christoph Von Furer-Haimendorf, *Caste and Kin in Nepal, India and Ceylon.* (Bombay : Asia Publishing House, 1966) p. 8.

25. *Ibid.*, p. 9.

voluntary associations attended female *bhajana* associations.[26] These women, however, represented only a very small proportion of South Indian women in the neighbourhood, and I found little evidence that such participation affected their status as women in a broader sense.

Another aspect of religion which may be of no small importance in India is the difference between popular Hinduism and Sanskritic Hinduism in their consequence for women. The tendency of those discussing religious ideology, beliefs and attitudes is to assume that the norms of what we might call the "high religion" are equally applicable to all people. It is well known, however, that there has long been differential access to religious knowledge among Hindus with the Brahmins having almost total monopoly over access to the Sanskritic texts and the right to interpret them. In popular Hinduism there is an emphasis on female deities, spirit possession and supernatural cures which are quite different from the beliefs and practices of Brahmanical Hinduism. Harper notes the high incidence of spirit possession among young married Brahmin women in a Mysore village and suggests that possession represents one means of coping with the tremendous strains inherent in this structural position. (Other solutions include fasting and suicide.)[27] The consequences of most of these popular beliefs and practices for women in the society, however, are not adequately understood.

In the realm of ritual beliefs and practices, two other important topics come to mind. The first is the concept of pollution. Beliefs and practices regarding pollution in India have received wide attention by anthropologists, many of whom consider concepts of female susceptibility to pollution to be central to the structure of the whole society.[28] Another aspect of ritual which has so far received very little attention

26. Andrea Menefee Singh, *Neighbourhood and Social Networks in Urban India : South Indian Voluntary Associations in Delhi* (Delhi : Marwah Publications, 1975).

27. Edward B.Harper, "Spirit Possession and Social Structure," in Bala Ratnam (ed.), *Anthropology on the March* (Madras : Social Science Association, 1963), pp. 165-177.

28. See Nur Yalman, *op. cit.* and Mary Douglas, *Purity and Danger* (New York : Praeger Publications, 1966).

is the different roles played by males and females in ritual performances. It appears that in ritual performances, as in many other areas of social life, there is a dichotomy between male and female spheres of activity. LaBrack suggests that in Hinduism female ritual activity focuses around the domestic hearth, while male ritual activity involves a more public role.[29] In only a few ritual activities do men and women participate together, but even then they rarely share an equal ritual role. This is a dimension of religion which needs more study.

Another question is the extent to which Hindu beliefs and practices have influenced other religions in India. We know, for example, that caste is not limited to Hindus, although caste is usually considered a Hindu structure. There is a need to know more about actual beliefs and practices and how they differ from religious ideology among the non-Hindu religions. This is important in trying to assess differences according to religion in the status of women within India, as well as when making cross-cultural comparisons.

There are a few studies of women which have taken religion into consideration, but the treatment has been brief and generally superficial. Census figures and demographic surveys tell us that fertility rates, urban residence and income differ for the major religions in India, but as yet we do not know the causes of these differences nor their consequences for the status of women. In a study of working mothers in white collar occupations in Madras it was found that Christian women had a much higher rate of participation in white collar occupations than Hindu women and that Muslim women had a much lower rate.[30] The authors suggest that Christians

29. Bruce La Brack, "Male and Female Ritual Roles in Khalapur," Paper presented at the Fourth Annual Meeting of the Pacific Coast Association for Asian Studies, Los Angeles, June 21, 1971. Ursula Sharma, "The Problem of Village Hinduism: Fragmentation and Integration," *Contributions to Indian Sociology* (New Series), IV (December, 1970), pp. 14-15, differentiates between individual and public ritual and notes the absence of women in the latter. See also Pauline Mahar Kolenda, "Religious Anxiety and Hindu Fate," in Edward B. Harper (ed.), *Religion in South Asia* (Seattle: University of Washington Press, 1964), p. 78, for examples of female ritual concerns in Khalapur. La Brack's analysis was based on Kolenda's field notes.

30. Madras School of Social Work, *op. cit.*, p. 18.

place fewer restrictions on the activities of women than other religions, and, therefore, Christian women have acquired more education and vocational training than women of other communities.[31] Hate found similar religious differences in rates of participation of working women in Bombay and Poona but offers a different explanation.[32] She claims that since there is no joint family system among the Christians, women work out of necessity or the expection of the eventual need to be self-supporting.[33] Both studies attribute the low participation of Muslim women to greater conservatism.[34] This question calls for more rigorous attention from researchers.

Too often the religious factor is left out altogether. Cormack, for example, tells us that her sample of Indian women studying at Columbia University includes Christians and Muslim women, but goes on to title her book *The Hindu Woman* and omits any further reference to the religion of her subjects.[35] In a study of marital adjustment among working women, Kapur includes non-Hindus in her sample but dismisses it as irrelevant to marital adjustment[36]; in another study she says that she excluded non-Hindus "In order to have a homogeneous group for study and also to delimit the scope of the study",[37] but elsewhere she says she included Sikhs, Buddhists and Jains in her definition of Hindu since these religions come under the jurisdiction of the Hindu Marriage Act of 1955.[38]

CASTE

There are a number of factors related to caste in India which clearly affect the position of women in society. Srinivas

31. *Ibid.*, p. 11.
32. Chandrakala A. Hate, *Changing Status of Women* (Bombay: Allied Publishers, 1969), pp. 36-37.
33. *Ibid.*, p. 38.
34. Madras School of Social Work, *op. cit.*, p. 11; Hate, *ibid.*
35. Margaret Cormack, *The Hindu Woman* (New York : Columbia University Press, 1953).
36. Promilla Kapur, *Marriage and the Working Woman in India* (Delhi : Vikas Publications, 1970), p. 59.
37. Promilla Kapur, 1973 *op. cit.*, p. 15.
38. *Ibid.*, p. 12.

and Beteille suggest that among the poor and low castes the relationship between men and women is more egalitarian than among the higher castes, and that when lower castes try to raise their status through Sanskritisation one of the consequences is lowering of the status of women, making them subordinate to men in moral, economic and ritual terms.[39] Stokes, in her study of a Bihar village, found Harijan women more open, expressive, joking and willing to mix freely than upper caste women.[40] One of her informants, a *Dai* (midwife), in fact, expressed very little envy of upper caste women, who, according to her, have nothing to do except fight with each other.[41] Thus it would seem that the differences between high caste women and low caste women are great.

There are a number of caste-related factors in addition to the general concept of the relative freedom of women that can be gleaned from the literature, but of special importance are differences in kinship and marriage practices. A very interesting example of how these may differ within a particular region is the case of the Nayars and Namboodiris of Kerala. In a traditional society, Nayars maintained a matrilineal system of descent whereby status and property were inherited through the maternal line. They also practised natolocal residence where brothers and sisters stayed together with their mother, mother's sisters and their children and maternal uncles; husbands had visiting privileges only. Namboodiri Brahmins, on the other hand, maintained a strict patrilineal system with inheritance passing through the male line and patrilocal residence where only the eldest son was allowed to marry and inherit property. Other sons were free to form alliances with Nayar women in marriage ceremonies which were considered legitimate by the Nayars, but not recognised by the Namboodiris. Among other things, this led to large numbers of Namboodiri women who were

39. M.N. Srinivas, "Status of Women in India : I—Tradition and Folk Norms," *The Times of India* (New Delhi), April 18, 1975; Andre Beteille, "The Position of Woman in Indian Society," in Devaki Jain (ed.), *op. cit.*

40. Olivia Stokes, "Women of Rural Bihar," in Devaki Jain (ed.), *op. cit.*, p. 218.

41. *Ibid.*

unable to marry. Thus there was a structural relationship between these two castes in which the position of women was entirely different. While this is probably a unique case, there is little doubt that differences in kinship systems, marriage practices and patterns of residence among castes in other regions of India have very important consequences for the status of women.

We also find caste differences throughout most of India relating to the giving of dowry or bride price in marriage, both of which have very limiting consequences for women. The ease with which divorcee may be achieved, the possibility of remarriage for widows and divorces, the extent to which women are allowed to move out of their house or caste cluster, the possibility of working and what types of work are considered appropriate to the women of the caste—all these things are defined by caste and are basic to the consid-deration of the position of women in society.

Of course, these things may also be subject to the influence of other factors such as religion or region. Nearly all castes in South India, for example, find cross-cousin marriage acceptable while hardly any North Indian castes would dream of such a marriage. As Kolenda ,points out, the incidence of bride price, divorce and remarriage varies in practice from region to region, despite differences in the ideal among castes within one region.[42] Still, it is important to consider caste-related differences when one sets out to discuss social change. Depending on caste tradition, actual change may be in two different directions, or even irrelevant. One might expect that even among educated women, caste tradition would be an important factor in shaping attitudes.

Another interesting question regarding caste is the extent to which caste background affects the woman's self-image and influences her selection of a role model or reference group. As Beteille and Srinivas point out, when the lower and middle castes imitate the Brahmins, the position of women may be adversely affected.[43] But it is not at all certain that Brahmins provide the only or even the most common

42. Pauline M. Kolenda, 1967, *op. cit.*
43. M.N. Srinivas, *op. cit.* ; Andre Beteille, *op. cit.*

reference group for non-Brahmin women. It is possible that as the Brahmins are progressively stripped of their traditional powers, other important role models will emerge. In fact, one can question the validity of this model in the past in North India where Brahmins have long occupied a lower status in society than Brahmins in the South. Another important question is who provides the reference group for Brahmin women? It is interesting to note that both Goldstein[44] and Vreed-De Stuers,[45] in studies of changing attitudes among female college students, found Brahmin women constituted the majority of their sample. Thus the change in attitudes they found are all the more interesting for what it tells us about Brahmin women in modern society. All this suggests that the dynamics of upward mobility for females as well as males is more complex than most writers have assumed.

In the urban arena, caste continues to operate as an important factor. The caste system—i.e., inter-dependence of castes at the village level—may be largely irrelevant to the social life of the city, but caste continues to be a primary marker of social identity. In a study of middle class South Indians in Delhi, I found that caste was one of the most important factors in the formation of social networks and in organising voluntary associations.[46] It also appeared to be related to the types of occupations women pursue and whether they would work before marriage or after marriage. At the middle class level, however, it was found that only a small portion of women are employed. In a study of lower class migrants in Delhi which is now in progress,[47] I have found that a much higher proportion of women are employed. Even at this level, however, caste and region play an important part in determining whether a woman will work or not and what type of employment she will take up if she does work. On the one hand, traditional caste occupation plays an important role in evaluating the suitability of different types of work and

44. Rhoda L. Goldstein, *op. cit.*

45. Cora Vreede-De Stuers, "Attitudes of Jaipur Girl Students Towards Family Life," in Dhirendra Narain (ed.), *op. cit.*, pp. 151-162.

46. Andrea Menefee Singh, *op. cit.*

47. The research project, "The Position of Women in Migrant Bastis in Delhi," is being carried out by the Indian Social Institute, New Delhi.

providing training and skills which might be adaptable to the urban situation; and, on the other hand, caste and village networks provide the mechanisms through which women are recruited to certain kinds of employment in the city. Bellwinkel has discussed these mechanisms with regard to Rajasthani contract labour in Delhi[48] and Lubell notes a similar tendency for migrants from certain castes and regions to dominate specific areas of employment in Calcutta.[49] The importance of caste as a vehicle to employment for women in urban areas needs more study. It is unfortunate that most studies dealing with occupational mobility, especially those that contrast traditional village occupations with modern urban occupations, focus only on men.[50] The occupational mobility of women should be considered just as important.

FAMILY STRUCTURE

Studies of women in South Asia have tended to focus on attitudes towards the family and marriage as an indicator of the changing position of women. One of the reasons for this has been the assumption that the forces of modernisation and urbanisation will lead to the breaking down of the joint family as well as an increasing number of unarranged marriages (or at least a larger degree of choice in arranged marriages). Because of this focus I have chosen here to discuss some of the aspects of family structure and marriage that might be of particular relevance to the status of women in society.

To begin with, it is necessary to take a careful look at the assumption that joint families are on the decrease. A number of recent studies lead us to question this assumption. In a comparison of family structures in a village near Poona in

48. Maren Bellwinkel, "Rajasthani Countract Labour in Delhi: A Case Study of the Relationship between Company, Middleman and Workers," *Sociological Bulletin*, 22 (March, 1973). pp. 78-79.

49. Harold Lubell, *Calcutta: Its Urban Development and Employment Prospects* (Geneva: International Labour Office, 1974), pp. 60-63.

50. See, for example, G.N. Ramu and Paul D. Wiebe, "Occupational and Educational Mobility in Relation to Caste in India," *Sociology and Social Research*, 58 (n.l., 1973), pp. 84–94, and Gene Kassebaum and N.E.C. Vidya Sagar, "A Survey of Caste and Occupational Mobility in a Small City in India," *Man in India*, 54 (n. 4, Oct-Dec, 1974), pp. 253-269.

1819, 1958 and 1967, Kolenda found that the joint family, if anything, is increasing—even after she manipulated the data from 1819 to show the maximum number of possible joint families and the modern data to show the minimum number.[51] Singer notes that among the industrial elite in Madras city, the joint family is both structurally and functionally compatible with the requirements of modern industry and urban life.[52] Other authors have found "limited change" in the direction of nuclear families, but this seems to be conditioned by the extent to which occupation requires geographic mobility rather than purely urban residence.[53] Nuclear family living may be out of necessity or expediency in such cases rather than the result of changing attitudes or ideas. In my own research I found a higher incidence of joint families among long-time Punjabi residents in Karol Bagh, most of whom were self-employed businessmen, than among South Indian migrants, most of whom were in salaried white-collar occupations.[54] Thus it would appear that the pressures of urbanisation and modernisation do not have equal impact or consequences for all segments of the population, whether we are speaking of the rural or the urban setting.

The next question, then, is how do these changes, when they do happen, affect women, and its corollary, how do changes in the traditional position or roles of women affect the stability of the joint family. Most researchers have assumed that changes in the attitudes and status of women, especially those associated with the pursuit of higher education and the opening of new avenues of employment, are related to the breaking down of the joint family. But the evidence of such a direct relationship between attitudes and conse-

51. Pauline Mahar Kolenda, "Family Structure in Village Lonikand, India: 1819, 1958 and 1967," *Contributions to Indian Sociology* (New Series), IV(Dec. 1970), pp. 50-72.

52. Milton Singer, "The Indian Joint Family in Modern Industry." in Milton Singer (ed.), *Structure and Change in Indian Society* (Chicago: Aldine Publishing Co., 1968).

53. See, for example, M.S. Gore, *Urbanisation and Family Change* (Bombay: Popular Prakashan, 1968) and Sylvia Vatuk, *Kinship and Urbanisation : White Collar Migrants in North India* (Berkeley, Los Angeles: University of California Press, 1972).

54. Andrea Menefee Singh, *op. cit.*

quences can be questioned. While Kolenda suggests that a woman may exert a deciding influence over joint family living, she argues that her bargaining power must be

> institutionalised in such cultural practices as a wife's right to a legal divorce, bride-price negotiation of marriage, economic and social support to a couple from the wife's natal family or lineage.[55]

The key point is whether the husband gets economic or social support from the wife's kin that might modify or override the advantages of joint family living. She also dismisses the argument that power derived from making an economic contribution to the family income through working is related to jointness since there is a high incidence of joint families among castes whose women work in the fields in some regions and not in others.[56] One might add that working women do not necessarily maintain full control over their own incomes. Goldstein found that 77 per cent of the employed women in her sample of highly educated women turned over more than half their earnings to their families.[57] In fact, she found that the majority of her respondents, whether married or not, felt that education would *help* them fit into a joint family, that it "will not cause them to challenge the traditional expectations of obedience to husbands and in-laws, but will enable them to handle role requirements better".[58]

Whether or not a woman lives in a joint family, however, may have important consequences for her position in society and the opportunities that are open to her. There is no doubt that in many cases joint family living restricts the freedom of women (especially younger women), with regard to movement outside the home, decision making in financial matters or running of the household, and even in the dress she may wear. But the nuclear family has its own problems in India. When geographic mobility necessitates the establishment of

55. Pauline M. Kolenda, 1967, *op. cit.*, p. 216.
56. *Ibid.*, p. 215.
57. Rhoda L. Goldstein, *op. cit.*, p. 282.
58. *Ibid.*, p. 284.

a neolocal residence, the joint family may continue to be the ideal, carrying with it obligations such as remittance of a significant part of the couple's income, participation in family ceremonies (sometimes at great cost if the distance is great), care for the aged or disabled, maintenance or supervision of family property, and so on. This, combined with the lack of other members of the family to share domestic chores and child-rearing responsibilities, or to provide adult company to alleviate the drudgery of household work may be far more limiting in the end than joint family living.

It sometimes happens, in fact, that joint family living frees women for employment who would otherwise find it impossible to handle both an outside job and domestic and child-rearing responsibilities. In the Madras study, it was found that half of the women who had once worked but withdrew from employment later did so due to increased child care and household responsibilities at home.[59] At the lower class level, although it is common for female construction workers and domestic workers to carry at least their youngest children with them to work, joint family living may case the burden of working women and increase the quality of child and household care. Mody and Mhatre describe a ease where a 45-year old woman living in a large Bombay slum was looking forward to the arrival of a new daughter-in-law to free her from the household work and enable her to return to selling vegetables in the market place.[60] Thus it is not just the younger female members of the joint family who may benefit; older women may also find greater freedom. This type of sharing of female role responsibilities appears more acceptable and perhaps more realistic in the Indian setting than the Western alternative of shared responsibilities be-ween husband and wife, although the Madras study has shown that even in India, husbands of working women participate in household tasks to a far greater extent than husbands

59. Madras School of Social Work, *op. cit.*, p. 34.

60. Susan N. Mody and Sharayu Mhatre "Slum Women of Bombay," in Devaki Jain (ed.), *op. cit.*, p. 241.

of non-working women.[61] Of course it can be argued that as long as domestic and child-rearing chores are considered beneath the dignity of men, women cannot achieve equality. But we must also point to the alternatives of the joint family and, for middle and upper class women of hiring full-time domestic workers (many of whom are men) in the Indian setting which are not usually realistic possibilities for women in the West.

I have touched here on only a few of the aspects of family structure which are of importance to the study of women in India. It is clear that we need much more information than is presently available on the dynamics of family life in both rural and urban situations, and the consequences of family structures for women in society.

KINSHIP AND MARRIAGE

I shall not go into detail here about the great variety of systems of kinship and marriage found in South Asia since I have alluded to many of these differences above as they relate to region, religion and caste. Whether inheritance passes through the paternal line or the maternal line of descent, whether dowry or bride price is given at the time of marriage (and who maintains control over these assets), whether cousin marriage is preferred or considered incestuous, whether the custom of levirate is practised, whether polygamy or polyandry are acceptable forms of marriage, whether hypergamous unions or marriages between men and women of equal status are preferred, where one draws the lines of endogamy and exogamy, and under what circumstances deviance from these norms are allowed—all of these things are clearly of immense importance to the understanding of the position of women in the society. In much of the general theory on kinship and marriage systems, it is significant that women are treated as pawns in the system, being "exchanged" or cementing "alliances" between males in the system. *Ego*, the person from whom descent or marriage patterns are traced, is always a male (which is often

61. Madras School of Social Work, *op. cit.*, p. 59; see also Hate, *op. cit.*, p. 86. Hate reports that many of her responders would not have been able to work were it not for their living in a joint family.

confusing to female students when personal pronouns are used to describe the action). Anthropologists have even gone to great lengths to explain how men in matrilineal systems continue to be the dominant force in the system. In India, one can find nearly every system of kinship and marriage which is described in the literature and it would seem to be an ideal setting for research into these systems from the female point of view. Nonetheless, the large body of literature on the subject which already exists should be examined by any researcher concerned with problems relating to the position of women in society, or with their changing roles and attitudes.[62]

One aspect of marriage which cuts across specific systems of kinship and marriage in India, and which has been widely discussed in studies of changing roles and attitudes of women, is the system of arranged marriages. Arranged marriages are practised by nearly all segments of the society, with the partial exception of portions of the Anglo-Indian community who find unarranged marriages acceptable, but also practise arranged marriages. It is significant that the Indian view of "love marriages" is filled with as much awe (if not thinly veiled disapproval) as the Western view of arranged marriage. This is clearly an emotion-tinged subject which makes objectivity difficult. Nonetheless, the system of arranged marriage certainly has important consequences for the position of women in society and it seems worthwhile to take note of some of the issues involved.

Recent studies have not found much change in attitudes towards arranged marriage among college students: there is some evidence, in fact, that modern women are more in favour of arranged marriages than they were ten years age.[63] This finding suggests that the system is not necessarily linked to the individual's level of education or the wider processes of urbanisation and modernisation.

Higher education, however, may have the effect of limiting marital choices for women where it is considered imperative

62. See for example, Irawati Karve, *op. cit.*, and Veena Das, "Marriage among the Hindus," in Devaki Jain (ed.), *op. cit.*, pp. 69-86.

63. Comment made by Promilla Kapur in a panel discussion, "The Problems of Working Mothers," India International Centre, August 13, 1974.

that the husband have equal, and preferably more, education than his wife.[64] Still, we cannot assume (as most researchers have) that this is a universal norm. Among the Punjabi business community in Delhi, for example, daughters often receive higher education than sons, higher education for males being considered of no great importance in developing business skills and an early entrance into the business being deemed more important to success in business than continuing education. Parents of these young men, however, often seek out girls with B.A.s or M.A.s who, it is expected, will bring "culture" into the household and will be better able to guide the children in their studies.[65] It would seem that factors related to region, caste, and occupation need greater consideration in analysing new trends in arranged marriages.

We know, in fact, very little about the elements of personal preference which enter into the negotiations for marital matches, and how or why these are likely to vary. It is common to note trends in the marriage advertisements of a well-known newspaper, but it is not clear to what extent these preferences are representative of the wider population (most of whom manage to arrange marriages without the help of classified ads) or to what extent, for the matter, the stereotyped descriptions ("beautiful homely girl"; "highly qualified boy") are accurate descriptions. The language used in classified ads includes "code words" such as "decent marriage" which may be taken to mean an elaborate ceremony and dowry included, but "caste no bar" cannot be taken literally since there are probably a host of considerations which are qualifications for going beyond the boundaries of caste and a limit to which caste boundaries will be crossed. The classified ads represent only an initial screening process for those unable to find suitable matches elsewhere or those wishing to broaden their choice. We need to know more about what happens after contact is made, whether through advertisements, paid marriage brokers or through more traditional channels.

The system of arranged marriages functions in many ways to limit the life-chances and options of males as well as females

64. Rhoda L. Goldstein, *op. cit.*, p. 272.

65. K.R. Unni also noted this tendency among businessmen in Old Delhi (private communication with the author, October 1969).

in the society. It makes young people in South Asia highly dependent on their parents at a time when young people in the West are usually independent and in pursuit of their own careers and life styles. It prevents them from trying out new roles and experiences which their elders believe would harm their marriage chances, creating pressure for conformity to traditional roles and expectations. At the same time it reinforces and supports the persistence of caste and ethnic groups within the wider society by eliminating marriage contact across these boundaries.

Many people seem to believe that dowry and bride price can be eliminated without changes in the system of arranged marriages, but despite legislation this has not occurred. One could argue that as long as marriages are arranged in a highly limited and competitive market through negotiations between elders (who, it may be assumed, have their own interests to look after in addition to whatever considerations they may have for the preferences of their children), dowry and bride price are bound to enter into the negotiations. It is interesting to note that the Chinese, in the Marriage Law of 1950, abolished arranged marriages along with wife-buying, polygamy, infanticide and child marriage, and legalised divorce and widow remarriage, in the belief that all of these practices were inextricably linked.[66] The result has not been the emergence of a Western-type system where marriage is based primarily on romantic love, apparently, but a situation where young couples agree to marriage on the basis of both traditional and modern Chinese values, keeping in mind their parents' preferences and advice.[67]

This system is not, however, without its benefits for women, and does have a number of advantages over the *laissez-faire* system of the West. First, a dowry, which usually includes moveable property of some value such as furniture, saris and jewellery, provides a certain basic security (to the extent that the girl can maintain control over these assets) that she can fall back on under adverse conditions. Second, it is quite

66. Carol Tavris, "Women in China: the Speak-Bitterness Revolution," *Psychology Today* 7 (n. 12., 1974), p. 49.

67. *Ibid.*

likely that parents, where their daughter's happiness is their overriding consideration, because of their long experience in marriage and their intimate knowledge of their daughter's strengths and weaknesses, may be able to make a far wiser choice of a life-long mate for their daughter than if she were left to make the choice wholly on her own. Third, it is possible that the modern Indian girl is free to pursue higher education and career opportunities single-mindedly to an extent that her Western counterpart is not since she can take comfort in the knowledge that her parents will take up the time-consuming task of finding her a satisfactory mate when the time is right.[68] There are other advantages to the system, no doubt, but these are enough to demonstrate that care must be taken in interpreting attitudes toward arranged marriages as typically modern or even in the best interest of the educated or working women.

The system of arranged marriages appears to be at the core of the society's ability to sustain traditional images and roles for women, despite the revolutionary changes in the economic and political spheres of the wider society. Regionalism, caste, religion, and, to some extent even the joint family, find reinforcement through this practice. The complex interrelationship of all these factors is a condition specific to the Indian situation and deserves special attention by those interested in the study of women in the Indian society.

In sum, India, with all its cultural diversity, provides us with a fertile ground for the study of women. At present we know relatively little about Indian women due to the tendency of researchers either to exclude them from analysis, or to focus only on limited samples of women who are not necessarily representative of women in the wider society. I have argued that a more integrated approach to the study of women would greatly enhance our understanding of her position in society. Studies of women have typically focused on attitudes and beliefs without reference to actual behaviour and without careful delineation of the relevance of important social and

68. Marjorie R. Wood noted this advantage in a panel discussion on "The Problems of Working Mothers" see n. 63.

cultural variables such as religion, caste, region, family structure or systems of kinship and marriage. Such knowledge is essential for the understanding of the special problems of women in Indian society and would seem to be a prerequisite for arriving at solutions and policy decisions meant to alleviate these problems and to create an atmosphere of greater equality.

APPENDIX

*Draft International Plan of Action**

I. BACKGROUND TO THE PLAN

1. In subscribing to the Charter, the peoples of the United Nations undertook specific commitments: "To save succeeding generations from the scourge of war . . . , to reaffirm faith in fundamental human rights, in the dignity and worth of the human person, in the equal rights of men and women, and of nations large and small, . . . and to promote social progress and better standards of life in larger freedom."

2. Many conventions, declarations, formal recommendations and other instruments have been adopted since then reinforcing and elaborating these fundamental principles and objectives. Some of them seek to safeguard and promote the human rights and fundamental freedoms of all persons without discrimination of any kind. Some have the specific aim of eliminating sex discrimination and promoting the equal rights of men and women. Others deal with general concepts of economic and social progress and development and include international strategies, programmes and plans of action.

3. In these various instruments the international community has condemned sex discrimination as fundamentally unjust,

*This Draft International Plan of Action (E/CONF. 66/CC/2 of Feb. 8 1975) was submitted for the consideration of the Consultative Committee for the World Conference of the International Women's Year.

an offence against human dignity and an infringement of human rights. It has proclaimed that the full and complete development of a country, the welfare of the world and the cause of peace require the maximum participation of women as well as men in all fields. It has declared that all human beings without distinction have the right to enjoy the fruits of social progress and should, on their part, contribute to it. It has included the full integration of women in the total development effort as a stated objective of the decade of the 1970s.

4. More recently, at the World Population Conference and the World Food Conference, both held in 1974, explicit recognition was given to the need to improve the situation of women as a significant factor in the solution of problems of population and world food shortages.

5. The international community has thus concerned itself with the status of women from the viewpoint both of human rights and social justice and of its implications for social progress and development.

6. Despite these solemn pronouncements and notwithstanding the work accomplished by the United Nations Commission on the Status of Women and the specialised agencies concerned, the progress made in translating these accepted principles into practical reality has been slow and uneven.

7. It was this situation which prompted the United Nations to proclaim 1975 as International Women's Year, and to call for intensified action to promote equal rights, opportunities and responsibilities of both sexes, to ensure the full integration of women in the total development effort, and to involve women widely in international co-operation and the strengthening of world peace.

8. Discrimination against women has existed throughout history and in most societies, manifesting itself in different ways, both overtly and covertly, and in differing degrees. The causes are complex. The biological factor of child-bearing and women's traditional role of child-rearing have often been used to justify discrimination against women. Political, economic, social, cultural and psychological factors also play a significant role, however, and the question should be considered as a multidimensional, multifaceted issue.

9. There are basic similarities, and major differences in the status of women in different countries and regions of the world, rooted in the political, economic and social structure and in the cultural framework of each country. There are also marked differences in the needs and problems of different categories of women within countries, which must be properly assessed and taken into account.

10. In general, it can be said that, on a global basis, substantial advances have been made in the legal field and the principle of equality of both sexes before the law has been written into the basic laws of a great number of countries. Nevertheless, discriminatory laws, customs, practices and attitudes persist in many parts of the world, and the gap between the *de jure* and *de facto* situations of women, especically in the political, economic and social fields, is very wide. In many instances, also, women have remained outside the mainstream of progress and development, and their talents and abilities have not been utilised in the promotion of better standards of living for all.

11. The resurgence of women's movements in the past decade in many countries has brought the question of sex discrimination to the forefront of public awareness. While these movements cannot in any sense be described as homogeneous, one result of their activities is that many women have become more conscious of their own lack of opinions and aware of instances of subtle as well as overt discrimination practised in long-established social institutions, such as the family, school and university, the work place, the law courts and the mass communications media.

12. Many nations are at present facing urgent and pressing social and economic problems that demand solution, if the very survival and well-being of their citizens is to be safeguarded. These include: high rates of unemployment and under-employment; mass poverty; rapid population growth; food shortages; malnutrition and starvation; under-development; inadequate school and health facilities; lack of trained manpower; shortages of housing and lack of amenities; and undesirable side effects of rapid urbanisation and social change. Each one of these problems is complex in itself, and their solution is rendered more difficult because they are interrelated

and often found simultaneously, the presence of one aggravating the other. There is growing evidence, moreover, that the status of women and many of these problems are interrelated and that improvements in the situation of women may be a vital factor in the alleviation of the problems.

13. For example, rural women represent between 70 per cent and 90 per cent of the female population in the developing world, and, because of their major and important role in agricultural production, preparation, processing and marketing of food, they constitute substantial economic resources. Yet, it is in this sector that in many countries women's status is lowest and, because they are ill-equipped with the tools of development, their agricultural productivity is seriously affected, and efforts that could help the prevailing world food shortage are largely dissipated.

14. From the demographic point of view women are 50 per cent of the world's population, and approximately 70 per cent of the total female population of the world is estimated to be living in the developing countries. Within this group, there are over 500 million girls under 15 years of age, constituting some 40 per cent of all females in the developing countries. The reproductive patterns that these girls will follow will be a significant determinant of the future rate of population growth in these countries.

15. Illiteracy, lack of education and of training in basic skills is one of the causes of the vicious circle of under-development and low productivity, poor conditions of health and welfare, which has most serious implications not only for women but for society as a whole and for future generations. Illiteracy rates are higher for women than for men, especially in some regions where they are more than 20 or 30 percentage points lower for men than women.

16. As societies evolve from a traditional economy to various levels of modernisation and industrialisation, women may, initially, be adversely affected by the process. For example, their roles may become less defined, their spheres of economic activity as producers of food and handicrafts may be reduced; their recognised rights to the use of land may be abolished; and their living standards may be lowered by migration to overcrowded urban areas. Hence, it is essential that

Governments take specific steps to avoid these and other negative effects when planning for the integration of women in development.

17. Planning should also take full account of the important factors affecting development, on the one hand, and the relationship of those factors to the status of women, on the other. Such interrelationship may include the link between the condition of women, population factors and overall development. High fertility usually goes hand in hand with low status of women, lack of educational and employment opportunities for them and conditions of poverty, overwork and drudgery. Another interrelationship is that which exists between the mother's level of education and the child's subsequent receptiveness to learning. This determines the degree to which the child is able to exercise a wider range of options for work and higher education in later life. Yet another link exists between the mother's level of health and nutrition, on the one hand, and the mortality rate of her children, on the other. Furthermore, women's level of education and the nature of their occupation affect the extent to which they themselves can participate effectively in political and economic life.

18. Recent years have seen the emergence of new approaches to and concepts of social progress and development, and a growing awareness that States are inter-dependent. If a new world order is to be established on the principle of equity and social justice among and within nations, and solidly anchored in conditions of peace and stability, then women must share as equals with men in its creation as well as its benefits.

19. It is in this perspective that the Plan has been prepared, in full recognition of the wide inequalities which exist among countries at different stages of development, and of the wide divergencies in social and economic conditions within individual countries.

II. SCOPE AND PURPOSE OF THE PLAN

20. The Plan is based on principles long recognised by the international community in existing international instruments, programmes and strategies. It is not intended as a substitute for these, but is aimed rather at stimulating the

national and international action required to give practical effect to their provisions, and to achieve the goals of International Women's Year within a broad and multidisciplinary framework, which has hitherto been lacking.

21. The Plan endorses programme and strategies setting forth similar or related objectives; in particular, the International Strategy for the Second United Nations Development Decade, the programme of concerted international action for the advancement of women, the World Population Plan of Action, the recommendations of the World Food Conference, and the regional plans of action for the integration of women in development, adopted in 1974 for the regions of the Economic and Social Commission for Asia and the Pacific and the Economic Commission for Africa. Many provisions of the present Plan are based on the recommendations of those global and regional plans.

22. The achievement of equality between women and men implies that both should have equal rights, opportunities and responsibilities to enable them to develop their particular talents and capabilities for their own personal fulfilment and the benefit of society. The Plan does not profess a preferential role for women, but it does imply the re-examination and reassessment of the functions and roles traditionally allotted to each sex within the family and the community at large.

23. The integration of women in development calls for a widening of their political and economic activities, the provision of the necessary skills to make their contribution more effective in terms of productivity, and their greater participation in decision-making, planning and implementation of all policies, programmes and projects. Full integration also implies that women receive their share of the benefits of development, thereby helping to ensure a more equitable distribution of income among all segments of the population.

24. Sustained international co-operation of all countries and peoples is required to achieve peace, which is not just the absence of conflict but depends upon the establishment of justice and equity for all. To this end, the Plan calls for the full participation of women in all efforts to promote and maintain peace, to eliminate racial discrimination and colonialism

in all its forms, and to contribute to the realisation of self-determination.

25. A further aim of the Plan is to ensure that the actual and potential contribution of women is not overlooked in existing concepts and strategies for development and a new world economic order. Recommendations for national and international action are proposed with the primary aim of accelerating progress in areas where women have been especially disadvantaged.

26. The Plan provides recommendations for action over the 10-year period, 1975 to 1985, as part of a sustained, long-term effort to achieve the objectives of the International Women's Year and future United Nations development decades. The action taken will be subject to periodic review and appraisal.

27. It stresses especially action at the national level, supported by the international community through global and regional action programmes. While the recommendations for national action are addressed primarily to governments, the full support of all public and private institutions, employers, trade unions, non-governmental organisations and other groups and individuals will be required to carry them out.

28. At the international level, the recommendations envisage that all organisations of the United Nations system should take separate and joint action to implement the Plan, including the relevant United Nations organs and bodies, especially the regional commissions, the United Nations Children's Fund, the United Nations Development Programme, the United Nations Fund for Population Activities, the United Nations Industrial Development Organisation, the United Nations Conference on Trade and Development, the United Nations Institute for Training and Research, the specialised agencies, and other intergovernmental and non-governmental organisations.

29. The Plan stresses the need for commitment on the part of governments and the international community to accord importance and priority to measures to improve the situation of women, both as a means of achieving the goals of social progress and development and as an end in itself.

III. RECOMMENDATIONS FOR ACTION

A. National Action

30. Governments should establish their own priorities and specific targets for achieving the goals of the Plan during the 10-year period, 1975 to 1985. Quantitative targets should be linked to those set out, in particular, in the International Development Strategy, and the World Population Plan of Action.

31. While integrated programmes for the benefit of all members of society should be the basis for action in implementing this Plan, special measures on behalf of women may be necessary where their status is particularly low and where discriminatory attitudes towards them are strong. These measures should be for an interim period only and should be appropriately phased out as their objectives are achieved.

32. The Plan recommends general measures on administrative and organisational matters, legislation, data collection and research, and the mass communications media. The specific areas selected in the Plan are not intended to be exhaustive but are considered to be the main areas for priority action, namely, international co-operation and peace, political participation, education and training, employment, health and nutrition, family and population change. In implementing the Plan, governments should pay special attention to improving the situation of women in rural areas.

33. It is recognised that some of the objectives of the Plan have already been achieved in some countries, while in others they will only be progressively accomplished. Moreover, some measures by their very nature will take longer to implement than others. Governments are urged to plan to achieve certain targets by the end of the first five-year period, 1980, such as a marked increase in literacy, the extension of vocational training in basic skills, parity of enrolment at the primary level of education, the establishment of infrastructural services in rural areas, the enactment of legislation on voting and eligibility for election, and on equal pay for equal work, and increased participation of women in policy-making positions at the local, national and international levels.

34. Many of the measures suggested in the Plan could be implemented by a change of emphasis and priorities in national plans and programmes without necessarily incurring additional expenditure. Governments should, however, explore all available sources of support to ensure adequate allocation of funds, including community resources and those of various private funding agencies. Evidence of government funding would enhance the possibilities of attracting international and bilateral assistance.

1. *General measures*

(a) Policy, administrative and organisational measures

35. As a matter of general policy there should be a clear commitment on the part of governments to take specific action within the framework of national planning and programmes to set up appropriate machinery for this purpose where it does not already exist.

36. The establishment of multisectoral machinery within government such as national commissions, women's bureaux and other bodies can be an effective transitional measure for accelerating the achievement of equal opportunities for women and their full integration in national life. Such bodies should include both women and men, representative of all groups of society responsible for making and implementing policy decisions in the public sector. Government ministries and departments (especially those responsible for education, health, labour, justice, communications, industry, trade, agriculture, rural development, social welfare, finance and planning) as well as appropriate private and public agencies should be represented.

37. The functions of such bodies should include the investigation of the situation of women at all levels, recommendations for needed legislative and other measures, including policies and programmes, and the evaluation of the progress achieved in meeting the targets established by governments to implement the Plan. The activities of such bodies should be co-ordinated as far as possible with similar regional and international bodies. These national bodies should also encourage the co-ordination of the activities of non-governmental organisations undertaken on behalf of women, and self-help programmes devised by women themselves.

(b) Legislative measures

38. Constitutional and legislative guarantees of the principle of non-discrimination on grounds of sex and of equal rights of women and men are essential. Equally important is the general acceptance of the principles embodied in such legislation. The adoption and enforcement of legislation is a significant means of influencing public attitudes and values. Wherever necessary, therefore, legislation should be enacted to bring national laws into conformity with the relevant international instruments and adequate provision made for their enforcement especially in each area dealt with in the Plan. International conventions relating to the status of women should be ratified where this has not yet been done.

39. Official bodies, such as law commissions, should be established where they do not exist and entrusted with the responsibility of modernising laws and regulations and of keeping them under review. Appropriate bodies should be set up to ensure that the provisions of the law are applied without discrimination. These could include human rights commissions, civil liberties unions, appeals boards and the office of *ombudsman.*

40. Provision should also be made for informing women of their legal rights, of how they may seek redress and for legal aid, where possible free of charge. For this purpose special counselling offices could be established.

(c) Data collection, research and analysis

41. In view of the lack of data and research on many aspects of the situation of women in the context of overall political, economic, social and cultural development, the scope of inquiry and research should be widened, and a scientific and reliable data base established for the purpose of formulating policy, evaluating progress and analysing differences between countries. National statistical offices should adhere to the standards followed by the United Nations and its specialised agencies for collecting and tabulating statistical data.

42. All census and survey data relating to the demographic, social and economic characteristics of individuals (e.g., urban/rural residence, age, marital status, literacy, education, income, level of skills and participation in both modern and traditional

economic activities) and to household and family composition should be reported and analysed by sex.

43. The value of the actual contribution of women to the national economy should be recognised whether or not their contribution is reflected in the national statistics on the economically active population. Many women are automatically excluded from this category because they are regarded only as homemakers, and homemaking is nowhere considered to be an economic activity. It should also be recognised that in many instances the head of a household or of a family may be a woman; it should never automatically be assumed that a woman can be the head only in the absence of any man. Another large group of women are erroneously classified as homemakers because it is assumed that women do not have an economic activity and therefore their status is not carefully investigated. This is particularly important in the less developed countries where women make a significant contribution, particularly as unpaid family workers in agriculture. These groups should therefore be included in national data gathering and statistics.

44. The extent of women's activities in food production (cash crop and subsistence), water and fuel supply, marketing, transportation and participation in local and national planning and policy-making in all sectors of national life should be measured.

45. Data collection should also seek to elicit information on the quality of life, such as satisfaction with job, income and family relations, use of leisure time and perception of self.

46. Suitable indicators should be developed to evaluate the contribution of women and assess the effectiveness of programmes and policies.

47. Special attention should be given to these broad areas of research:

(i) Inquiries into customs, traditions, practices, attitudes and values which impede or promote the exercise of equal rights of women and men, and which constrain or increase women's contribution to development;

(ii) The assessment and evaluation of women's current and potential contribution to the various sectors of national life in relation to the country's overall development plans and programmes including political life;

(iii) The interrelationship of the condition of women, demographic patterns and changes, and economic and social development;

(iv) The extent and nature of women's participation in the labour force; special attention should also be given to the agricultural and service sectors of the economy and the contribution of co-operatives;

(v) The influence of scientific and technological developments on the position of women and their integration into the development effort;

(vi) The changing status and roles of women in the family and society and their relationship to sexual behaviour;

(vii) The appropriate technology, including intermediate technology required to maximise employment opportunities and enable women to contribute more efficiently towards overall economic activity and reduce the negative aspects of modernisation with due regard to overall productivity;

(viii) The extent and causes of female mortality in countries where it is higher than male mortality, with a view to recommending appropriate medical and social action;

(ix) The division of labour and the time-budgets for women and girls compared to men and boys, with regard to both economic and household activities.

(d) Mass communications media and attitudes towards women's roles.

48. A major obstacle in effecting changes in the status of women lies in public attitudes and values regarding women's roles in society. The mass communications media which at present tend to reinforce traditional attitudes have great potential as a vehicle for social change and could exercise a significant influence in helping to remove prejudices and stereotypes and in accelerating the acceptance of women's new and expanding roles. Mass media include not only press, radio, television and cinema but also traditional types of entertainment such as drama, story telling, songs and puppet shows, which are essential in reaching the rural areas of many countries.

49. Governments should encourage the carrying out of investigations and surveys of the positive and negative influences exerted by the mass media in relation to national goals and the changing roles of women and men. Such investigations and surveys should examine the various functions of the media: dissenimation of information; education; entertainment; and advertising.

50. Those in control of the media should raise public consciousness with respect to the changing roles of women and men and the serious concern that both have about important issues that affect their families, communities and society at large. They should be urged to project a more dynamic image of women as well as men, and to take into account the diversity of women's roles and their actual and potential contribution to society.

51. Women should be appointed in greater numbers in media management decision-making and other capacities, as editors, columnists, reporters, producers and the like, and should encourage the critical review, within the media, of the image of women projected.

2. *Specific areas*

(a) International co-operation and the strengthening of peace

52. In order to involve more women in the promotion of international co-operation and the strengthening of peace and in combating colonialism, neo-colonialism, foreign domination and alien subjugation, *apartheid* and racial discrimination, the peace efforts of women as individuals and in groups, in national and international organisations should be encouraged.

53. Women should be given equal opportunity to represent their countries in all international forums and especially in the delegations to the United Nations family of organisations. Women should have equal opportunity to serve in the principal organs and committees of the United Nations, including the Security Council and all conferences on disarmament and peace.

54. The efforts of non-governmental and intergovernmental organisations having as their aim the strengthening of international security and the furthering of peaceful co-existence

should be supported and women should be given every encouragement to participate actively in their endeavours.

55. A special day devoted to peace should be celebrated nationally and internationally. Meetings and seminars should be organised for this purpose by interested individuals and groups and should have wide coverage in the press and other media. Women should lend their full support to these objectives and explore, together with men, ways to overcome existing obstacles to peace and international co-operation.

56. Measures should be taken to facilitate the free flow of information and ideas among countries, having due regard for their sovereignty and the principle of non-intervention in their domestic affairs, and to promote the exchange of visits between women of different countries to study common problems. Educational, cultural, scientific and other exchange programmes should be expanded and new forms developed in order to facilitate mutual understanding between peoples, particularly the young, and promote the principle of peaceful coexistence. For these purposes the mass media should be utilised fully.

57. Women and men should be encouraged to instill in their children values of mutual respect and understanding and the desire to maintain peace.

(b) Political participation

58. The goal under this part of the Plan is to afford equal opportunity for women to participate in public life and make them aware of their responsibilities as citizens.

59. The right to vote, to be eligible for election and to hold all public offices and exercise the public functions should be enjoyed by women on equal terms with men at the national, local and community levels. Where legislation guaranteeing these rights does not exist efforts should be made to adopt it by the end of the first biennium of this Plan, in 1978. Where special qualifications are required, they should apply to both sexes equally and should relate only to the expertise necessary for performing the specific functions.

60. Governments should establish specific quantitative targets for increasing the number of women in public office and public functions at all levels, including policy-making, and special efforts should be made to meet them.

61. Such special efforts could include the following: (i) the official stand towards equal political participation of women should be reaffirmed and widely publicised; (ii) special governmental instructions for achieving a fair representation of women in public office should be issued and government departments dealing with personnel questions should compile periodic reports on the number of women in the public service and their levels and areas of work; (iii) drives for the recruitment, nomination and promotion of women, particularly to fill important positions, should be undertaken until equitable representation of the sexes is achieved; (iv) educational and informational activities should be undertaken to enlighten the female electorate on political issues and on the need for their active participation in public affairs.

62. Special drives should be undertaken to encourage the increased participation of women and girls in rural, community and youth development programmes, and their access to related training for leadership in those programmes.

63. In order to increase the participation of women as well as other under-represented groups in the political system of each country, nation-wide voluntary contributions of a minimum flat sum could be included in the existing system of taxation to help defray the campaign expenses of all political candidates.

(c) Education and training

64. Equal opportunities for basic education and literacy should be provided on a formal and non formal basis, according to national needs. This objective is not only a basic right in itself but can be a powerful instrument for social mobility and for reducing gaps between social groups and between the sexes, since it confers the potential for obtaining gainful employment. Governments should relate educational priorities to population projections and to employment opportunities. Programmes should also be related to the culture of the communities concerned.

65. Measures should be taken to promote equality of opportunity for both sexes at all levels of education and training within the context of lifelong education. These measures should conform to the existing international standards and, in particular, to the Convention and Recommendation against Dis-

crimination in Education, 1960, and to the revised Recommendation on Technical and Vocational Education, 1974, of the United Nations Educational, Scientific and Cultural Organisation. All legal and practical discrimination in access to all forms of education and training at all levels should be abolished.

66. Programmes, curricula and standards of education and training should be identical for the two sexes, even where separate institutions exist for girls and women and boys and men, respectively. Courses for both sexes should include agriculture and other employment-oriented subjects, responsible parenthood, family life and nutrition. Co-education and mixed training groups should be actively encouraged.

67. Dynamic programmes for eradicating illiteracy should be adopted and target dates established for its elimination. Literacy campaigns should include basic training in agricultural, technical, entrepreneurial and co-operative skills or training for a variety of paraprofessional roles in health, nutrition, family planning and education.

68. The provision and effective enforcement as quickly as possible of free and compulsory primary education for girls on an equal basis with boys should be made. Parity of enrolment for the sexes should be accompanied by a revision of the content and structure of education such as to ensure that it is relevant to national needs and that it prepares the individual adequately for future life.

69. Every effort should be made to overcome high dropout rates amoung school-age girls and to enable women to participate in literacy and basic skills programmes. Inexpensive child care and other arrangements should therefore be organised to coincide with school or training hours to free women and girls from confining domestic work. Special programmes for continuing education on a part-time basis should also be arranged to ensure retention of what has been learned at school.

70. Existing and newly established vocational programmes of all types should be widely diversified, to equip girls and boys for a wide choice of employment opportunities and to match national needs and job opportunities, and should be equally accessible to both women and men.

71. Special programmes need to be established or developed for those living in rural areas, to enable women to participate fully in programmes for social and economic development , to encourage a self-reliant and self-help approach to life and give basic agricultural training including extension work and employment-oriented skills.

72. Special measures should be developed to assist women who wish to return to work after a comparatively long absence, owing in particular to family responsibilities, or who wish to take up employment for the first time at a more mature age to do so.

73. Informational and formal and non-formal educational programmes are required to make the general public, parents, teachers, counsellors and others aware of the need to provide girls with a solid initial education and adequate training for occupational life and ample opportunities for further education and training. This can be partially achieved by widespread mass media programmes to eliminate prejudices and modify traditional practices which automatically accord a secondary role to women and girls in learning or employment situations.

74. Special orientation, counselling and guidance arrangements should be made available to girls to make them aware of the opportunities for education, training and employment open to them and of the education and training required to take full advantage of the opportunities available. Girls should also have equal access with boys to all educational and vocational guidance facilities, and should be encouraged to choose a career according to their real aptitudes and abilities rather than on the basis of deeply ingrained sex stereotypes.

75. Research activities should be promoted which are designed to identify discriminatory practices based on sex with regard to education and training and to ensure educational equality.

(d) Employment and economic roles

76. The goals in this sector are to achieve equality of opportunity and treatment for women workers and their integration into the labour force and to provide them with equal access to the necessary skills. Governments should formulate policies and action programmes directed expressly towards

equality of opportunity and treatment for women workers and overcoming the present disequilibrium in their integration in the work force, thereby enhancing their contribution to development. Such policies and programmes, which should be in conformity with the standards relating to the employment of women elaborated by the United Nations and the International Labour Organisation, should include legislation stipulating the principle of non-discrimination on the grounds of sex or marital status, guidelines for implementing the principles, appeals procedures, and effective targets and machinery for implementation.

77. Training and education policies should be related to existing and projected job opportunities. In attempting to deal with problems of unemployment and underemployment, special efforts should be made to create a variety of economic roles for women and men and to encourage and support self-employment and self-help activities. Together with such measures, efforts should be made to foster positive attitudes towards the employment of women, irrespective of marital status, among employers and workers and among women and men in society at large, and to eliminate obstacles based on sex-typed divisions of labour.

78. In order to extend women's range of economic roles, co-operatives and small-scale industries can be developed and encouraged with the necessary help and support of government. For example, where co-operatives already exist, women should be encouraged to take an active part in them. New co-operatives, and, where appropriate, women's co-operatives, should be organised, especially in areas where women play a major role, such as food production, marketing, housing, nutrition and health. Co-operatives may also be the most appropriate and feasible arrangement for child-care to enable women and girls to obtain gainful employment.

79. Essential to the effective implementation of the above is the provision of adequate training in co-operatives and entrepreneurial skills, access to credit and necessary seed capital for improved tools; assistance with marketing, the provision of adequate rural social services and amenities, decentralised development of town in rural areas and basic

infrastructural arrangements, such as child care arrangements, transportation and conveniently situated water supplies.

80. Because of the high proportion of women in the agricultural sector in many countries, it is particularly important that efforts be made to increase their participation at the national planning level in the formulation of integrated employment policies for the agricultural and rural sectors. These policies should include projects for diversification, import substitution and expansion of rural activities for farming, forestry, fisheries, animal husbandry and agro-industries.

81. In urban areas in particular, efforts should be made to provide for the needs of migrant women and low-income working women and their families who live in slums and squatter settlements by providing training, job counselling, child care facilities and financial aid.

82. Access to skills and the provision of institutional and on the job training should be open to women in the same way as to men in every sphere and on the same conditions so as to make them equally eligible for promotion. Training should also be offered to enable women to re-enter the labour force or to enter it at a more mature age.

83. Special attention should be given to more flexible working hours and part-time work for women and men, with a view to facilitating the combination of household tasks and work responsibilities.

84. All women workers should have the right to maternity protection including maternity leave with a guarantee of returning to their former employment and to nursing breaks, in keeping with the principles laid down in the International Labour Organisation's Maternity Convention (Revised) and Recommendation, 1952.

85. Protective legislation applying to women only should be reviewed in the light of scientific and technological knowledge and revised, repealed or extended to all workers as necessary.

86. Measures should be taken to eliminate to the maximum possible extent discriminatory treatment of women in national social security schemes. Women workers should be covered equally with men by all aspects of such schemes.

87. Governments should encourage and stimulate concerted efforts, in particular on the part of employers' and workers'

organisations, to bring about a marked improvement in the position of women in employment and occupation and should co-operate with all voluntary organisations concerned with the status of women workers in economic life and in society as a whole.

88. Trade unions should adopt policies to increase the participation of women in their work at every level of the hierarchy, including the higher echelons. They should have special programmes to promote equality of oppportunity for jobs and training for women workers and leadership training for women. They should play a leading role in developing new and constructive approaches to problems faced by workers paying special attention to the problems of women workers.

(e) Health and nutrition

89. While everyone has an undeniable right to health, conditions have often precluded the actual enjoyment by women of this right equally with men. The situation becomes more accentuated in societies with considerable shortages of health personnel and facilities and constitute a high cost to the family, society and development by impairing the productivity of women. Women also need special care during pregnancy, delivery and lactation.

90. Attention should be given to the development of comprehensive simple community health services in which the community identifies its own health needs, takes part in decisions on delivery of health care in different socio-economic contexts, and develops primary health care services within easy access of every member of the community. In the development of primary health care for the entire population, provision should be made to ensure that women have the same rights and access to that care as men.

91. Within the context of health services, governments should pay special attention to women's specific health needs by provision of pre-natal and post-natal and delivery services; gynaecological and family planning services during the reproductive years; comprehensive and continuous health services directed to all infant, pre-chool children and schoolchildren without prejudice on grounds of sex; specific

services for pre-adolescent and adolescent girls and for the post-reproductive years and old age.

92. Particular attention should be paid to the reduction of certain risks which affect the health of women and their children, including too many pregnancies or pregnancies at too close intervals or at too early or too late an age. Governments should promote the provision of family planning education and services as a means of reducing the above risks and improving the status and health of women. It would also enable women to exercise equally with men their right to decide how many children they will bear, thereby aiding the community to implement national policies in the population field and further the integration of women into development.

93. Easily accessible water supplies should also be provided (including wells, dams, catchments, piping, etc.) for safe potable water as well as sewerage and other sanitation measures to improve health conditions and reduce the burden of carrying water which falls mainly on women and children.

94. In view of women's importance not only as users but as providers of health care, steps should be taken to incorporate them as fully informed and active participants in the health planning and decision-making process at all levels and in all phases. Efforts should be made to encourage women to participate actively in community efforts, to provide primary health care and improve coverage. Moreover, women should have the same right of access as men to any training establishment or course for any health profession and to continue to the highest levels. Practices which exclude women from certain health professions on traditional, religious or cultural grounds should be abolished. Women should also be trained as paramedics and encouraged to organise health co-operatives.

95. In national food and nutrition policies governments should give priority to the consumption by the most vulnerable groups in the population (adolescent girls, pregnant and lactating women, and young children) of certain types of food produce such as milk and milk products and specially enriched foods. The practice of breast feeding and good feeding practices for the weaning period should be encouraged. Supplementary food programmes for the mothers and child-

ren in need and for children at imminent risk of malnutrition should be introduced and nutritional deficiencies should be prevented through fortification of staples or other widely consumed foods.

96. Techniques and equipment for food processing, preservation and conservation at the local village level should be improved and made available to rural women. Co-operatives for the production, quality control and distribution of food should be organised to give impetus to this effort and, where appropriate, campaigns to educate the consumer should be organised.

97. Opportunities should be created for women to contribute more efficiently to the production of proper types of food through vegetable gardens in rural aud urban areas through the provision of better tools, seeds and fertiliser. Girls and boys should also be encouraged to grow food in school gardens the produce of which could be used to supplement daily school meal programmes.

98. Mass communications media compaigns on nutrition education should be launched to explore the most effective techniques for introducing previously unacceptable nutritious foods into the daily diets of people. These campaigns should also inform women how to use the family income most economically towards the purchase of more nutritious foods. The exchange of experience on effective nutrition programmes through seminars, informal visits and the publication of suitable menus should be arranged.

(f) The roles of women and men in the family

99. The goal under this part of the Plan is to enable the family to adjust to economic, social and cultural change, to ensure the dignity, equality and economic security of both spouses and create conditions conductive to the balanced development of the child.

100. In the total development process the role of women, along with men, needs to be considered in terms of their contribution to the family as well as to society and the national economy. Higher status for this role in the home—as a parent, spouse and homemaker—can only enhance the personal dignity of a man and a woman. Household activities have generally been perceived as having a low economic and social prestige.

However, they are valued by all societies because procreation and the rearing of children are basic functions for the maintenance and perpetuation of the family group.

101. Legislation relating to marriage should ensure that women and men have the same right to free choice of a spouse and to enter into marriage only with their free and full consent, that marriage below the age of 18 is prohibited to enable a longer period of education for girls and boys, but particularly girls, for personal development and work prior to marriage. Official registration of marriages should be made compulsory and all institutions and practices which infringe upon these rights should be abolished, in particular, child marriage and the inheritance of widows.

102. Legislative and other measures should be taken to ensure that both spouses enjoy full legal capacity and the exercise thereof relating to their personal and property rights, including the right to acquire, administer, enjoy, dispose of and inherit property (including property acquired during marriage). Limitations, where such exist, should apply to both spouses alike. During marriage the principle of equal rights and responsibilities would mean that both spouses should perform an active role in the home, taking into account the importance of combining home and work responsibilities, and share jointly decision-making on matters affecting the family and children. At the dissolution of marriage, this principle would imply that procedures and grounds of dissolution of marriage should be liberalised and apply equally to both spouses; assets acquired during marriage by either or both should be shared on an equitable basis; appropriate provisions should be made for the social security and pension coverage of the work contributed by the homemaker; and decisions relating to the custody of children should be taken in consideration of their best interests.

103. In order to assist in the solution of conflicts arising among members of the family, adequate family counselling services should be set up wherever possible and the establishment of family courts staffed with personnel trained in law as well as in various other relevant disciplines should be considered. Free legal aid and assistance should be made available to needy litigants.

104. Programmes of education for personal relationship, marriage and family life, including psycho-sexual development, should be integrated into all school curricula at appropriate levels and into programmes for out-of-school education to prepare young people of both sexes for responsible marriage and parenthood. These programmmes should be based on the ideals of mutual respect and shared rights and responsibilities in the family and in society.

105. In recognition of the growing number of single-parent families, additional assistance and benefits, wherever possible, should be provided for them. The unmarried mother should be granted full-fledged status as a parent, and children born out of wedlock should have the same rights and obligations as children born in wedlock. Special nursing homes and hostels should be established for married and unmarried mothers in need, before and after delivery.

106. Social security programmes should, to the maximum extent possible, include children and family allowances in order to strengthen the economic stability of family members. They should be granted directly to the spouse who is actually taking care of the children.

107. Women should have full opportunity to participate in the planning of urban and housing development as well as human settlements. Planning for housing should take into account the size of the family as well as the need to make provision within easy reach of dwellings for the necessary social services and facilities for family and community life, including playgrounds, creches, day-care centres and shops.

(g) Population

108. The position of women in the family and in society is inextricably linked with the demographic processes of growth and decrease, including fertility, mortality, migration and urbanisation. To alter the pattern whereby women are denied full participation in the development process involves a change in certain crucial demographic variables, such as age at marriage, age at birth of first child, total number of children and the interval between births, and age at termination of child-bearing. Further, the status of women and in particular their educational level, whether or not they are employed, the nature of their employment and their position within the

family are all factors which significantly influence family size. Conversely, the right of the woman to decide freely and responsibly on the number and spacing of her children and to the means to enable her to exercise that right has a decisive impact on her ability to take advantage of educational and employment opportunities.

109. The Plan endorses the recommendations of the World Population Plan of Action, especially those relating to the status of women, in view of the interrelationship of the status of women, demographic factors and development. Governments are urged to ensure balanced demographic, economic and social development by closely relating population policies and programmes with measures to improve the status of women.

110. All individuals and couples should have access, through an institutionalised system, such as a family planning programme, to the information and means to enable them to determine freely and fully the number and spacing of their children, and all obstacles to the dissemination of family planning knowlege and services, including legal, social and financial obstacles, should be removed.

111. Both women and men equally should be the target groups of family planning programmes which should be integrated and co-ordinated with health and other services designed to raise the quality of family life. Family planning information services should be included in any organized services that have the confidence and support of the people.

112. Programmes should be formulated for the reduction of infant, child and maternal mortality by means of improved nutrition, sanitation, maternal and chilth health care and maternal education. Social service and health programmes should also be devised to meet the needs of the elderly and particularly women, who form the majority of that group.

B. International action

1. *Global action*

113. International action in support of national efforts to achieve the objectives of the Plan will require the co-operation

of the entire United Nations system of organisations, properly co-ordinated through the existing machinery, especially the Economic and Social Council and the Administrative Committee on Co-ordination, which should be strengthened appropriately.

114. Women should be fully involved in policy-making at the international as well as the national level, and be equitably represented among the principal delegates to all international bodies, conferences and committees, including those dealing with political and legal questions, economic and social development, disarmament, planning, administration and finance, science and technology, the environment and population. The secretariats of the international organisations should set an example by eliminating any provisions or practices in their employment policies which may be discriminatory to women. Quantitative targets to achieve an equitable balance of male and female employees at all levels should be established on a biennial basis throughout the decade 1975-1985. This should apply to all substantive areas, and to field posts where operational programmes are initiated and carried out.

115. International action should support existing programmes and expand their scope in the following main areas: drawing up standards to provide the framework for national policies; data collection, analysis and research; operational activities furnishing technical and material assistance to governments; and exchange of knowledge and experience.

(a) Formulation and implementation of international standards

116. The preparation of international conventions, declarations and formal recommendations, and the development of reporting systems and other procedures for their implementation are important elements of international programmes and should be continued.

117. High priority should be given in 1976 to the preparation and adoption of the convention on the elimination of discrimination against women, with effective procedures for its implementation.

118. Studies should be undertaken of the effectiveness of the implementation of existing instruments and periodic reviews made to determine their adequacy in the light of changing

conditions in the modern world, and of experience gained since their adoption.

119. The need for the development of new standards in new fields of concern to women should be kept constantly under review in relation to the implementation of the present Plan.

(b) Data collection, research and analysis

120. The primary aim of international action should be to assist countries in the systematic collection of adequate data on women, and provide the basis for cross-cultural analysis and comparisons. An index of relevant social and economic indicators should be prepared not later than 1980, in co-operation with the interested specialised agencies, the United Nations Research Institute for Social Development, the regional commissions and other relevant bodies.

121. The Plan also gives high priority to research activities on all aspects of the situation of women. Cross-cultural studies, especially of the causes of discriminatory practices and attitudes and of the mechanisms of change are considered important. Research oriented towards the specific problems of countries and regions should have high priority and be carried out by competent women and men especially acquainted with national and regional conditions.

122. Every effort should be made to promote the exchange of information and research findings making maximum use of existing national and regional research institutes and universities, in order to build up a network for the regular exchange of information. These institutions should include the United Nations University, the United Nations Institute for Training and Research, the United Nations Research Institute for Social Development and the United Nations Social Defence Institute.

(c) Operational activities for technical co-operation

123. Concerted efforts of all organisations in the United Nations system are needed to implement the Plan effectively, through the means of technical co-operation programmes.

124. The United Nations Development Programme, the United Nations Fund for Population Activities, the United Nations specialised agencies, including the International Bank for Reconstruction and Development and the International Monetary Fund, the regional commisions, intergovernmental organisations, the bilateral assistance agencies and foundations,

and the international and regional development banks, all carry out their work through projects that are highly specific in terms of the objectives to be reached, the resources to be employed, and the target areas and populations for which they are intended. Given the scope and diversity of the world-wide system of assistance agencies, action can be initiated in a large number of areas without delay once the needs are understood and diffused throughout the United Nations system.

125. A deliberate and large-scale effort should therefore be made to ensure that high priority and attention are given to programmes, projects and activities which give women the skills, training and opportunities necessary to improve their situation and enable them to participate fully and productively in the total development effort.

126. Field surveys should be undertaken in each region to assist governments and the international community by establishing the necessary data base to develop projects which will implement the objectives of the Plan.

127. Existing plans and projects should be scrutinised with a view to extending their sphere of activities to include women, and new and innovative projects should also be developed, especially in such key areas as :

(i) Agricultural development, with special attention to women's role as producers, processors and vendors of food;

(ii) Integrated rural development, stressing training of women and girls in improved methods of farming, marketing, purchasing and sales techniques; basic accounting and organisational methods; fundamentals of hygiene and nutrition; training in crafts and economy;

(iii) Health and reproduction, including family health and child health, family planning, nutrition and health education;

(iv) Education and training at all levels, geared to the opportunities for employment and related economic roles of women;

(v) Public administration, with the aim of preparing women to participate in development planning and policy-making, especially in middle- and higher-level posts ;

(vi) Youth projects, which should be examined to ensure that they include adequate emphasis on the needs and participation of young women.

128. The resident representatives of the United Nations Development Programme should play a key role in helping governments to formulate requests for such assistance within the framework of country programming. Advisory services provided by the specialised agencies in the form of special consultants or task forces could also render assistance in the formulation of project requests. Periodic reviews could be initiated to suggest crucial areas where special support might be needed.

129. Women should participate fully in planning and implementing UNDP country programmes as well as regional, interregional and global projects.

(d) Exchange of information and experience

130. The exchange of information and experience at the international level is an effective means of stimulating progress and encouraging the adoption of measures to eliminate discrimintion against women and encourage their wider participaation in all sectors of national life. Countries with different political, economic and social systems and cultures and at differing stages of development have benefited from the common knowledge of problems, difficulties and achievements and from solutions worked out jointly.

131. Meetings and seminars, especially those organised under the technical co-operation programme of the United Nations in conjunction with host countries, have proved to be most valuable in extending this type of exchange and experience and should be continued.

132. Educational and informational programmes supported by the international community are needed to make all sectors of the population aware of the international norms established, the goals and objectives of this Plan of Action, and the findings of research and data envisaged under the relevant sections of the Plan.

133. International organizations, both governmental, and non-governmental, should strengthen their efforts to distribute information on women and related matters, particularly through periodic publications on

the situation of women, their changing roles and their integration into the development effort through planning and implementation policies, as well as the utilisation of communications media and aids, and the wide distribution of newsletters, pamphlets, visual charts and similar material on women.

2. *Regional action*

134. The United Nations regional commissions for Africa, Asia and the Pacific, Europe, Latin America and West Asia should stimulate interest in the Plan and provide national governments and non-governmental organisations with the technical and informational support they require to develop and implement effective strategies to further the objectives of the Plan in the regions. Where they have not already done so, the regional commissions should establish appropriate machinery for the purpose. This might include a regional standing committee of experts from countries of the region to advise the commission on its activities directed towards the integration of women in development in relation to those of governments and other agencies in the region. The committee's functions should be:

(a) To initiate country studies and assist national institutions to identify the types of information needed for a proper understanding of the situation of women and the factors facilitating or limiting their advancement;
(b) To assit with the design and implementation of surveys for collection of data and other information;
(c) To give leadership in the methods of reporting on the situation of women and in the development of indicators for assessing the progress made towards the scales of this Plan in conjunction with regional statistical bodies and international efforts to this end;
(d) To provide a clearing-house for exchange of information which would facilitate co-ordination and mutual support between programmes for the advancement of women at various levels, and for the sharing of relevant experience among the countries of the region.

135. States, members of the regional commissions, in requesting technical and financial assistance, should endeavour to raise the priority accorded to projects to enhance opportunities for women and to increase recognition of the importance of these projects for overall development in consultation with UNDP regional offices.

136. The regional commissions should provide assistance to governments and non-governmental organisations to identify needed action, develop policies, strategies and programmes for strengthening women's role in national development, and formulate requests for technical and financial assistance for such programmes. They should encourage training institutions in the region to expand their curricula to encompass topics related to the integration of women in development, and assist in the development of training programmes, particularly those whose initial aim is to increase women's potential for leadership and develop the cadres for formulating the programmes and implementing the activities indicated by this Plan.

137. The commissions should also promote technical co-operation between the developing countries of the region, utilising the existing talent available. Trained women could, for example, offer short-term assistance to women in countries other than their own on a voluntary basis, or as part of a special task force. Special advisers should be attached to the regional field officers in order to strengthen the regional field structure and carry out more effectively the functions and aims described above. They could also seek to stimulate increased contributions of funds for financing programmes for the advancement of women from existing sources of multilateral and bilateral assistance, and to secure new sources of funds, including the establishment of revolving funds at the national and local levels.

138. In implementing the Plan, special efforts should be made by the commissions and other United Nations bodies having regional offices to co-ordinate their programmes with existing United Nations and other regional centres whose fields of competence relate to the aims of this Plan, such as centres for research and training in development training,

literacy, social welfare, social defence, employment, health and nutrition, and community development.

139. Regional development banks such as the African Development Bank, the Asian Development Bank and the Inter-American Development Bank as well as sub-regional banks, such as the Central American Bank for Economic Integration and the East African Development Bank, and bilateral funding agencies should be urged to accord high priority in their development assistance to projects which include the integration of women in the development effort and the achievement of equality. Such assistance would stimulate national support for innovative national and local programmes, including self-help activities.

IV. REVIEW AND APPRAISAL

140. It is essential to review and appraise progress made in meeting the goals of this Plan. Such an exercise should be part of the procedures for the review and appraisal of progress made under the International Development Strategy of the Second United Nations Development Decade. This has already been provided for by the General Assembly in its resolution 3276 (XXIX) of 10 December 1974, by which it decided to consider relevant recommendations of the Conference at its seventh special session and thirtieth regular session in 1975. The Plan should also be considered at the first regular session of the Economic and Social Council in 1976. Provision should also be made for the regular review of the implementation of the Plan by the General Assembly and the Council every two years.

141. The Plan as adopted should also be considered by the regional commissions, the United Nations Development Programme, the United Nations Children's Fund, the United Nations Industrial Development Organisation, the relevant specialised agencies and other intergovernmental and non-governmental organisations at their meetings following the World Conference. The discussions and decisions of these bodies concerning the Plan should be submitted to the Economic and Social Council and its relevant functional commissions and advisory bodies (the Commission on the Status

of Women, the Commission for Social Development, the Population and Statistical Commissions, the Committee on Development Planning, and the Committee on Review and Appraisal) at their sessions in 1976 and 1977. An item on action on the implementation of the Plan should be included in the agenda of the sessions of all these bodies at intervals of no longer than two years.

142. At the regional level, the regional commissions should assume responsibility for monitoring progress towards the greater and more effective participation of women in all aspects of development efforts. Such monitoring should be carried out within the framework of the review and appraisal of the Strategy for the Second United Nations Development Decade. The commissions should include information on the integration of women in development in their reports to the Economic and Social Council on the social and economic situation in the regions. They should also discuss at appropriate intervals (such as every two years) the progress made towards achieving the aims of the Plan of Action. They should encourage governments to provide equal opportunities for women to be represented on their delegations to the sessions of the commissions and to other relevant meetings.

143. At the national level, governments are encouraged to undertake their own regular review and appraisal of progress made to achieve the goals and objectives of the Plan and to report to the Economic and Social Council in conjunction, where necessary, with other existing reporting systems, e.g., those of the International Development Strategy, the World Population Plan of Action, the recommendations of the World Food Conference, the implementation of the Declaration on the Elimination of Discrimination against Women, and of the Programme of Concerted International Action for the Advancement of Women.

144. International organisations should review the implications of the Plan in the context of their own programmes, and should make appropriate recommendations to their governing bodies on any revisions of their financial and administrative arrangements that may be required to implement the Plan.

145. It is suggested that the programme should be organised around the following six basic areas: (a) data collection and research; (b) elaboration and ongoing review of international standards; (c) technical co-operation, training and advisory services including co-ordination with national and regional activities of organisations within the United Nations system: (d) review and appraisal including monitoring of progress made in achieving the aims and' objectives of the Plan; (e) dissemination and exchange of information and liaison with non-governmental organisations and other groups; and (f) executive and management functions including overall co-ordination, within the United Nations system, with national and regional machinery referred to in the Plan.

SELECT BIBLIOGRAPHY

Ackerman, Winona B. "The Man-Made Woman", *Teachers College Record,* 76 (February, 1975), 449-459.

Ahmad, Karuna. "Women's Higher Education : Recruitment and Relevance", in Amrik Singh and Philip G. Altbach (eds.), *The Higher Learning in India.* Delhi : Vikas Publishing House, 1974.

Asthana, Pratima. *Women's Movement in India.* Delhi : Vikas Publishing House, 1974.

Aurora, G.S. *The New Frontiersmen.* Bombay : Popular Prakashan, 1967.

Barnabas, A.P. "Population Growth and Social Change : A Note on Rural Society", *Social Action,* 24 (Jan-March, 1974), 25-32.

Bernard, Jessie. *The Future of Marriage.* London : Souvenir Press, 1972.

Beteille, Andre. "The Family and Social Change in India and Other South Asian Countries", *The Economic Weekly,* 16 (n. 5-7, 1964), 237-244.

Bhasin, Kamla (ed.). *The Position of Women in India.* Bombay: Leslie Sawhney Programme of Training in Democracy, 1973.

Bose, Ashish. "A Demographic Profile of Indian Women," in Devaki Jain (ed.), *Indian Women.* New Delhi : Ministry of Information and Broadcasting, Government of India, 1975.

Chakravorty, Shanti. "Farm Women Labour: Waste and Exploitation," *Social Change,* 5 (March-June, 1975), 9-15

Chandrasekhar, S. *Infant Mortality, Population Growth and*

Family Planning in India. London : George Allen and Unwin, 1972.

Consultative Committee for the World Conference of the International Women's Year. *Draft International Plan of Action.* New York: United Nations Economic and Social Council, E/CONF. 56/CD/2, February 8, 1975.

Cooney, Rosemary S. "Female Professional Work Opportunities : A Cross-National Study", *Demography*, 12 (February, 1975), 107-120.

Cormack, Margaret. *She Who Rides a Peacock: Indian Students and Social Change.* Bombay: Asia Publishing House, 1961.

———*The Hindu Woman.* Bombay: Asia Publishing House, 1961.

D'Souza, Anthony A., and de Souza, Alfred (eds.). *Population Growth and Human Development.* New Delhi : Indian Social Institute, 1974.

———Anthony A. "The Indian Family in the Seventies : An Integrated Family Policy," *Social Action,* 22 (Jan-March, 1972), 1-15.

Dube, Leela. "Woman's Worlds : Three Encounters", in Andre Beteille and T.N. Madan (eds.), *Encounter and Experience.* Delhi : Vikas Publishing House, 1975, 157-177.

Dube, S.C. "Men's and Women's Roles in India : A Sociological Review," in Barbara Ward (ed.), *Women in the New Asia.* Paris : UNESCO, 1973.

Dumont, Louis. "Marriage in India : The Present State of the Question—III : North India in Relation to South India", *Contributions to Indian Sociology,* 9 (1966).

———"Dowry in Hindu Marriage : As a Social Scientist Sees it", *The Economic Weekly,* 11 (n. 15, 1959), 519-521.

Epstein, Cynthia F. *Woman's Place : Options and Limits of Professional Careers.* Berkeley : University of California Press, 1970.

Friedan, Betty. *The Feminine Mystique.* New York : W.W. Norton and Company, 1963.

Gandhi, M. K. *Women and Social Justice.* Ahmedabad: Navajivan Publishing House, Fourth ed., 1958.

Goldstein, Rhoda L. *Indian Women in Transition : A Bangalore*

Case Study. Metuchen, N.J. : The Scarecrow Press, 1972.

———. "Tradition and Change in the Roles of Educated Indian Women", in Dhirendra Narain (ed.), *Explorations in the Family and Other Essays*. Bombay : Thacker and Company, 1975, 268-287.

Gore, M.S. *Urbanisation and Family Change*. Bombay : Popular Prakashan, 1968.

Gulati, Leela. "Female Work Participation: A Study of Inter-State Differences", *Economic and Political Weekly*, X (Jan 11, 1975), 35-42.

Gupta, Giri Raj. *Marriage, Religion and Society : Pattern of Change in an Indian Village*. Delhi : Vikas Publishing House, 1974.

Hate, Chandrakala. *Changing Status of Woman*. Bombay : Allied Publishers, 1969.

Indian Social Institute. *The Indian Family in the Change and Challenge of the Seventies*. New Delhi : Sterling Publishers, 1972.

International Labour Office. *Women Workers in a Changing Society* (Employment of Women with Family Responsibilities). Geneva, 1964.

Jahan, Rounaq. "Bangladesh: the Hidden Millions", *People* (International Women's Year issue), 2 (n. 2, 1975), 18-19.

Jain, Devaki (ed.). *Indian Women*. New Delhi : Publications Division, Ministry of Information and Broadcasting, Government of India, 1975.

John, DeWitt. *Indian Workers' Associations in Britain*. London : Oxford University Press, 1969.

Kapadia, K.M. *Marriage and Family in India*. Bombay: Oxford University Press, 1958.

Kapur, Promilla. "Myth or Reality?" *World Health* (January, 1975), 8-11.

———. "The Changing Role and Status of Women", in *The Indian Family in the Change and Challenge of the Seventies*. New Delhi : Sterling Publishers, 1972.

———. *Marriage and the Working Woman in India*. Delhi : Vikas Publications, 1970.

———. *The Changing Status of the Working Woman in India*. Delhi : Vikas Publishing House, 1974.

Kapur, Rama. "Role Conflict among Employed Housewives", *Indian Journal of Industrial Relations*, 5 (July, 1969), 39-76.

Karve, Irawati, *Kinship Organisation in India*. Bombay : Asia Publishing House, 1965.

———. "Family in India," in Baidyanath Verma (ed.), *Contemporary India*. Bombay : Asia Publishing House, 1964.

Kolenda, Pauline M. "Region, Caste and Family Structure : A Comparative Study of the Indian Joint Family," in Milton Singer and Bernard Cohn (eds.), *Structure and Change in Indian Society*. Chicago : Aldine Publishing Company, 1968, 339-396.

———. "Religious Anxiety and Hindu Fate", in Edward B. Harper (ed.), *Religion in South Asia*. Seattle : University of Washington Press, 1964, 71-81.

———. "Family Structure in Village Lonikand, India : 1819, 1958 and 1967", *Contributions to Indian Sociology* (New Series), IV (1970), 50-72.

Krauss, Wilma Rule. "Political Implications of Gender Roles : A Review of the Literature", *American Political Science Review*, LXVIII (December, 1974), 1706-1723.

Madras School of Social Work. *Working Mothers in White Collar Occupations*. Madras, 1956.

Mamdani, Mahmood. *The Myth of Population Control : Family, Caste and Class in an Indian Village*. New York : Monthly Review Press, 1973.

Mandelbaum, David G. *Human Fertility in India*. Berkeley, Los Angeles : University of California Press, 1974.

Meher, M.R. "Problems of Women's Employment", *The Indian Journal of Social Work*, 32 (July, 1971), 129-135.

Mukherjee, B.N. "Status of Women as Related to Family Planning," *Journal of Population Research*, 2 (Jan-June, 1975), 5-33.

———. "Status of Married Women in Haryana, Tamil Nadu and Meghalaya", *Social Change*, 4 (1974), 4-17.

Nath, Kamla. "Urban Women Workers: A Preliminary Study", *The Economic Weekly*, 17 (Sept. 11, 1965), 1405-1412.

Papanek, Hanna, "Men, Women and Work : Reflections on the Two-Person Career", in Joan Huber (ed.), *Changing Women in a Changing Society*. Chicago : University of Chicago Press, 1973, 90-110.

Punekar, Vijaya. "Fertility, Education and Social Change", *Sociological Bulletin*, 23 (March, 1974), 99-111.

Ramanujam, B.K. "The Indian Family in Transition : Changing Roles and Relationships", *Social Action*, 22 (Jan-March, 1972), 16-25.

Report of the Committee on the Status of Women in India. *Towards Equality*. New Delhi : Department of Social Welfare, Ministry of Education and Social Welfare, Government of India, 1974.

Ritter, Kathleen V, and Hargens, Lowell L. "Occupational Positions and Class Identifications of Married Working Women: A Test of the Asymmetry Hypothesis", *American Journal of Sociology*, 80 (January, 1975), 934-948

Ross, Aileen D. *The Hindu Family in its Urban Setting*. Bombay : Oxford University Press, 1961.

Seear, B.N. *Re-Entry of Women to the Labour Market after an Interruption in Employment*. Paris : Organisation for Economic Co-operation and Development, 1971.

Sen Gupta, Padmini. *Women Workers in India*. Bombay : Asia Publishing House, 1960.

Shah, A.M. "Changes in the Indian Family", *The Economic and Political Weekly* 3, (n. 1-2, 1968), 127-135.

———. *The Household Dimension of the Family in India*. Delhi : Orient Longman, 1973.

Sharma, Ursula. "The Problem of Village Hinduism : Fragmentation and Integration," *Contributions to Indian Sociology* (New Series), IV (December, 1970), 1-21.

Singh, K. P. "Women's Age at Marriage", *Sociological Bulletin*, 23 (September, 1974), pp. 236-244.

S.N.D.T. University. *Women in India*. Bombay, 1975.

Status of Women. A Symposium on the Discriminated Section of Society. *Seminar*, 165 (May, 1973).

Strober, Myra. "Women Economists : Career Aspirations, Education and Training", *American Economic Review*, LXV (May, 1975), 92-99.

Szalal, Alexander, "The Situation of Women in the Light of Time-Budget Research". World Conference of the International Women's Year. New York: United Nations, E/CON. 66/BP/6, April 15, 1975.

Takahashi, Nobuko. "Women's Wages in Japan and the Question of Equal Pay", *International Labour Review*, III (January, 1975), 51-68.

Tellis-Nayak, J. "Women's Welfare Services", in *The Indian Family in the Change and Challenge of the Seventies*. New Delhi : Sterling Publishers, 1972.

Vatuk, Sylvia. *Kinship and Urbanisation : White Collar Migrants in North India*. Berkeley, Los Angeles : University of California Press, 1972.

Vreede-De Stuers, Cora. *Parda: A Study of Muslim Women's Life in Northern India*. Assen: Van Gorcum and Company, 1968.

———. "Attitudes of Jaipur Girl Students Towards Family Life", in Dhirendra Narain (ed.), *Explorations in the Family and Other Essays*. Bombay : Thacker and Company, 1975.

Wasi, Muriel (ed.). *The Educated Woman in Indian Society Today*. New Delhi : Tata McGraw-Hill, 1971.

Zachariah, K.C. and Sebastian, A. "Juvenile Working Migrants in Greater Bombay", *The Indian Journal of Social Work*, 27 (October, 1966), 255-262.

Zuckerman, Harriet and Cole, Jonathan R. "Women in American Science", *Minerva* XII (Spring, 1975), 82-102.

INDEX